Cognitive neuropsychol
Is pessimisr

Tim Shallice

*Institute of Cognitive Neuroscience, University College, London, UK
and SISSA, Trieste, Italy*

The paper considers the possible role that cognitive neuropsychology might play in neuropsychological rehabilitation. Issues specifically considered include (i) under what conditions can alternative systems substitute for an impaired one, (ii) the potential efficacy of direct retraining, (iii) the acquisition and voluntary application of new schemes.

Over the past 30 years cognitive neuropsychology has increasingly provided us with an excellent theoretical framework for characterising the cognitive deficits that result from neurological disease. It is therefore rational to consider whether it can provide a basis not only for the static picture of the patient's deficit but also for improving its dynamic trajectory. This special issue contains seven impressive papers, a subset of those given at the Milan conference on the relation between cognitive neuropsychology and aphasia rehabilitation. On the whole, at the meeting, the idea that the relation between the science and this clinical application has and can be productive was not strongly supported. Thus the papers range from only a single, if impressive, example of the clearly productive use of cognitive neuropsychological theory, where the evidence essentially supported the predictions (Luzzatti, Colombo, Frustaci, & Vitolo) to one paper explicitly sceptical about the approach (Basso & Marangolo). Moreover, the tone of the conference itself was rather pessimistic about the possibility of a form of rehabilitation likely to prove productive being based on a theoretical understanding derived from a cognitive neuropsychological analysis of the nature of the patient's underlying deficit.

Requests for reprints should be sent to Tim Shallice, Institute of Cognitive Neuroscience, University College London, Alexandra House, 17 Queen Square, London WC1N 3AR, UK.

© 2000 Psychology Press Ltd
http://www.tandf.co.uk/journals/pp/09602011.html

My aim in this paper is to consider from the perspective of theoretical cognitive neuropsychology a question posed explicitly at the conference by the paper of Basso and Marangolo concerning the likely effectiveness of theoretically based rehabilitation for disorders such as agrammatism. It was implicitly answered rather negatively by the tone of the meeting. The question is, can cognitive neuropsychology be relevant as a "rational starting point" to use Basso and Marangolo's phrase, for determining what form of rehabilitation is a promising candidate for a patient, if any? Clearly, in the practical situation these issues cannot be isolated from other factors, in particular the social organisation of the rehabilitation process and the family support structure. Thus Schwartz (personal communication) argues community sites that rehabilitation should be extended into the chronic phase by establishing community sites that feature computerised therapy software and therapeutic conversation groups. Moreover, families should be involved as much as possible. However, as a simplification I will consider the cognitive factors only.

Before directly discussing the question it is necessary to consider some preliminary issues. First, as Basso and Marangolo point out, it is inappropriate to treat syndromes as though they reflected a preferred means of characterising disorders in cognitive neuropsychology. Instead, a cognitive neuropsychological approach requires that the disorder be specified in terms of the loci and degrees of damage within a *model* of the operation of the cognitive system. Such models are of two types. In first-stage cognitive neuropsychology, one attempts to characterise the disorder in terms of damage to components or transmission routes with a model that specifies only the broad functional architecture of the cognitive system. Moreover, the components are characterised only by verbal labels, e.g., visual input lexicon (e.g., Shallice, 1988). However, since 1990 there has developed a second stage cognitive neuropsychology where the disorder is situated within a more detailed computational account of the function (e.g., Caramazza & McCloskey, 1991; Plaut & Shallice, 1993). Basso and Marangolo's call for the necessity of a more fine-grained analysis, which echoes the position of Hillis (1993), is, in my view, too strong a critique of the use for this purpose of first stage models. However, for some of the points discussed below second stage models may well prove more fruitful to act as a rational basis for rehabilitation.

More generally, Basso and Marangolo characterise cognitive neuropsychology as assuming that a "cognitive function is constituted by sub-functions that are computationally independent of one another and informationally encapsulated". In other words they take a symbolic-processing theoretical perspective. Even excellent second-stage theories of this type in cognitive neuropsychology—consider e.g., Caramazza & Miceli's (1990) account of graphemic buffer disorder—typically do not use any concepts which relate to how the system changes over time or how learning proceeds. Thus it remains unclear how one should make principled use of such theories in rehabilitation.

I would draw four initial conclusions from these considerations. First, a typical cognitive neuropsychological model is limited to the function itself, and for symbolic models to static characterisations of the function. However, the cognitive aspects of rehabilitation are inherently dynamic and involve many processes other than the damaged process itself. Second, following from this, use may have to be made of other branches of cognitive neuroscience in order to apply cognitive neuropsychology in a fully principled as opposed to an at least partly pragmatic fashion. Third, as pointed out by Baddeley (1993), a theoretically based rehabilitation practice will require a theory or theories of learning.

The fourth point is that one needs to situate how one views cognitive neuropsychology with respect to the ideological split that exists within it over cognitive theory. There are two extreme positions. Theorists such as Chomsky and Fodor reject connectionist theorising as quasi-behaviourist and incompatible with the major advances of the structuralist symbol-processing theoretical developments of the 1960s and 1970s. Cognitive neuropsychology theorists such as Caramazza and Coltheart, while not being so extreme, tend in this direction. By contrast Sejnowski and Churchland, for instance, would view any model using information-processing or other structural concepts as a pre-scientific conceptual framework that will be undercut by a connectionist approach.

I will adopt a middle position, holding that the standard information-processing computational approach is a valid and useful means of understanding the gross functional organisation of the cognitive system, but that the most promising means of understanding how individual sub-systems work is the connectionist one. In particular, in Shallice, Glasspool, and Houghton (1995) it was argued that cognitive functions differ in the number of additional specific assumptions that must be added to a prototypic multi-layer network in order for them to be effectively simulated. For instance it was argued that functions which require serial ordering of elements such as phonological short-term memory or the mapping from an orthographic word-forin onto letter units in spelling is best carried out in an architecture where there is some type of representation of serial order (e.g., distance from beginning of sequence, distance from end). It will be argued that the presence of these additional specific requirements for the effecting of particular functions may well have considerable relevance for rehabilitation.

These initial considerations lead to four types of theoretical questions:

Can any alternative system substitute for the impaired one?

This is clearly a potentially attractive possibility. There are two possible ways it might prove relevant. One possible approach is to train up the use of alternative "routes" within a multiple route model (see e.g., Derouesne &

Beauvois, 1982). This is the procedure called by Grafman and Litvan (1999) *compensatory masquerade*. It has the obvious advantage that such models give rise to a principled hypothesis for how the function may be improved.

A critical issue for some syndromes, in particular aphasic ones, is the potential utility of a second approach. If a function was being carried out by a now damaged system in one hemisphere, then the issue is whether it might be possible to obtain a take-over of the function by an analogous system in the other hemisphere, which in the normal subject is not fully operative. This has been called *homologous adaptation* by Grafman and Litvan. In this respect, a critical line of evidence, as Cappa's paper in this issue makes clear, will be derived from broader cognitive neuroscience methods, such as functional imaging, rather than cognitive neuropsychological ones. Cappa's important, if interim, conclusion is that recovery, for instance in aphasia, does not generally make major productive use of systems in the other spared hemisphere. This does not entail that some specific training regime might not use such a process when this does not normally occur in recovery of function at present. However, it makes somewhat less plausible the attempt to produce relateralisation of function as a form of rehabilitation (but see also the Springer, Huber, Schlenck, & Schlenck's paper in this issue).

Can the operation of individual damaged subsystems or pathways be improved by retraining on particular input stimuli-output action pairings?

In this respect it now seems, from the cognitive neuroscience perspective, that the potential for plasticity is greater than might have been anticipated in the heyday of cognitive neuropsychology through what Grafman and Litvan call *map enhancement* and *cross-modal reassignment* (e.g., Buonomano & Merzenich, 1998; Kaas, 1994; Ramachandran, Rogers-Ramachandran, & Stewart, 1992). Moreover, functional imaging studies suggest that such processes are relevant in some patients for processes such as recovery of motor functions from stroke (Weiller et al., 1993). However, to be able to assess in a given patient whether such processes could be effectively used, one needs to model them, which in my view currently implies a connectionist perspective. Such a perspective leads to two further types of question.

What regime of input–output training should be used? Here the most promising theoretical approach known to me, since it links naturally to one part of a theory of learning, is that of Plaut (1996) on generalisation in surface dyslexia of the type studied by Coltheart and Byng (1989) (see the paper by Best & Nichels, this issue). It aims to retrain the function directly by mimicking part of the initial learning process but using a particular subset of stimuli. Stimuli are presented to the patient and errors are corrected. The model is used to guide theoretically the selection of the most appropriate stimuli to use for direct retraining so that generalisation to non-trained examples will be greatest.

What types of process are most appropriate for this connectionist retraining approach? The modified connectionist position of Shallice, Glasspool, and Houghton (1995) discussed above holds that some cognitive processes such as the mapping from orthographic to semantic representations can be well modelled by standard recurrent feed-forward connectionist nets with an attractor structure (see Plaut & Shallice, 1993, for discussion). In such cases the direct retraining of the type modelled by Plaut (1996) would be the principled application of cognitive neuropsychological theory. However, the Shallice, Glasspool, and Houghton position also holds that there are other types of cognitive process where additional elements are required in the simulation which are specific to the particular cognitive process. For example, a plausible model of the phonological buffer (Burgess & Hitch, 1992) which uses an overall connectionist framework involves so-called "temporal context nodes" and an "output competitive filter". These temporal context nodes and output competitive filters are part of the architecture of the network. They are not altered by any types of input to the net or any type of reinforcement. On the model, retraining of the type discussed above does not affect how they operate. If the simulation is a good model of the processes involved in retaining phonological input over short intervals of time, then these aspects can be assumed to correspond to specific innate properties of the system or to processes developed early in life, and not to be easily reproduced by simple retraining of input–output mappings. I will call these components of models *special components*.

These considerations have major implications from a rehabilitation perspective. They suggest that some types of network will be much more easily retrained after damage than others. In particular, if one separates out these special components from other more standard aspects of the network, then the following property will presumably generally hold: The more complex the processes carried out by the special components of the network implementing the function the more difficult it would be to approximate grossly to the set of input–output mappings it had prior to damage by retraining after the damage. From this perspective, partial disconnections of, say, orthographic-to-semantic or orthographic-to-phonological representations, of a given level of severity (i.e., of a given resource loss in the terminology of Shallice, 1979, 1980) should be easier to rehabilitate by connectionist retraining than, say, phonological short-term memory, or syntactic or episodic memory processes where the degree of damage is comparable. This is because the orthographic-to-semantic or orthographic-to-phonological mappings would have none of these special components but the other three types of function seem likely to require them. Intuitively, this justifies why sound-to-speech procedures may be especially appropriate to attempt to rehabilitate (see paper by Luzzatti et al., this issue). Moreover, the success of certain rehabilitation procedures for neglect, such as those of Robertson, Hogg, and McMillan, 1998, may rely on particular mechanisms of vistio-spatial attention being internally of rather simple structure as a model such as that of Pouget and Sejnowski (1997) would suggest.

How easily can the patient acquire and use a novel action or thought schema which will be required in a rehabilitation procedure?

Rehabilitation procedures frequently require that the patient internalise a particular strategy (see many of the papers). In addition to the instruction and training involved there may well be many processes used which relate to those required in the acquisition of a new schema without instruction (see Shallice & Burgess, 1996), in which case the prefrontal cortex would be strongly involved. Thus, the presence of damage to the supervisory system may result in otherwise satisfactory retraining procedures not being practicable. In particular, one needs to be concerned not just with whether a particular procedure would lead to improved operation of the damaged system but also with what strategic-level demands such retraining will place on the patient.

Will a newly acquired schema requiring voluntary application lead to eventual effective automatic use?

There is a further issue which is liable to be empirically critical in rehabilitation of some processes. Assume that rehabilitation training of the sort referred to above is successful in inducing the patient to develop new action or thought schemas, to use the conceptual framework of Shallice and Burgess (1996). These will be initially represented as temporary schemas and require supervisory system control. To automate them will presumably necessarily entail much practice. Can the processes be useful even if they are operating slowly and somewhat inaccurately? Take a process such as the carrying out of syntactic operations (see Mitchum, Greenwald, & Berndt, this issue). To be useful, the process must be dovetailed with many others including phonological input or output processes, semantic processes, and whatever cognitive processes the meaning of the sentence relates to. Consider a situation in which the syntactic process were to be grossly impaired following a stroke, but to improve somewhat after training but still operate much more slowly than before. Then to utilise them effectively may still not be possible because they do not dovetail effectively with the processes with which they must necessarily operate. By contrast such considerations seem less likely to be critical for a process such as writing or other simple motor acts where explicit use of a learned procedure could enable the process to work in an effective if slow fashion. Thus the patient will be motivated to continue to try to improve.

The processes relevant to the last two questions are poorly understood from a cognitive neuropsychological perspective. However, difficulties at these levels—which relate to executive functions seem to be linked to the failure of patients to recover from their impairment in some sorts of syndrome. Thus Robertson et al. (1997) have shown the existence of strong correlations between neglect and failure on a vigilance task closely related to one specifically affected by right prefrontal lesions (Wilkins, Shallice, & McCarthy, 1987) (see also Robertson et al., 1998). Moreover, Burgess, and Alderman (1990), Von Cramon and Mathes-Von Cramon (1994), and Alderman, Fry, and Youngson (1995) have developed rehabilitation procedures based on theoretical models in the executive function domain, so the cognitive neuropsychological approach is relevant in this domain too.

These initial conclusions and questions posed for cognitive neuropsychological theory are derived from a purely theoretical perspective. They are not informed by knowledge of the detailed practice of cognitive rehabilitation. My aim in raising them is to outline the necessary complexity of the rehabilitation process from the perspective of cognitive neuropsychology. In particular, if one uses cognitive neuropsychology to inform some part of a rehabilitation procedure and the overall process is not successful, then it would be premature to argue that the use of cognitive neuropsychology is inappropriate. First, as Hillis has argued, the cognitive neuropsychology theorising on the primary impaired function may be too primitive, or the impairment may be quantitatively too severe. Second, wider cognitive neuropsychology considerations may suggest that the function is not ideal for an attempt at direct recovery. It should not be assumed that all functions are equally suitable for rehabilitation. Also, the aim of the rehabilitation attempt may be too ambitious. Third, the overall failure may be due to a failure in one of the other parts of the process which would, in our current state of knowledge, necessarily be pragmatically guided. The utility of using a cognitive neuroscience account of the impaired processes in providing a rational basis for rehabilitation can only be properly assessed in the context of an adequate theory of the other key elements of the overall processes. Fourth, cognitive neuropsychological theorising may have to be combined with more basic neuroscience approaches before an effective procedure is possible.

Possibly, the challenge posed by Basso and Marangolo's question will help to lead to more satisfactory multi disciplinary theories of the rehabilitation process as a whole. It would be a mistake to answer the question negatively just because particular initial attempts to use cognitive neuropsychology fail.

REFERENCES

Alderman, N., Fry, R.K., & Youngson, H.A. (1995). Improvement of self-monitoring skills, reduction of behaviour disturbance and the dysexecutive syndrome: Comparison of response cost and a new programme of self-monitoring training. *Neuropsychological Rehabilitation, 5,* 193–231.

Baddeley, A. (1993). A theory of rehabilitation without a model of learning is a vehicle without an engine: A comment on Caramazza and Hillis. *Neuropsychological Rehabilitation, 3,* 235–244.

Basso, A., & Marangolo, P. (this issue). Cognitive neuropsychological rehabilitation: The emperor's new clothes? *Neuropsychological Rehabilitation, 10,* 219–229.

Best, W., & Nickels, L. (this issue). From theory to therapy in aphasia: Where are we now and where to next? *Neuropsychological Rehabilitation, 10,* 231–247.

Buonomano, D.V., & Merzenich, M.M. (1998). Cortical plasticity: From synapses to maps. *Annual Review of Neuroscience, 21,* 149–186.

Burgess, P.W., & Alderman, N. (1990). Rehabilitation of dyscontrol syndromes following frontal lobe damage in a cognitive neuropsychological approach. In R. L. Wood & I. Fussey (Eds.), *Cognitive rehabilitation in perspective.* Hove, UK: Psychology Press.

Burgess, N., & Hitch, G.J. (1992). Toward a network model of the articulatory loop. *Journal of Memory and Language, 31,* 429–460.

Cappa, S.F. (this issue). Neuroimaging of recovery from aphasia. *Neuropsychological Rehabilitation, 10,* 365–376.

Caramazza, A., & McCloskey, M. (1991). The poverty of methodology. *Behavioural and Brain Sciences, 14,* 444.

Caramazza, A., & Miceli, G. (1990). The structure of graphemic representations. *Cognition, 37,* 243–297.

Carlomagno, S., Blasi, V., Labruna, L., & Santoro, A. (this issue). The role of communication models in assessment and therapy of language disorders in aphasic adults. *Neuropsychological Rehabilitation, 10,* 337–363.

Coltheart, M., & Byng, S. (1989). A treatment for surface dyslexia. In X. Seron & G. Deloche (Eds.), *Cognitive approaches in neuropsychological rehabilitation.* (pp. 159–174). Hillsdale, NJ: Erlbaum.

Grafman, J., & Litvan, I. (1999). Evidence of four forms of neuroplasticity. In J. Grafman & Y. Christen (Eds.), *Neuronal Plasticity: Building a bridge from the laboratory to the clinic.* (pp. 131–139). Berlin: Springer.

Hillis, A.E. (1993). The role of models of language processing in rehabilitation of language impairment. *Aphasiology, 7,* 5–26.

Kaas, J.H. (1994). The reorganisation of sensory and motor maps in adult mammals. In M.S. Gazzaniga (Ed.), *The cognitive neurosciences.* (pp. 51–71.) Cambridge, MA: MIT Press.

Luzzatti, C., Colombo, C., Frustaci, M., & Vitolo, F. (this issue). Rehabilitation of spelling along the sub-word-level route. *Neuropsychological Rehabilitation, 10,* 249–278.

Mitchum, C., Greenwald, M., & Berndt, R.S. (this issue). Cognitive treatments of sentence processing disorders: What have we learned? *Neuropsychological Rehabilitation, 10,* 311–336.

Plaut, D.C. (1996). Relearning after damage in connectionist networks: Toward a theory of rehabilitation. *Brain and Language, 52,* 25–82.

Plaut, D.C., & Shallice, T. (1993). Deep dyslexia: A case study of connenctionist neuro-psychology. *Cognitive Neuropsychology, 10,* 377–500.

Pouget, A., & Sejnowski, T.J. (1997). A new view of hemineglect based on the response proper-ties of parietal neurons. *Philosophical Transactions of the Royal Society of London Series B-Biological Sciences, 352,* 1449–1459.

Ramachandran, V.W., Rogers-Ramachandran, D., & Stewart, M. (1992). Perceptual correlates of massive cortical reorganisation. *Science, 258,* 1159–1160.

Robertson, I.H., Hogg, K., & McMillan, T.M. (1998). Rehabilitation of unilateral neglect: Reducing inhibitory competition by contralesional limb activation. *Neuropsychological Rehabilitation, 8,* 19–30.

Robertson, I.H., Manly, T., Beschin, N., Daini, R., Haeske-Dewick, H., Homberg, V., Jehkonen, M., Pizzamiglio, L., Shiel, A., & Weber, E. (1997). Auditory sustained attention is a marker of unilateral spatial neglect. *Neuropsychologia, 35,* 1527–1532.

Shallice, T. (1979). Case study approach in neuropsychological research. *Journal of Clinical Neuropsychology, 1,* 183–211.

Shallice, T. (1988). *From neuropsychology to mental structure.* Cambridge: Cambridge University Press.

Shallice, T., & Burgess, P.W. (1996). Domains of supervisory control and the temporal organisation of behaviour. *Philosophical Transactions of the Royal Society of London Series B, 351,* 1405–1412.

Shallice, T., Glasspool, D.W., & Houghton, G. (1995). Can neuropsychological evidence inform connectionist modelling: Analyses of spelling. *Language and Cognitive Processes, 10,* 195–225.

Springer, L., Huber, W., Schlenck, K.-J., & Schlenck, C. (this issue). Agrammatism: Deficit or compensation? Consequences for aphasia therapy. *Neuropsychological Rehabilitation, 10,* 279–309.

Von Cramon, D.Y., & Matthes-Von Cramon, C. (1994). Back to work with a chronic dysexecutive syndrome? (A case report) *Neuropsychological Rehabilitation, 4,* 399–417.

Weiller, C., Ramsay, S.C., Wise R.S.J., Friston, K.J., & Frackowiak, R.S.J (1993). Individual patterns of functional reorganisation in the human cerebral cortex after capsular infarction. *Annals of Neurology, 33,* 181–189.

Wilkins, A., Shallice, T., & McCarthy, R. (1987). Frontal lesions and sustained attention. *Neuropsychologia, 25,* 359–365.

Manuscript received October 1999

NEUROPSYCHOLOGICAL REHABILITATION, 2000, *10* (0), 219–229

Cognitive neuropsychological rehabilitation: The emperor's new clothes?

Anna Basso

Milan University

Paola Marangolo

IRCCS S. Lucia, Rome

It has often been claimed that cognitive neuropsychology allows a far better diagnosis and understanding of the nature of a patient's language disorder than classical clinical diagnoses, and that a theoretically-driven therapeutic intervention can only be based on a cognitive diagnosis. In this paper we argue that: (1) Cognitive neuropsychologists have fostered and made explicit knowledge about the nature of aphasia which can be a rational starting point for intervention; however, former aphasia therapy was not atheoretical, but always based on existent theories of aphasia. (2) The new cognitive dyslexia and dysgraphia syndromes are perhaps more homogeneous than the classical diagnoses but no more informative or useful for rehabilitation planning. (3) Due to the modularity assumption, cognitive rehabilitation has sometimes been planned with only the damaged module/s being taken into consideration. We argue that the whole functional structure of the model adopted should be addressed because it can dictate the focus of rehabilitation.

We conclude that cognitive neuropsychology allows a more detailed analysis of the functional damage but provides no indication as to how to implement rehabilitation for a given patient—even if it does evidence the lack of rationality of many interventions.

Cognitive neuropsychologists have often claimed that any attempt to treat a cognitive disorder should have as a starting point a secure model of the cognitive function to be restored. A correct and detailed diagnosis consists of identifying which aspects of the cognitive function to be restored are impaired and which are intact, the functional diagnosis being the only reasonable starting

---

Requests for reprints should be sent to Anna Basso, Neurological Clinic, Via F. Sforza 35, 20122 Milan, Italy.

© 2000 Psychology Press Ltd

http://www.tandf.co.uk/journals/pp/09602011.html

point of any intervention. However, as Howard and Hatfield (1987) put it, "too often ... the relationship between deficit and treatment is based on some implicit idea of how treatment has its effects, which has no good justification or scientific support" (p. 106).

In this paper we argue that speech pathologists have always based their interventions on existent theoretical views of aphasia even if it has sometimes taken some time for new knowledge about aphasia to be introduced into therapeutic practice. We also claim that the new syndromes proposed for reading and spelling disorders are neither theoretically well defined nor useful for rehabilitation planning.

Lastly, we briefly consider the *philosophy* of cognitive neuropsychological rehabilitation as may be inferred from published cases, and we argue that some general principles to guide aphasia therapy can be derived from cognitive neuropsychological models.

CLASSICAL APHASIA THEORY AND THERAPY

After the Second World War and notwithstanding decade after decade of discussion about it, aphasia remained a somewhat mysterious entity. Many aphasiologists, among whom we may recall Wepman (1951), Schuell (1974; Schuell, Jenkins, & Jimenez-Pabon, 1964), and Bay (1964), claimed that aphasia was a unique disorder which could only vary in severity. Schuell et al., (1964) defined aphasia "a general language deficit that crosses all language modalities and may or may not be complicated by other sequelae of brain damage" (p. 113). As for aphasia rehabilitation, Schuell (1974) stated that until the efficacy of any approach is unequivocally demonstrated, what we do must at least be defensible on theoretical grounds (p. 138). Given that aphasia is regarded as a unidimensional, multimodality impairment (that is, all language modalities are impaired in aphasia and tend to be impaired to about the same degree), it makes sense to treat the patient through a single modality. For Schuell, this modality was the auditory modality because auditory processes are at the apex of the interacting language systems. Schuell (1974) considered the notion of intensive auditory stimulation to be "the most important clinical discovery that we ever made" (p. 112) and this belief has been bolstered by the observation that for many patients the recovery of auditory functions preceded the recovery of other language functions (Basso, Capitani, & Zanobio, 1982; Hanson & Cicciarelli, 1978; Kertesz & McCabe, 1977).

On the other hand, the classical localisationist doctrine sustained that there are different types of aphasic disorders, and that different patterns of impairment can be traced back to specific lesion sites. The clinical observation that aphasic symptoms consistently cluster in fairly distinct patterns led many researchers to speak about "the aphasias" (Damasio, 1991; Kertesz,

1979). In very general terms, aphasia was defined (Kertesz, 1979) as a "neurologically central disturbance of language." (p. 2). The analysis of the nature of language made by aphasiologists was rather crude and language was simply considered the sum of all possible verbal behaviours: comprehension and production of oral and written language, repetition, reading aloud, copying, and writing to dictation. Moreover, it was thought that each verbal behaviour could be analysed at different linguistic levels: phonemes, words, and sentences.

The disruption of language in aphasia was believed to fall into the same pattern: Phonemes, words, and sentences could be differently impaired in each modality and verbal behaviours differently impaired in the various aphasias. Transcortical sensory aphasia and conduction aphasia, for instance, were held to differ because of the relative impairment of auditory comprehension (relatively spared in conduction aphasia) and repetition (spared in transcortical sensory aphasia). Accordingly, aphasia rehabilitation proceeded from phoneme to word to sentence, and from comprehension to production to reading and to writing. At that time, many manuals for aphasia therapy were published describing exercises for comprehension, production, and reading and writing of words, sentences, and paragraphs (see, for instance, Ducarne de Ribaucourt, 1986; Shewan & Bandur, 1986). Contrary to common belief, this type of intervention was not atheoretical; but based on an implicit theoretical view about the nature of aphasia shared by many. In short, when theories of aphasia were dominated by the view that aphasia is a unique disorder, the theoretical content of therapeutic approaches was similarly underspecified. When this view of aphasia was rejected and the classical localisationist theories were rediscovered, it was argued that therapy must be based on diagnostic groups defined by the relative impairment of language behaviours. In line with the diagnosis of aphasia, aphasia therapy endeavoured to rehabilitate production in Broca aphasics, comprehension in Wernicke's aphasics, and so on.

Many years have gone by and our knowledge about the nature of aphasia has increased. Even more importantly, what has changed is the point of view from which aphasia is now studied. The main interest of cognitively-minded aphasiologists is no longer the study of relationships between cognitive functions and cerebral areas. Instead, the formal characterisation of the mental structures underlying human cognitive capacities has become a major endeavour for many cognitive neuropsychologists. Detailed cognitive models have been developed and have been used to interpret impaired performance. This has afforded for greater insight into the nature of language and of the aphasic disorders. Today's understanding of language processes is more sophisticated and more explicitly defined than it was some years ago. Speech pathologists must take this increased knowledge into account when treating aphasic patients but this should make their task easier rather than more difficult, because they now have more clearly defined guidelines.

COGNITIVE NEUROPSYCHOLOGICAL DIAGNOSES

Classical diagnoses were essentially descriptive and taxonomic whereas cognitive neuropsychological diagnoses are aimed at identifying the functional locus of impairment. The advantage of cognitive neuropsychological diagnoses over the older clinical ones is argued to be that the former are based on a model of normal processing and that they help to localise the functional damage, and thus allow for a theoretically-informed approach to rehabilitation. However, this is not always so. In the case of reading and writing disorders, a cognitive diagnosis (such as deep dyslexia, surface dysgraphia, etc.) is of no help to rehabilitation. Briefly, most models of the lexical-semantic system postulate at least two distinct routes for converting a written word into phonology, and two routes for converting a heard word into the corresponding orthographic form. The two reading routes diverge after the visual analysis of the printed word is achieved; reading by the lexical route involves recognition of the to-be-read word (in the orthographic input lexicon), and activation of the corresponding semantic representation (in the semantic system) which in turn activates the stored phonological representation (in the phonological output lexicon) (Figure 1).

The sublexical route involves a different process: The orthographic input is converted into a plausible phonological representation by the conversion procedures. Very similar routes are described for writing. According to whether one or the other route (or both) is impaired, we have surface, phonological, or deep dyslexia (or dysgraphia). Reading and spelling, however, are complex processes and identification of the damaged route is not the same as identification of the damaged process. We need a more fine-grained analysis to understand why the patient cannot read (or spell). More importantly, from the therapeutic point of view, except for the conversion rules, the routes are not dedicated to reading and spelling. Integrity of the input lexicons, besides being necessary to recognise heard and written words in the spelling and reading process, is also necessary for comprehension; integrity of the output lexicons is necessary for naming, speaking, repeating, *and* reading (or spelling). Finally, an intact semantic system is necessary both for correct comprehension and production. To say that a patient has dyslexia or dysgraphia draws attention to just one aspect of the patient's disorder and shifts the focus away from others.

We will illustrate our point with one often quoted example of cognitive rehabilitation: patient EE described by Coltheart and Byng (1989). EE was a 40-year-old left-handed postal worker who had a right temporoparietal evacuation of an acute subdural haematoma and haemorrhagic contusions following head trauma. He was first tested by Coltheart and Byng 5 months post-onset and was found to have surface dyslexia: In short, better reading of regular than irregular words with many regularisation errors. Nonlexical

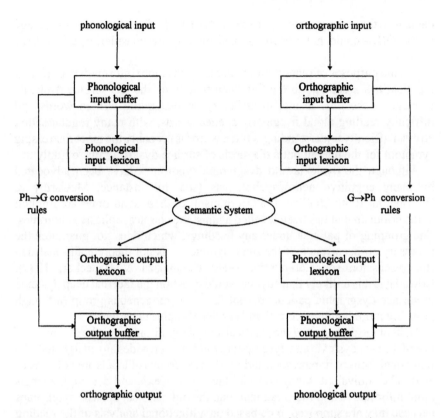

Figure 1.   Schematic representation of the functional structure of the lexical/semantic system.

procedures for reading were also damaged. Coltheart and Byng decided to treat his lexical reading but did not know how to proceed because surface dyslexia, according to Coltheart and Funnell (1987), can arise in different ways. It may arise: "If processing of words by a visual-recognition system fails . . . If . . . communication from this system to a phonological output lexicon (via a semantic system, for example) fails . . . If retrieval of phonological word forms from a phonological output lexicon fails . . . one is an orthographic deficit, one involves semantic impairment, and one is an anomia" (Coltheart & Byng, 1989). Coltheart and Byng conclude that "theoretical interpretation is still not specific enough to guide one's choice of treatment" (pp. 163–164). However, it is not the "theoretical interpretation" that is not specific enough; it is the syndrome of surface dyslexia that lacks a sound theoretical basis. And, as Coltheart and Byng clearly state, the very reason of this is that qualifying a patient as surface dyslexic does not say where the functional damage lies. In fact, they do more than classify EE as a surface dyslexic; based on an analysis of EE's results, they reach the conclusion that EE's surface dyslexia is due to damage to the orthographic input lexicon (OIL). The final diagnosis — damage to the OIL—could have been reached directly by considering all of EE's deficits.

For the purposes of rehabilitation planning it is more informative to say that a patient has a damage to the OIL than that he or she has surface dyslexia. Damage to the OIL results in difficulty understanding written words and difficulty reading aloud irregularly spelled words, with many regularisation errors. Difficulty understanding written words is probably the more distressing symptom for the patient but a diagnosis of surface dyslexia fails to imply it.

Although the dyslexia and dysgraphia syndromes have been advocated by many cognitive neuropsychologists (see, for instance, McCarthy & Warrington, 1990; Shallice, 1988), criticisms of these syndromes are implicit in the criticism that has been levelled against the classical aphasia syndromes: The grouping of patients under any headings, which does not guarantee the necessary co-occurrence of the same symptoms, is not theoretically justified (for discussion see Caramazza, 1986; Caramazza & Badecker, 1989). Nowadays, it is unlikely that anyone would question the fact that deep dyslexia or surface dysgraphia patients do not form a homogeneous group (although probably more homogeneous than Wernicke's aphasia patients).

Neither the diagnosis of the classical aphasia syndromes nor the diagnosis of one of the new dyslexia and dysgraphia syndromes provides any insight into the functional locus of impairment, and yet the two groups of labels are not considered to be equivalent. Many consider the new dyslexia and dysgraphia labels more informative and more rational than the old classical aphasic syndromes because they are supposed to be based on a functional analysis of the reading and spelling mechanisms and thus to refer, in a more or less precise way, to a functional damage that should explain the patient's performance. We sustain that they are neither more informative nor rational; on the contrary, we argue that they are more misleading. The label of Wernicke's aphasia, for instance, tells us something about the locus of the lesion, the presence of other neurological disorders, the type of speech production, and so on; it is a descriptive label which does not pretend to offer an interpretation of the disorder. The label of surface dyslexia, on the other hand, does not say anything about the possible presence of other language disorders but is considered a functional diagnosis of the reading disorder. This is misleading because, as already said, it draws attention from other disorders which necessarily coexist in the dyslexias and dysgraphias resulting from damage to the lexical routes. Deep and surface dyslexia and dysgraphia cannot in fact exist alone, other language impairments are always present because the damaged lexical reading (and writing) routines are not dedicated to reading (or writing). Only damage to the conversion mechanisms is confined to reading or writing and patients can present isolated phonological dyslexia (or dysgraphia).

COGNITIVE NEUROPSYCHOLOGY'S RATIONALE
FOR REHABILITATION

According to cognitive neuropsychologists, any cognitive function is constituted by sub-functions that are computationally independent of one another and informationally encapsulated. This is a strong version of modularity which would not be accepted by everyone; a weaker version of modularity admits different degrees of functional independence. It is our opinion that, even if one accepts a strong version of modularity, in case when there is damage to two or more modules, considering together all the patient's deficits can help in providing a more rational intervention because the functional structure of the model adopted can dictate the choice of what must be re-educated first. It is self-evident that an intact component cannot operate normally if the inputs to it are not normal, as would occur if they are the outputs of a damaged component. However, there is no such simple rule as: "Always begin by retraining the damaged component that comes first in the information processing chain". We will give two examples of choices determined by the structure of the assumed model as represented in Figure 1. In the first example, damage to the central component should be retrained before retraining of both the higher or lower component; in the second example we argue that the lower component in the chain of information processing should be retrained first.

Let's imagine a patient with damage to the semantic system (SS) and any one of the four lexicons. As it can be seen in Figure 1, the semantic component is central and necessary for the comprehension and production of words; the lexical components are more peripheral and specific for phonology and orthography and for input and output. This being the case, damage to the SS and damage to one lexicon cannot be considered equivalent from the point of view of rehabilitation planning. Coexisting damage to any lexicon and to the SS suggests that the SS is rehabilitated first because damage to it will have repercussions on all lexicons. If, for instance, the SS and the phonological input lexicon are damaged, recovery of the input lexicon would not be of much help to the patient. Because of the damaged SS, the patient will fail to understand words correctly, even if they are now recognised as words. By way of example, on hearing the word *table*, the patient will know it is a word and attribute it the meaning of *chair*. If, however, the SS recovers first, the patient will at least be able to understand written words (and speak), and we are now entitled to rehabilitate the input lexicon which, on improving, will enable the patient to correctly understand spoken words as well.

The same reasoning is valid for damage to an output lexicon coexisting with damage to the SS. It is not much use to the patient to be able to find the phonological form of the word *cat*, say, when what he or she is trying to say is *dog*. Recovery of the damaged SS would allow the patient to understand, which is in itself an important achievement; subsequent recovery of the output lexicon will allow the patient to find the phonological form of the word he or she really wants to say and not of a semantic paraphasia.

Our second example of a choice dictated by the proposed structure of the lexicon is damage to one output lexicon and the corresponding buffer. Consider the case of a patient with damage to the phonological output lexicon (POL) and the phonological buffer. Damage to the phonological buffer will prevent him or her from correctly saying, repeating, and reading words and non-words, depending on their length. Damage to the POL implies that (some) phonological representations are inaccessible or disrupted. In the case considered here of damage to the POL and the buffer, previous (and successful) rehabilitation of the POL would enable the patient to access the correct phonological representation in the lexicon but not to produce it correctly because of damage to the buffer. On the other hand, successful rehabilitation of the buffer would enable the patient to repeat and read (regular) words and non-words, and to correctly produce those words for which the lexical phonological representations are accessible or undamaged. Successive recovery of the POL would enable the patient carefully to produce words. Moreover, rehabilitation of the lexicon before rehabilitation of the buffer is made difficult by coexisting damage to the buffer which prevents the patient from producing any correct response (obviously depending on the severity of the damage) in any situation. On the other hand, notwithstanding damage to the POL, it is not impossible to enhance the capacity of the buffer through the conversion mechanisms which are, by hypothesis, undamaged.

When no suggestion can be derived from the model, therapy should be planned in such a way as to give the highest benefit to the patient. In other words, we cannot consider the patient as the sum of interconnected modules but as a person eager to communicate. Let's imagine an aphasic patient with damage to one lexicon and to one conversion procedure (Phoneme-to-Grapheme [Ph→G] or Grapheme-to-Phoneme [G→Ph]). Again the order in which the rehabilitation interventions are carried out is important. In the above example, recovery of the lexicon should be pursued first because its recovery is more important for the patient than recovery of the conversion procedures. Damage to the POL will prevent the patient from finding words he or she wants to say and from reading irregular words. Damage to Ph→G mechanisms only prevents him or her from writing unknown words to dictation, and damage to G→Ph conversion procedures only prevents the patient from reading unknown words. However, priority of rehabilitation of the lexicon is opportune only if its recovery is likely. If this is not the case, the patient should be trained to use the output from the supposedly undamaged POL and use the recovered G→Ph conversion procedures (which are now the primary goal of rehabilitation) in order to produce a plausible rendition of the word.[1]

Needless to say, these are very abstract considerations which may not hold in any specific case. When it comes to making decisions about a real patient we cannot be satisfied by simply stating that there is functional damage here and there. To give but one example, when two or more modules are damaged, besides the simple fact that they are damaged, the relative degree of their impairment must be considered in planning therapy. Moreover, these considerations are valid only if we know nothing about whether a specific impairment has more or less chance to be remediated than another. They derive from the structure of the lexicon and do not consider what we might know about the possible effect of specific therapeutic interventions. Simply stated, our argument is that the structure of the lexicon cannot be ignored when planning rehabilitation.

So far we have always referred to damage and therapy of lexical–semantic disorders. Cognitive neuropsychological models of the lexical–semantic system are not identical but there is general agreement on their basic structure. This is obviously convenient when planning rehabilitation because one does not have to chose between competing models. But what happens when patients have disorders at the sentence level? Models of sentence production and comprehension are not as detailed as models of the lexicon and there is no general agreement on one or the other. Just consider how many different interpretations of agrammatism have been offered (provided agrammatism were a sentence-level disorder). In the case of a patient with sentence production deficits, one can try to locate the deficit with reference to Garrett's (1975; 1980) model, for instance, but even if this endeavour is successful, the speech pathologist will have only rather general guidelines for planning intervention.

CONCLUSION

Summing up, we have argued that: (1) Speech therapy has sometimes been intuitive and imprecise but in most cases based on a definite—albeit vague—theoretical position. (2) The new dyslexias and dysgraphias are misleading; besides subsuming patients with deficits to different cognitive components, they lead to some aspects of the patient's disorder being ignored and should not be considered when planning rehabilitation. (3) Even if it were true that modules are functionally independent, the organisation of the lexicon and the relevance of the various disorders to the patient dictate some priorities.

---

[1] We are grateful to Argye Hillis for having attracting our attention to this question.

The unsolved question is: Can treatment be guided by cognitive theory? An easy answer is *no*. Cognitive neuropsychology does not indicate what should be done or how it is to be done. As Caramazza (1989) puts it "The promise of cognitive neuropsychology as a guide for the choice of intervention strategies is still largely unfulfilled" (p. 396). Cognitive neuropsychology has fostered and made explicit knowledge about the nature of aphasia. Its contribution has been invaluable and a cognitive neuropsychological evaluation can disclose quite detailed and specific aspects of the dysfunction in need of remediation; however, the contribution of cognitive neuropsychology to aphasia therapy does not consist in new and explicit guidelines for the remediation of the various disorders.

That being said, the answer to the question of whether treatment can be guided by cognitive theory can also be *yes*, because the more you know about the disorder the better you are equipped to treat it. Our assumptions about the structure of the cognitive apparatus and its processing mechanisms invite a principled approach to treatment. The most important contribution of cognitive neuropsychology to aphasia therapy lies in the massive reduction of the theoretically-motivated choices left open to the therapist. Clearly articulated and detailed hypotheses about representations and processing of cognitive functions allow rejection of all those strategies for treatment that are not theoretically justified. The more detailed the cognitive model, the narrower the spectrum of rationally motivated treatments; whereas the less fine-grained the cognitive model, the greater the number of theoretically justifiable therapeutic interventions.

Our point here is that, in the absence of any hypothesis about whether and how intervention can modify a damaged function and about which cognitive processes are modifiable, the most rational way to proceed is to implement a therapeutic programme coherent with what we know about the damaged component(s). We are not saying that detailed models of cognitive functioning are by themselves sufficient to dictate the choice of the only possible therapeutic intervention; models cannot dictate what to do but they help us to establish whether or not there is a theoretical rationale for a given approach.

To conclude, the emperor is not naked but his new clothes can only be perceived with considerable sagacity and skilfulness. And last but not least, therapy is not synonymous with the task. Therapy takes place at the interaction between the aphasic patient and the speech pathologist. The patient is not a passive recipient of therapy and the therapist is not a machine. They must continually adapt their behaviour to what the partner does and says. But that is another story.

REFERENCES

Basso, A., Capitani, E., & Zanobio, M.E. (1982). Pattern of recovery of oral and written expression and comprehension in aphasic patients. *Behavioural Brain Research, 6,* 115–128.

Bay, E. (1964). Principles of classification and their influence on our concepts of aphasia. In A.V.S. de Reuck & M. O'Connor (Eds.), *Disorders of language.* (pp. 122–142). London: Churchill.

Caramazza, A. (1986). On drawing inferences about the structure of normal cognitive systems from the analysis of patterns of impaired performance: The case for single-patient studies. *Brain and Cognition, 5,* 41–66.

Caramazza, A. (1989). Cognitive neuropsychology and rehabilitation: An unfulfilled promise? In X. Seron & G. Deloche (Eds.), *Cognitive approaches in neuropsychological rehabilitation.* (pp. 383–398). Hillsdale, NJ.

Caramazza, A., & Badecker W. (1989). Patient classification in neuropsychological research. *Brain and Cognition, 10,* 256–295.

Coltheart, M., & Byng, S. (1989). A treatment for surface dyslexia. In X. Seron & G. Deloche (Eds.), *Cognitive approaches in neuropsychological rehabilitation.* (pp. 159–174). Hillsdale, NJ.

Coltheart, M., & Funnell, E. (1987). Reading and writing. One lexicon or two? In D.A. Allport, D.G. MacKay, W. Prinz, & E. Scheere (Eds.), *Language perception and production: Shared mechanisms in listening, reading and writing.* London: Academic Press.

Damasio, H. (1991). Neuroanatomical correlates of the aphasias. In M.T. Sarno (Ed.) *Acquired Aphasia.* (pp. 45–71) New York: Academic press (2nd edition).

Ducarne de Ribaucourt, B. (1986). *Rééducation sémiologique de l'aphasie.* Paris: Masson.

Garrett, M. F. (1975). The analysis of sentence production. In G.H. Bower (Ed.), *The psychology of learning and motivation,* Vol. 9 (pp. 133–177). New York: Academic Press.

Garrett, M.F. (1980). Levels of processing in sentence production. In B. Butterworth (Ed.), *Language Production,* Vol. 1.(pp. 177–220) New York: Academic Press.

Hanson, W.R., & Cicciarelli, A.W. (1978). The time, amount, and pattern of language improvement in adult aphasics. *British Journal of Disorders of Communication, 3,* 59–63.

Howard, D., & Hatfield, F.M. (1987). *Aphasia therapy: Historical and contemporary issues.* Hove, UK: Psychology Press.

Kertesz, A. (1979) *Aphasia and associated disorders: Taxonomy, localization and recovery.* New York: Grune & Stratton.

Kertesz, A., & McCabe, P. (1977). Recovery patterns and prognosis in aphasia. *Brain, 100,* 1–18.

McCarthy, R.A., & Warrington, E.K. (1990). *Cognitive neuropsychology. A clinical introduction.* San Diego: Academic Press.

Schuell, H. (1974). The treatment of aphasia. In L.F. Sies (Ed.) *Aphasia theory and therapy: Selected lectures and papers of Hildred Schuell.* Baltimore: University Park Press.

Schuell, H., Jenkins, J.J., & Jimenez-Pabon, E. (1964). *Aphasia in adults.* New York: Harper & Row.

Shallice T. (1988). *From neuropsychology to mental structure.* Cambridge: Cambridge University Press.

Shewan, C.M., & Bandur, D.L. (1986). *Treatment of aphasia: A language-oriented approach.* London: Taylor & Francis.

Wepman, J.M. (1951). *Recovery from aphasia.* New York: Ronald.

Manuscript received October 1999

NEUROPSYCHOLOGICAL REHABILITATION, 2000, *10* (3), 231–247

From theory to therapy in aphasia: Where are we now and where to next?

Wendy Best[1] and Lyndsey Nickels[1,2]

[1]Birkbeck College, University of London, UK and
[2]Macquarie University, Sydney, Australia

Language therapy for acquired aphasia has come under much scrutiny in recent years, with debate focusing on whether or not it is effective and how best efficacy can be measured. In this paper, we argue that although the efficacy of many different therapies has been clearly documented, there remain unanswered questions. In particular, it is still difficult to predict which therapeutic task or approach will be successful at remediating which particular disorders. We argue that this is particularly true in the rehabilitation of anomia, whilst in other areas (e.g., reading) the relationship between deficit, task, and outcome is easier to interpret. We discuss in detail the reasons for these differences arguing that specificity of theoretical models, complexity of therapeutic tasks, and a lack of (reporting of) comprehensive assessment of linguistic deficits all contribute to the problem. We conclude that research needs to perform a microanalysis of the interactions between tasks and deficits.

INTRODUCTION

Language therapy for acquired aphasia has a long history (Howard & Hatfield, 1987). The techniques used have been many and varied and some are still in use today. There has been much debate over the past few decades about whether or

Requests for reprints should be sent to Wendy Best, Department of Psychology, Birkbeck College, Malet Street, London WC1E 7HX (e-mail: w.best@bbk.ac.uk) or Lyndsey Nickels, Psychology Department, Macquarie University, Sydney, NSW 2109, Australia (e-mail: lyndsey@frogmouth.bhs.mq.edu.au).

We would like to acknowledge the help of RD, MF, JOW and PG and to thank them and their relatives for enthusiastic participation in the project. David Howard, Carolyn Bruce, and Claire Gatehouse were involved in the research with the computerised aid which was funded by the MRC and the Stroke Association. We would also like to thank the reviewers for helpful comments on an earlier draft. David Howard carried out the statistical analysis of the data for the study. Lyndsey Nickels was funded by a Wellcome Trust Fellowship during the preparation of this paper.

© 2000 Psychology Press Ltd
http://www.tandf.co.uk/journals/pp/09602011.html

not therapy for aphasia is effective. However, as Howard (1986) argues, this question is inappropriate and probably unanswerable. Rather, we need to consider whether a particular therapy can be shown to be effective in remediating an individual person's aphasia (or aspect of that aphasia). There have now been many reports, published within a cognitive neuropsychological framework, that show just that—a specific therapy task results in a clear improvement of a particular skill. For example, Hillis and Caramazza (1994) showed that matching a written word to the correct picture (from a large array) improved the ability of JJ, a person with aphasia, to find the names of pictures. Similiarly, De Partz (1986) showed that reteaching of the correspondence between letters and their realisation as sounds improved the reading ability of SP (with acquired dyslexia). In this paper we use "efficacy" in this limited sense of demonstrable improvement on a specific task, although generalisation to natural communication is obviously crucial.

Which therapy for which problem?

A key aim of research into the treatment of aphasic language is to be able to determine which therapy is most appropriate to remediate which particular language deficit. In other words if an aphasic person presents with problem X, then treatment Y is the most appropriate and this will produce result Z.[1] How far have we progressed towards this goal? We will take examples from two different areas of language processing—disorders of word production (anomia) and disorders of reading (acquired dyslexia).

First, in the case of anomia, it has been clearly demonstrated that several different tasks can improve naming for some aphasic people (e.g., word–picture matching, Marshall, Pound, White-Thompson, & Pring, 1990; reading aloud, Miceli, Amitrano, Capasso, & Caramazza, 1996). Is it possible to predict which people with which levels of breakdown in word production (for a model of speech production see, for example, Butterworth, 1989) will benefit from a particular therapy task? Nickels and Best (1996a,b) addressed precisely this issue, focusing particularly on word–picture matching. They found that from the (published) results of research, it was difficult to draw any clear conclusions. There were anomic people who appeared to have similar levels of breakdown (e.g., lexical–semantic deficits) but yet responded differently to therapy. They conclude that "it is still not clear exactly how the treatments are working, and how they relate to levels of deficit" (1996b, p. 134).

---

[1] Of course, we acknowledge that in clinical practice it is both the deficits and the areas of relative strength that are taken into account. However, in published research this is often overlooked with the emphasis being placed on the impairment(s).

The contrasts with the apparently clear findings from the remediation of acquired surface dyslexia. Weekes and Coltheart (1996) have recently reported a treatment study involving NW, a person with acquired dyslexia (specifically surface dyslexia). NW's difficulty in reading irregularly spelled words (e.g., yacht, colonel, pint) was identified as being due to a deficit in visual word recognition. (He was poor at visual lexical decision making with pseudo-homophones; e.g., Which is the real word: turtle/tertle?) Previously, Byng and Coltheart (1986; Coltheart & Byng, 1989) described a treatment programme involving EE who also had a problem in visual word recognition (resulting in surface dyslexia). Therefore, Weekes and Coltheart treated NW's difficulty in reading irregular words aloud using this same therapy technique. The treatment involved pairing the written word with a picture representing the word meaning (a pictorial mnemonic)[2]. The results of the therapy with NW were exactly the same as those found by Byng and Coltheart for EE: After therapy, both EE and NW showed a specific treatment effect (treated words were read better than untreated words), and generalisation (untreated words were read better than they were before therapy). These results seem promising—two people who were identified as having the same level of breakdown in reading, when given the same type of therapy, responded in the same way. However, what remains to be seen is whether the same pattern of results will occur when the same techniques are applied to other people in further replication studies. Indeed, evidence from the rehabilitation of anomia (and other areas such as sentence processing) suggests that the picture can become less clear as more case studies are reported.[3]

The problem of prediction

The example from Weekes and Coltheart (1996) illustrates the ideal—determine the level of breakdown in language processing, identify a therapy that is appropriate for that level of breakdown, predict the pattern of change, and obtain these results. Unfortunately, predicting the results of therapy is not always so straightforward. Nickels and Best (1996b) describe three people with anomia, all of whom were identified as having semantic deficits. All three were

---

[2] Unlike Byng and Coltheart, Weekes and Coltheart also included a further aid—a letter string, whose pronunciation via conventional letter-sound rules was the pronunciation of the word being learned, was also printed on each card.

[3] The difference between the domains of reading and word production may also be important. Reading is a late acquired skill (in comparison to word production) and may be "relatively" modular—and hence more predictable in its breakdown and subsequent remediation. In comparison, word production relies heavily on many other domains and the complexity of interactions between domains may be part of the difficulty in interpreting both disorders of word production and the effects of therapy on this skill.

given the same type of therapy—word–picture matching with semantic distractors. Far from the results being predictable each of the three responded in a different way to the therapy. Why is it that the outcome of therapy can be so hard to predict? We will begin our discussion by using as an example a series of studies concerned with the remediation of reading in deep dyslexia.

Treatment of deep dyslexia

De Partz (1986) described a therapy programme for SP who was deep dyslexic. SP made semantic errors in reading aloud and was unable to read aloud non-words or even provide a sound for a written letter. De Partz retaught SP to assemble the phonology of non-words (i.e. read them aloud) by using a sequence of therapy tasks starting with the relearning of letter–sound (grapheme–phoneme) correspondences. At the conclusion of the therapy, SP's reading of words has improved substantially (with a reduction in semantic errors) and he was able to read aloud non-words (which had previously ben impossible). Nickels (1992, 1995) used the same technique with TC, another deep dyslexic, who, like SP, was unable to read aloud non-words. However, although after therapy TC's word reading was greatly improved and there was a reduction in the incidence of semantic errors, he remained unable to read non-words. This contrasts with SP who was able to read non-words after treatment.

Why did SP and TC show different patterns of improvement—in other words why were the results of therapy not predictable for TC? The first point to note is that the therapy was effective for both SP and TC—they both showed improved reading of words (and, more importantly, could use this to help their spoken naming). However, this improvement had been achieved in different ways. After therapy SP, when unable to read aloud a word, would assemble the phonology of that word (using the taught grapheme–phoneme corres-pondences to identify the phonemes and then blend these together to form a syllable). In contrast, when TC was unable to read a word aloud he would identify only the first phoneme of the word (using the taught grapheme–phoneme correspondences), this phoneme then served as a phonemic cue, enabling him to read the word aloud (by facilitating retrieval of the phonolog-ical form from the lexicon). Thus, the same therapy task was effective in improving SP and TC's reading by rather different means (assembling the phonology vs. self-cueing). It follows, then, that some of the difficulty in predicting the results of therapy is because that even for those with apparently the same level of deficit, the same task can work in different ways (which may lead to different results).

There is a further lesson to be learned from these studies of the remediation of non-lexical reading, relating to the level of detail of the deficit analysis which precedes therapy. In order to read aloud non-words, it is not sufficient to know grapheme–phoneme correspondences, one must also be able to assemble (blend) the phonemes into a syllable. The reason that TC (Nickels, 1992) did not benefit from relearning grapheme–phoneme correspondences in the same way that SP (De Partz, 1986) had, was that he was unable to blend the resulting phonemes into syllables (and also unable to relearn this ability). Thus, for TC there were two levels of disruption to the non-lexical reading route: Loss of knowledge of grapheme–phoneme correspondences and impaired blending procedures. In other words, the initial assessment of TC's reading problem was not sufficiently detailed to fully specify the nature of the breakdown in non-lexical reading. This, then, is a further complication in our attempts to predict the results of therapy: Although SP and TC did have identical deficits at one level, a more detailed analysis would have revealed that they were indeed different. Berndt and Mitchum (1994; Mitchum & Berndt, 1991) demonstrate the advantages of, and necessity for, this more detailed analysis in another study aimed at remediating non-lexical reading. They identify that deep dyslexic, LR, had a number of difficulties in the component processes involved in non-lexical reading and took these deficits into account in the therapeutic procedure (readers are referred to the original papers for details).

Finally, the difference between SP and TC was not restricted to the fact that TC had an additional blending deficit. His response to therapy was also different because of the effectiveness of phonemic cues in helping to produce a response. In other words, the presence of one strength (cueability) affected the results of therapy as much as the absence of another skill (blending). If TC had been unable to make use of a phonemic cue, obtaining the phonemes derived from the letters of the written word would not have influenced his ability to say that word aloud—in other words his reading would not have improved.

Clearly, the formula that was our original goal (problem X + treatment Y = result Z) needs amending. The situation is far more complex, and problem X simply cannot be considered in isolation.[4] Rather, the amended formula might read:

$$(\text{problem } X \; [+ \text{ skills a,b,c}; \; - \text{ skills d,e,f}] + \text{treatment } Y = \text{result } Z)$$

That is, given problem X in the presence of skills a, b, c and absence of skills d, e, f; then if you do therapy y, you should get result Z.

What we are arguing, therefore, is that to gain the maximum (clinical) benefit from research into remediation we need to be clear about the relationship between therapy and outcome. The earlier example, illustrates that we

---

[4] We make a distinction between the broader strengths and weaknesses that are routinely taken into account in clinical practice and the very specific linguistic skills (a, b, c) and deficits (d, e, f) that become clear only with very detailed analyses of language processing. Examples are given in the main text.

need detailed analyses of the language skills of the aphasic person, in order to be able to interpret which skills impact on the results of therapy. At a gross level, therapy studies clearly do take a person's skills into account—for example, no clinician would use auditory word–picture matching as a therapy task with a person who had severe peripheral auditory and/or visual processing problems. However, a more detailed analysis of impaired and retained skills has often not been reported in the literature. We would suggest that without this information, it is impossible to understand exactly why one person responded in a certain way to a therapy, and why another person with (at a gross level) a similar problem responded differently. For example, in early studies of the treatment of anomia little attention was given to the other skills of the anomic people involved (e.g., Howard et al., 1985). This was despite the fact that the therapy tasks used necessitated the use of many processing components not involved in word production (the problem being treated). For example, word–picture matching, one task that has been used in many studies, must also involve input processes in reading comprehension (where a written word is used), picture recognition processes, plus processes involved in reading aloud (where the word is read aloud before selection). Thus, differences in the pattern of strengths and weaknesses of processes across these areas could impact on the effect of this task on subsequent naming. Furthermore, in addition to the basic processing elements involved in a task, there are clearly other skills and factors that will impact on the effects of therapy: For example, to correctly perform word–picture matching, the person must be able to "hold", "compare", and "decide" between the semantically related items. All these factors make it less surprising that Nickels and Best (1996a,b) found it difficult to interpret the pattern of results from using therapy of this kind with different anomic subjects. Moreover, word–picture matching is a relatively simple therapy task compared to many that are used (e.g., cueing hierarchies).

We conclude by presenting data from a therapy study which illustrates many of the points discussed above. This study began by using previous research to develop a clear set of predictions regarding the efficacy of a therapy task depending on both the deficits and intact skills of some people with anomia. However, these predictions were not supported. Nevertheless, with the detailed analysis of a broader range of skills and consideration of the processes involved in the (complex) therapy task, the reason for the failure of these predictions becomes clearer.

TREATMENT STUDY

We present here an outline of a study that illustrates the main points of our paper. Detailed information on the treatment study is provided elsewhere (Best, Howard, Bruce, & Gatehouse, 1997).

Much of the research into treatment for anomia has focused on tasks involving semantic processing such as word-to-picture matching. In contrast, the focus of this study is on using orthographic cues to help word retrieval.

Bruce and Howard (1988) ask the question, why don't aphasic speakers cue their own word finding? That is, why don't they use any retained knowledge of initial letters to help access spoken word forms? Bruce and Howard worked with 20 people with anomia and asked three questions which reflect three skills necessary to self-cue word finding:

1. Can people indicate the initial letters for words they cannot produce?
2. Can they convert letters to sounds?
3. Does naming benefit from phonemic cues (over and above extra time)?

Unsurprisingly, the participants did not all show the same pattern (e.g. only half benefited from initial phoneme cues). However, importantly, none of the 20 people had all three skills that would be necessary in order to self-cue their word finding. Five people had skills (1) and (3), i.e. they were able to point to the correct initial letter for some words even when unable to produce the spoken form and they were better at finding words when initial phoneme (plus schwa) cues were provided. If they had possessed skill (2) they might have been able to convert the initial letters into phonemes to cue their word finding.

In order to make the link between letters and sounds (step 2 above) Bruce and Howard (1987) devised a computerised aid that converted letters to sounds. They worked with the five people who were able to select initial letters for pictures they could not name and who benefited from initial phoneme cues. When taught to use the aid (in a picture naming paradigm) they found all five people's word finding improved (the pattern of improvement varied and readers are referred to the original article for details).

In the 1990s a research project was set up to replicate and extend these findings. In particular, one aim of the study was to determine for whom the aid was most appropriate in order to make recommendations for efficient use of the aid in clinical practice.

In relation to our formula

(problem X [+ skills a,b,c; – skills d,e,f] + treatment Y = result Z)

we worked with people with anomia (X), providing treatment with the computerised aid (Y) with the aim of improving word finding (Z). The difference from the original study was that people varied in the skills that they retained in relation to their word finding. While Bruce and Howard included only people who had both some letter knowledge and benefited from cues, we also included people who did not have letter knowledge and some who did not benefit from phonemic cues. Overall there are four possible combinations of these abilities (see Table 1).

TABLE 1
Possible combinations of abilities with predicted outcome

Benefit from cues	Letter pointing	Predicted benefit from aid treatment
Yes	Yes	Yes
No	Yes	No
Yes	No	No
No	No	No

For the purposes of this paper we select only 4 of the 13 people included in the study, one to represent each of the previous patterns of skills.[5]

Background information and performance on naming tasks is provided in Table 2. All the patients were male and aged in their 60s. All had suffered a left hemisphere cerebrovascular accident. All had adequate comprehension for single concrete words as reflected in the scores on the word-to-picture matching task. Good performance on this task is also suggestive of relatively intact picture processing. However, all four had considerable word finding problems in conversation. This is reflected in the proportion of items correct in the picture naming task. The individual descriptions below discuss the skills predicted to be important for successful use of the aid (cf. the final two sections of Table 2). In addition to these assessments, the errors made and variables influencing naming were investigated for each individual.[6] Unfortunately, in common with many people with anomia, all four showed a complex pattern of naming breakdown and a clear single functional lesion within a model such as that of Butterworth (1989) is hard to determine. In each case, however, word finding problems formed a major part of their aphasia.

---

[5] In fact, of the 13 people treated with the aid, 12 showed at least some benefit. We are restricting the cases considered here to 4 in order to make clear the difficulty in predicting results of treatment.

[6] Each person made some semantic and some phonological errors in picture naming. In each case there were numerically more semantic than phonological errors (proportion of responses semantic error, phonological error: RD 0.11, 0.07, MF, 0.36, 0.14; JOW, 0.16, 0.03; PG 0.10, 0.01). The influence of variables was investigated using matched sets of items (see Best, 1996 for details). None of the four showed any influence of semantic category (living/non-living), operativity, or age of acquisition on performance. MF was significantly worse at naming 3 syllable items (1 syllable, 0.58, 2 syllable, 0.67, 3 syllable, 0.38), none of the other three was influenced by length. PG and RD were significantly better at naming high than low frequency (/familiarity) items (PG high frequency/familiarity 0.37, low frequency/familiarity 0.26; RD high frequency/familiarity 0.15, low frequency/familiarity 0.03). MF and JOW were not influenced by frequency. Thus, interpretation of the naming impairments in relation to a single functional deficit in a model of production is far from straightforward, e.g., RD is influenced by frequency/familiarity, perhaps suggesting a lexical deficit, yet he makes the second highest proportion of phonological errors, perhaps suggesting a difficulty post-lexically.

TABLE 2
Background data

Patient	Age (years)	Sex	Time post-onset (years)	Western Aphasia Battery		Word-to-picture matching		Picture naming			Letter pointing	
				Category	AQ	Auditory	Visual	No cue	Cue	Sig.	Proportion correct	Sig.
RD	62	M	2	Broca's	42	0.93	0.93	0.10	0.26	Y	0.20	Y
MF	67	M	1.5	Anomic	76	1.00	0.87	0.56	0.57	N	0.15	Y
JOW	62	M	4	Anomic	69	0.95	0.95	0.29	0.36	Y	0.10	N
PG	65	M	1	Transcortical sensory	72	0.93	0.85	0.39	0.36	N	0.00	N

Word-to-picture matching is from Kay, Lesser, & Coltheart (1992; $n = 40$), the figure shown is the proportion correct (controls range 0.88–1.00).

Picture naming shows the proportion of pictures named correctly (out of 194 items) in a no cue condition and in a cueing condition where an initial phoneme cue (plus schwa) was presented immediately after the picture. Y indicates significantly better performance in the cued condition (McNemar test, $p < .05$), N means the two conditions were not significantly different.

Letter pointing shows the proportion of pictures for which the correct initial letter was selected (from a choice of nine letters on a letter board) for items which were not named correctly within 5 seconds (from a set of 49 items). Significance of the proportion correct above chance is indicated as above by Y and N (Binomial test, $p < .05$).

Sig., Significant.

RD

RD's skills matched those of the original 5 people who were treated with the aid (Bruce & Howard, 1987). He was able to select from initial letters for pictures he was unable to name. In addition, his naming was improved by initial phoneme cues. The prediction was that he could learn to use the aid to provide the missing link between these two skills (converting initial letters into phonemes which could act as phonemic cues) thereby improving word finding.[7]

MF

MF's naming did not benefit from phonemic cues. However, he was able to chose from initial letters at greater than chance rates for items he was unable to name. Thus, whilst he might be able to select an initial letter and convert this to a sound using the aid, the prediction was that this would not help word finding as his naming was not helped by phonological cues.

JOW

JOW's skills show a double dissociation with those of MF. He did benefit from phonemic cues but was unable to chose from letters at greater than chance rates for items he was unable to name. So, the prediction was that JOW would be unable to chose from the letters on the aid and would not be able to use this to improve naming (Best et al., 1997 provide further details on this and other treatments for JOW's anomia).

PG

PG had neither of the key skills one would predict would be required to benefit from the aid. He neither selected initial letters for items he could not name nor benefited from phonemic cues. In this case the strong prediction can be made of no benefit from treatment with the aid.

In summary, on the basis of detailed assessment of naming abilities and related skills only 1 of the 4 people described above (RD) would be predicted to benefit from treatment involving a computerised aid which converts letters to sounds. The remaining 3 people all lack one or both of the skills thought to be necessary to benefit.

---

[7] In Bruce and Howard's original study the aid not only improved word finding (treated items were named better than control items) but also acted as a prosthesis. That is, after treatment, four people were better at naming with the aid present that without (the fifth's performance approached ceiling). Thus, it is possible for the aid to be effective in two ways. It may improve word finding abilities *per se*, it may also be needed as a prosthesis to aid word finding.

Treatment

A set of pictures was presented three times for baseline naming. From the original set, a set of treatment items ($n = 50$) and set of control items ($n = 50$, not to be seen during treatment) were selected individually for each participant. The treatment and control items were matched for number correct across baseline naming. Filler pictures ($n = 50$) which had had a high success rate during baseline naming were also included in order to provide encouragement.

This version of the aid had nine letters available which when pressed produced the appropriate phoneme (plus schwa). All the picture names began with one of these initial letters.

Treatment took place once a week, over 5 weeks, for about 1 hour on each occasion. During the first three sessions participants were instructed that they must use the aid prior to naming the picture. During the final two sessions use of the aid was optional. The same sequence was followed for each of the treated and filler pictures which were presented in a random order.

1. Press the initial letter—if failed go to step (4).
2. Encourage repetition of the cue.
3. Name the picture—if failed go to step (7).
4. Therapist points to three of the letters for participant to press the correct one—if failed go to step (7).
5. Encourage repetition of cue.
6. Name the picture—if failed go to step (7).
7. Therapist says the name and asks for repetition.

Results

The results of treatment with the aid are shown in Table 3. The results were not as predicted. In all four cases there was significant benefit from the aid (as reflected in improved picture naming): Performance at post-test 1 was significantly better than baseline naming.[8]

---

[8] Clearly, the only change of real value is change in word finding in real-life conversation. In the case of JOW a change in connected speech was clear. He was rated blind, by experienced therapists, as significantly better at both finding words and transmitting a message, after treatment (see Best et al., 1997 for details). RD continues to show carryover from the treatment to word finding in conversation and himself feels the aid was of considerable benefit. Bruce (1996) notes that RD continued to respond to phonological cues after treatment and suggests his problem may relate to initiating speech output. Treatment for his anomia has continued and he is now able to write initial letters to cue his word finding in conversation. In both cases the change in conversation was apparent without the aid present. However, neither MF nor PG showed lasting functional benefit from the treatment. We do not wish to draw strong conclusions from these findings as the treatment lasted only five sessions and there was no treatment directed at carry-over to conversation. Rather we would note that it is extremely positive that carry-over was found for RD and JOW.

TABLE 3
Results of the treatment

Patient	Mean of three baseline scores	Post-test 1 (without aid) Prop.	Sig.	Post-test 1 Effect of aid Effect	Sig.	Post-test 2 (without aid) Prop.	Sig.	Item set	Generalised? Pre.	Post-1	Post-2	Gensn.
RD	0.17	0.32	Y	0.10	Y*	0.38	Y	Treated	0.00	0.32	0.38	Partial**
								Controls	0.00	0.22	0.20	
MF	0.58	0.71	Y	−0.08	N	0.65	N	Treated	0.29	0.66	0.54	Partial**
								Controls	0.25	0.50	0.36	
JOW	0.34	0.54	Y	−0.06	N	0.53	Y	Treated	0.08	0.40	0.34	Full
								Controls	0.08	0.40	0.34	
PG	0.40	0.59	Y	−0.09	N	0.50	N	Treated	0.10	0.42	0.22	Full
								Controls	0.10	0.46	0.24	

Figures shown are proportion correct with the exception of the fifth column which shows the proportion of items successfully named with the aid minus those named without the aid. Throughout the table Y indicates statistical significance at $p < .05$ level and N indicates non-significance.
Post-test 1 was carried out immediately after the completion of treatment. The post-treatment score was compared with the 3 baseline scores using a Wilcoxon test. The first post-test was carried out using an ABBA design with and without the aid. The significance of the difference between these was examined using the McNemar test. For RD there was a significant effect of using the aid. * Detailed analysis showed that this was for the treated items.
Post-test 2 was carried out 5 weeks after post-test 1. Both MF and PG showed significant decline relative to post-test 1 (McNemar test).
The final section shows the data for two sub-sets of items: treated ($n = 50$) and control ($n = 50$) items. These were selected so as to be the most difficult items for each person as indicated by baseline naming.
** In two cases (RD and MF) the apparent partial generalisation to control items may simply reflect regression to the mean for those items that were initially selected to be poorly named. That is, if there is some variation in the items that are correct between occasions, and the set have selected to be poorly named on one occasion, they will, by chance alone, be better named on a subsequent occasion.
Prop., Proportion; Sig, Significant; Pre., pre-test; Post-1, Post-2, Post-test 1 and 2; Gensn., generalisation.

For RD the improvement had been predicted. However, MF, JOW, and PG all showed significant improvement after treatment despite not appearing to have the skills required to benefit from the aid. The results were very encouraging from one point of view, suggesting that it may be worth trying this type of treatment for many people with anomia. However, the findings confirm that the success or otherwise of treatments for anomia are hard to predict. With these results it is difficult to be clear about the theory of the therapy and impossible to make sensible recommendations as to whom the aid may be suitable for.

Our predictions clearly need refining. In fact, in the individual cases, taking account of the full complexity of the treatment task, one can devise plausible *post hoc* explanations for the findings. The important point for this paper, however, is that, even in this study which included related skills in assessment, we still could not predict the outcome of treatment without further detailed analysis.

One of the possible reasons for this is the complexity of the treatment. The treatment has many components including trying to name the picture, selecting from a choice of initial letters, hearing the letters converted to sounds, using cues to access spoken word forms, and producing the words. One possibility is that different components of the treatment were important for different people.

Microanalysis of the effects of treatment

RD

As it was predicted that RD would benefit and this turned out to be the case, perhaps in his case, additional consideration of how the treatment worked is not warranted. In fact a close examination of the results (Table 3) is informative. RD's naming improved greatly after treatment. In addition, he was better at naming the pictures with the aid present than without. The effect was probably limited to treated items (the partial generalisation to controls may be explained by regression to the mean, see table legend for further explanation) but it was a lasting effect. Thus RD was like the original aphasic people treated by Bruce and Howard (1987), the aid helped him access treated items and he was best able to do this with the aid present as a prosthesis after treatment (see Bruce 1996 for further discussion of the treatment of RD's anomia).

MF

As MF did not benefit from phonemic cues, it had been predicted that treatment with the aid would not improve naming. However, the results showed a significant improvement. As for RD the improvement in control items was less than for treated items and may simply reflect regression to the mean. The improvement was short lasting; MF's performance had significantly declined 5 weeks later. One reason for the item-specific, short-lasting effect of treatment, would be that MF *as predicted*, did not benefit from cues and therefore the aid was not useful to him. Instead, the final step in the treatment, repetition of the targets, may have helped him. Perhaps he did not have difficulty in accessing the word forms from a lexicon (the level at which cues could be of benefit) but rather with later stages of production. It is possible that he had accessed (at least some of) the phonological forms but could not assemble the phonology for production. There are two important lines of evidence in support of this proposal. First, in treatment sessions 4 and 5, when not required to use the aid, MF never chose to press the letters. Second, MF's naming was influenced by the length of the stimuli, he was worse on longer items, in line with a post-lexical effect on production (for a detailed description of MF's naming, see Best, 1996, but see also footnote 6).

JOW

As JOW could not select from nine initial letters for items he could not name it had seemed unlikely that he would be able to benefit from treatment with the aid. In fact he showed a significant improvement which both generalised fully to the untreated items and was maintained after the end of treatment. One reason for the success of the treatment probably lies in the fact that JOW's naming did benefit from a more restricted choice between three written letters. Also, in the treatment we incorporated a choice between a restricted set of three letters on the occasions when participants were unable to select from all nine letters (step 4, in the treatment). Thus, to understand how the treatment may have worked for JOW, we need to carry out a microanalysis of the treatment task as well as of his linguistic deficits and strengths. For further discussion of the ways in which the aid treatment may have worked for JOW see Best et al., 1997.

PG

PG neither benefited from phonological cues nor was able to select initial letters for words he could not find. Thus, the significant effect of the aid treatment is particularly difficult to explain. The effect was short lasting (with significant deterioration by post-test 2). However, there was full generalisation to the control items. PG's naming did not benefit from the aid being present after treatment. How then did it have its effect? One possibility is that, like JOW, PG was able to select from a set of initial letters restricted to three and that he was able to use orthographic information to address the speech output lexicon directly (Howard & Harding, 1998). Perhaps the therapy generally encouraged lexical access. One piece of information in line with this is that PG's naming was influenced by frequency and not be length which would fit with a lexical level deficit (Bruce, 1996). In addition, there was a non-significant trend for items that were correct in post-test 1 to be higher frequency than those that PG failed to name in post-test 1 (using treated and control items that were never correct during baseline assessment, log of lemma frequency from Celex database; correct x = 1.32, std = 0.48; incorrect x = 1.14, std = 0.62; unrelated t-test, $t(69) = 1.37, p < .1$, n.s.).

So, with a little creativity and a lot of detailed analysis it is possible to suggest plausible hypotheses for how the treatment may have worked in each case. This brings us back, from our example, to the main focus of the paper. It is only with such detailed microanalysis of deficits, strengths, and tasks, that we will further understand treatments for aphasia. In addition, the results of treatment should be examined relative to baseline scores and with respect to generalisation to untreated items or tasks, and maintenance of change. Finally, with respect to our "formula" for predicting the effects of treatment, we propose one further change highlighting the importance of task analysis

$$(\text{problem X } [+ \text{ skills a,b,c; } - \text{ skills d,e,f}]$$
$$+ \text{ treatment Y } [\text{with components i,j,k}] = \text{result Z}).$$

This is not a new suggestion but is something that is often not provided in published treatment studies.

CONCLUSIONS

In summary, consideration of studies of the treatment of acquired dyslexia and anomia show that it is possible to find the elusive link between therapy and outcome. So far this has been easier in the case of dyslexia but in both cases a microanalysis of the task alongside linguistic skills and deficits is necessary.

The data from the aid study illustrate the level of detailed analysis necessary to try to understand how a treatment works (particularly in the case of a multi-component treatment such as this). Nevertheless, clinically the results are very encouraging and suggest that this therapy may be able to help many people's word-finding. Because of this, and despite the problems in predicting the outcome, we would encourage therapists to include the aid (fairly easily accessible with today's technology) along with the range of other techniques available for the treatment of anomia.

Our understanding of treatment for aphasia will benefit from more studies in which there is detailed analysis of linguistic strengths and weaknesses and task demands. One way to achieve this would be using very simple treatment tasks (such as those used in facilitation studies) in research into treatment.

Clinically, in the meantime, therapists will continue to use a variety of broad-based tasks that work in different ways for different aphasic people but are very often effective. Examples of such treatments are semantically based tasks such as word-to-picture matching (Nickels & Best, 1996a) and sentence level tasks such as "mapping therapy" (Schwartz, Fink, & Saffran, 1995). The use of such treatments is justified in that they stand a very good chance of working for the maximum number of people. However, it is also important that we continue to develop our understanding of treatment and outcome so that precisely targeted therapy can be offered where possible.

REFERENCES

Berndt, R.S., & Mitchum, C.C. (1994). Approaches to the rehabilitation of "Phonological assembly": Elaborating the model of nonlexical reading. In M.J. Riddoch & G.W. Humphreys (Eds.), *Cognitive neuropsychology and cognitive rehabilitation*. Hove, UK: Lawrence Erlbaum Associates Ltd.

Best, W. (1996). When racquets are baskets but baskets are biscuits, where do the words come from? A single case study of formal paraphasic errors in aphasia. *Cognitive Neuropsychology, 13*, 443–480.

Best, W., Howard, D., Bruce, C., & Gatehouse, C. (1997). A treatment for anomia; combining semantics, phonology and orthography. In S. Chiat, J. Marshall, & J. Law (Eds.), *Language disorders in children and adults, psycholinguistic approaches to therapy.* (pp. 102–129). London: Whurr.

Bruce, C. (1996). *Sound effects: A new investigation of phonemic cues in aphasia*. Unpublished PhD Thesis, University College London.

Bruce, C., & Howard, D. (1987). Computer generated cues: An effective aid for naming in aphasia. *British Journal of Disorders of Communication, 22*, 191–201.

Bruce, C. & Howard, D. (1988). Why don't Broca's aphasics cue themselves? An investigation of phonemic cueing and tip-of-the-tongue information. *Neuropsychologia, 26*, 253–264.

Butterworth, B. (1989). Lexical access in speech production. In W. Marslen-Wilson (Ed.), *Lexical representation and process*. Cambridge, MA: MIT Press.

Byng, S., & Coltheart, M. (1986). Aphasia therapy research: Methodology requirements and illustrative results. In E. Hjelmquist & L.-G. Nilsson (Eds.), *Communication and handicap: Aspects of psychological compensation and technical aids*. New York: North Holland Elsevier Science.

Coltheart, M., & Byng, S. (1989). A treatment for surface dyslexia. In X. Seron & G. Deloche (Eds.), *Cognitive approaches in neuropsychological rehabilitation*. Hillsdale, N.J.: Erlbaum.

De Partz, M-P. (1986). Reeducation of a deep dyslexic patient: Rationale of the method and results. *Cognitive Neuropsychology, 3*, 149–177.

Hillis, A.E., & Caramazza, A. (1994). Theories of lexical processing and rehabilitation of lexical deficits. In M.J. Riddoch & G.W. Humphreys (Eds.), *Cognitive neuropsychology and cognitive rehabilitation*. Hove, UK: Lawrence Erlbaum Associates Ltd.

Howard, D. (1986). Beyond randomised controlled trials: The case for effective case studies of the effects of treatment in aphasia. *British Journal of Disorders of Communication, 21*, 89–102.

Howard, D., & Harding, D. (1998). Self-cueing of word retrieval by a woman with aphasia: Why a letter board works. *Aphasiology, 12*, (4/5), 399–420.

Howard, D., Patterson, K.E., Franklin, S., Orchard-Lisle, V., & Morton, J. (1985). The treatment of word retrieval deficits in aphasia: A comparison of two therapy methods. *Brain, 108*, 817–829.

Howard, D., & Hatfield, M.H. (1987). *Aphasia therapy*. Hove, UK: Lawrence Erlbaum Associates Ltd.

Kay, J., Lesser, R., & Coltheart, M. (1992). *Psycholinguistic Assessment of Language Processing in Aphasia (PALPA)*. Hove, UK: Psychology Press.

Marshall, J., Pound, C., White-Thomson, M., & Pring, T. (1990). The use of picture/word matching tasks to assist word retrieval in aphasic patients. *Aphasiology*, *4*, 167–84.

Miceli, G., Amitrano, A., Capasso, R., & Caramazza, A. (1996). The treatment of anomia resulting from output lexical damage: Analysis of two cases. *Brain & Language*, *52*, 150–174.

Mitchum, C.C., & Berndt, R.S. (1991). Diagnosis and treatment of "phonological assembly" in acquired dyslexia: An illustration of the cognitive neuropsychological approach. *Journal of Neurolinguistics*, *6*, 103–137.

Nickels, L.A. (1992). The autocue? Self-generated phonemic cues in the treatment of a disorder of reading and naming. *Cognitive Neuropsychology*, *9*, 155–182.

Nickels, L.A. (1995). Reading too little into reading? Strategies in the rehabilitation of acquired dyslexia. *European Journal of Disorders of Communication*, *30*, 37–50.

Nickels, L., & Best, W. (1996a). Therapy for naming disorders (Part 1): Principles, puzzles and progress, *Aphasiology*, *10*, 21–47.

Nickels, L., & Best, W. (1996b). Therapy for naming disorders (Part II): Specifics, surprises and suggestions, *Aphasiology*, *10*, 109–136.

Schwartz, M.F., Fink, R.B., & Saffran, E.M. (1995). The modular treatment of agrammatism. *Neuropsychological Rehabilitation*, *5*, 93–127.

Weekes, B., & Coltheart, M. (1996). Surface dyslexia and surface dysgraphia: Treatment studies and their theoretical implications. *Cognitive Neuropsychology*, *13*, 277–315.

Manuscript received October 1999

NEUROPSYCHOLOGICAL REHABILITATION, 2000, *10* (3), 249–278

Rehabilitation of spelling along the sub-word-level routine

Claudio Luzzatti[1], Camillo Colombo[2], Mirella Frustaci[3], and Francesca Vitolo[4]

[1]*Department of Psychology, University of Milan-Bicocca, Milan, and Aphasia Unit, Salvatore Maugeri Foundation, Montescano Medical Centre (Pavia)*
[2]*Passirana Rehabilitation Unit, G. Salvini Regional Hospital, Rho (Milan)*
[3]*San Carlo Regional Hospital, Milan, Italy*

Contemporary psycholinguistic models assume at least two routes in writing. These models have been verified on the basis of neuropsychological obser- vations of patients suffering from acquired dysgraphia. Many studies have discussed the architecture of the phonological and graphemic lexicons, their relations to semantic knowledge, and their disruption following neuropsycho- logical damage, but few have dealt with the nature of the sub-word level writing routine and its disruption. This may be due to the fact that, although this routine has importance in languages such as Italian, where orthography is much more regular and predictable, it appears to have a relatively reduced impact on the spelling abilities of educated English-speaking adults.

The present paper describes the rehabilitation of dysgraphia along the sub- word-level route in Italian dysgraphic patients. Particular emphasis is given to the treatment of the unit that allows the phonological analysis of the auditory string to be written. The treatment procedure was tested on two patients (RO, and DR suffering from severe dysgraphia. After treatment, the spelling ability of the two subjects was restored to practically normal levels on most subsets of items. Both patients were also able to apply the restored skills to spontaneous writing and to written naming tasks. Results are discussed in relation to the contemporary writing models and the principles of cognitive neurorehabilitation.

Requests for reprints should be sent to Claudio Luzzatti, Department of Psychology, University of Milan-Bicocca, Piazza dell'Ateneo Nuovo 1, 20126 Milano, Italy. E-mail: Luzz@.unimib.it

This research was supported by a grant from the Italian Ministero dell'Università e della Ricerca Scientifica e Tecnologica (MURST) to Claudio Luzzatti. The authors wish to thank Anna Basso for her helpful critical comments. We are also grateful to Frances Anderson for her careful review of the English version of the manuscript.

© 2000 Psychology Press Ltd
http://www.tandf.co.uk/journals/pp/09602011.html

INTRODUCTION

Contemporary cognitive psychology has demonstrated the need for at least two routes for the processing of written language. Neuropsychological cases showing double dissociation in reading and writing have been used to demonstrate two routine models, which explain how it is possible to read and write both words with irregular spelling and regular non-words. However, as interaction between cognitive psychology and cognitive neuropsychology is bi-directional, detailed cognitive models also permit a more accurate description of reading and writing disorders caused by cerebral damage. This should help to develop more focused approaches to the treatment of such disorders.

Many studies have discussed the architecture of representations in the phonological and graphemic input and output lexicons, their relations to semantic knowledge and their disruption in consequence of a neuropsychological disorder. Fewer studies, however, have dealt with the nature of sub-word level routes and their disruption, which may be explained by the relatively reduced impact these routes have on the reading and writing of educated English-speaking adults. In fact, while in English these routines seem to be relevant only when writing new words, they would appear to be more important in languages such as Italian, where orthography is much more regular and predictable.

When describing the sub-word-level writing route, major attention has been given to the phoneme-to-grapheme conversion unit. However, for conversion to be effective, the phonemic string must first be identified and segmented. This is practically the gamma unit described by Wernicke (1885/ 1886; De Bleser & Luzzatti, 1989) who believed that processing of written language would be possible by a sub-word-level route only, as opposed to an exclusive use of the lexical route for the processing of oral language.

As has already been implied, the importance of sub-word-level processing seems to vary from language to language, depending on the rate of regular spelling in the lexicon of each language. Lauria, Naydin, Tsvetkova, & Vinarskaya (1969), for instance, considered that, at least in Russian "the task of writing a given word (whether independently or from dictation) begins with the process of analysis of the phonetic composition of the word, or in other words with the breaking down of the phonetic stream of living speech into isolated phonemes" (p. 382).

Returning to contemporary information-processing models, it is reasonable to assume this processing unit is located at the acoustic-to-phonological conversion level. A similar level of analysis allows, however, some implications with respect to contemporary models of written language. In fact, if the level coincides with the acoustic-to-phonological conversion unit, spontaneous writing would require a feedback loop to the sub-word-level route, probably through the phonological output lexicon (and output buffer) and from there, back to the acoustic-to-phonological conversion unit. Furthermore, a spelling deficit following damage to this processing level would necessarily be accompanied by a deficit in repetition of non-words.

Cognitive models of written language and dysgraphia

The spelling deficits an adult patient may develop after a focal brain lesion are caused by impairment of the lexical and/or of the sub-word-level spelling routine. If we analyse the classical diagram for written language shown in Figure 1, the former follow damage to one of the processing units which connect the phonological input lexicon to the semantic system and subsequently to the graphemic output lexicon and the graphemic buffer. On the contrary, a deficit of the sub-word-level routine follows damage to one of the units which, starting from acoustic analysis, allow acoustic-to-phonological conversion of the perceived string of phones, its sequencing in the phonological buffer, the conversion of single phonemes in the corresponding orthographic representation and its sequencing at the graphemic buffer level.

This paper describes the rehabilitation of spelling deficits along the different processing units that make up the sub-word-level writing routine. Particular emphasis is given to the treatment of the acoustic-to-phonological conversion unit which allows the isolation and identification of the single phonemes which constitute the word to be written.

When analysing writing processing along the sub-word-level routine, one must keep in mind the following considerations:

1. Literate subjects usually write words along the lexical routine, i.e. by directly activating the appropriate representation in the graphemic output lexicon. Spelling disorders in aphasic patients usually follow damage to this routine. If patients are not able to retrieve a direct lexical representation, they will try to compensate the graphemic lexical damage using sub-word-level abilities. A patient who writes along the non-lexical spelling routine, however, will be able to write only regular words (and non-words) and will regularise words with irregular spelling. It is therefore to be expected that the efficacy of the routine will vary in relation to the orthographic regularity of each language.

2. Damage to the acoustic-to-phonological conversion process is implicated in the genesis of a spelling disorder. This is especially evident in languages where the sub-word-level routine is extensively used, such as Italian, while in languages with prevalent irregular, i.e. lexical, spelling, such as English or French, this level seems to be less relevant (Luria et al., 1969; Hatfield & Weddell, 1976). The identification of damage to the acoustic-to-phonological conversion—as opposed to the phoneme-to-grapheme conversion—is crucial for focused treatment of spelling deficits, as in the former case, the disorder is due to primary damage to phonemic analysis and identification. Abnormal

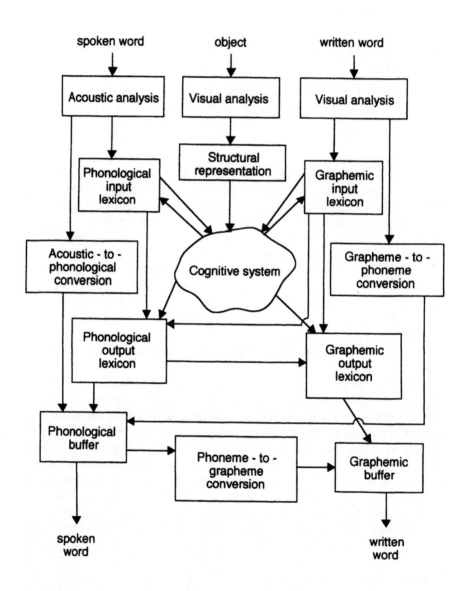

Figure 1.   Information processing model for picture naming, word naming, and spelling (adapted from Patterson, 1986).

analysis of the phonemic string will thus cause incorrect spelling even if the phoneme-to-grapheme conversion is unimpaired. Indirect proof of this hypothesis is constituted by the fact that, at least in Italian, in dysgraphic patients the phoneme-to-grapheme conversion skill (writing of single letters) is often quite intact, while the isolation and identification of each single phoneme to be converted is impaired. In this frame, it is worth remembering a further claim made by Luria et al. (1969):

> Before beginning the retraining of a patient it is essential to make a detailed neuropsychological analysis of the disturbance, to identify the primary defects responsible for it, to describe its neurophysiological structure accurately, and only when this has been done, to outline the plan of the necessary measures of rehabilitation ... It is quite clear, for example, that if a disturbance of writing is based on a defect on the phonematic analysis of the sound composition of speech, the problem of reconstructing the functional system will amount to the substitution of this primary defect, and any method which does not satisfy this demand ... will not produce the required result (p. 384).

3. Auditory analysis of the phonetic string composing a word is a quite simple task for a normal alphabetised adult subject. Such a phonological awareness however, is usually matured during acquisition of literacy (Wernicke, 1885/1886) and is severely impaired in aphasic patients. Phonological analysis is subject to certain variables which determine its complexity, such as the presence of consonant clusters and the phonetic-acoustic quality of the phones. With regards the phonetic aspects, it is easier to isolate and identify continuant phones, i.e., vowels and fricative ([f], [v], [s], [ʃ], liquid ([l], [r]), and nasal consonants ([n], [m], [ɲ], [ŋ]), that are susceptible to prolongation, for the simple reason that the analysis of their acoustic and stato-kinesthetic features may be carried out over a longer period and therefore with higher chance of success. Therefore, it is easier to analyse words which contain consonant-vowel (CV) sequences only (e.g., *ala*, wing), than words containing consonant clusters (e.g., *astro*, star), and words that only contain continuant phones (e.g., *limone*, lemon) are easier to analyse than words containing plosive phones (e.g., *patata*, potato). Thus, a spelling deficit following damage to this processing level is most likely to involve the realisation of consonants clusters and of plosive and affricate phones.

Studies on the efficacy of the rehabilitation of written language

In almost all aphasic patients oral language disorders are accompanied by a spelling deficit. Logotherapy, however, is usually focused on the treatment of the oral output deficit only (i.e., articulatory, phonological, lexical-semantic, or morpho-syntactic disorders, respectively). Writing is generally not treated directly, and is only used as a stimulation technique and as indirect support for the treatment of the oral language modality.

One of the main reasons that spelling disorders are usually not treated is that writing has often been considered secondary to the spoken language, and therefore susceptible to a recovery that is secondary to that of the spoken modality.

Furthermore, spelling deficits often remain untreated because written language is supposed to have less relevance in the everyday life of a patient and therefore not to be worth the cost of a specific rehabilitation programme. Apart from the ethical aspects of such a decision, the premise itself is open to criticism. Furthermore, written language may be selectively affected by cerebral damage. At least in these cases, spelling deficits must be considered for specific treatment.

Table 1 summarises the principal studies on the efficacy of rehabilitation of acquired spelling deficits. Columns 4 and 5 of the table summarise the type of therapy given to the patients. Column 6 indicates the efficacy of the treatment. Overall results lack homogeneity, ranging from no effect (–) through dubious effect or non-stable recovery which disappears a few months after the end of the treatment (±), to stabilised improvement that either involved exclusively the treated items (+), or extended to non-treated items (++). These differences may be attributed to the high number of variables involved including the severity of language disorders, types of dysgraphic impairment types and of treatment used.

Two early studies based on a non-specific rehabilitation programme developed outside a cognitive psychological frame (Pizzamiglio & Roberts, 1967; Schwartz, Nemeroff & Reiss, 1974) showed little effect on the patients involved.

Luria and coworkers (1969) made some suggestions that anticipated the modular fractioning of written language processing along the sub-word-level routine. They distinguished an acoustic analysis, a segmentation of the phonemic string, a phoneme-to-grapheme conversion level, a serial sequencing of letters, and a final activation of the appropriate sequence of motor patterns. Since one or more of these components may be disrupted in a dysgraphic patient, they suggested that the objective of the rehabilitative treatment has to be the remediation of the damaged units. The major limits of this view is that Luria et al. neither considered a lexical route of writing nor did they present empirical data in support of the efficacy of the proposed treatment procedures.

Hatfield and Weddel (1976) tested the effect of writing rehabilitation using an approach that clearly shows the influence of the mounting information-processing models. The purpose of their study was to demonstrate that a treatment of spelling disorders must be based on the mechanisms involved in the normal processing of written language, i.e., a dual-route model. Of the five patients included in the study, two were treated with a visual-kinesthetic (in fact

TABLE 1
Studies on writing rehabilitation

Author(s)	Cases	Dysgraphia	Therapy	Remediation/compensation	Results
Pizzamiglio & Roberts, 1967	...	...	Aspecific	...	±
Luria et al., 1969	...	...	Focused on specific damaged unit	R	No results are given
Schwartz et al., 1974	...	...	Aspecific	...	±
Hatfield & Weddel, 1976	1, 2 3 4, 5	...	Visual-lexical global SWL	...	± ± ±±
Seron et al., 1980	5 pts.	...	Visual-lexical	R/(C)	±/++
Hatfield, 1983	3 pts.	deep	Lexical (function words)	C	+
Hillis Trupe, 1986	1 pt.	deep	SWL	R	++
Behrmann, 1987	CC M	surface	Lexical	R	+(+)
Carlomagno & Parlato, 1989	OG	...	SWL	R	++
Hillis & Caramazza, 1994	SJD PM	(deep ?)	SWL	R	++ –
Ferrand & Deloche, 1991	1 pt.	phonological	Lexical	C	+
Zesiger & de Partz, 1991	1 pt.	surface	Visual-lexical	R	+ (±?)
Deloche et al., 1992	18 pts.	...	Visual-lexical	...	+(+)
Aliminosa et al., 1993	JES	mixed	Lexical		+
Deloche et al., 1993	2 pts.	...	Lexical	C R	+ ++
Carlomagno et al., 1994	6 pts.	...	Lexical + SWL (both)	...	3pt.: –/++ 1pt.: +(+)/– 2pt.: +/++
Carlomagno et al., 1996	2 pts.	...	Lexical	R	+(+)
Luzzatti et al., 1996	2 pts.	mixed	SWL	R	++

N, number of patients; SWL, sub-word-level treatment; R, remediation; C, compensation. Results: –, no effect; ±, dubious effect or non-stable recovery; +, stable improvement of the treated items; ++, recovery extended to non-treated items.

lexical) treatment, one with a global approach, and the remaining two patients were treated along the various steps of the sub-word-level routine. However, none of the methods was particularly efficacious and improvement lasted a few months from the conclusion of the treatment in only one of the three patients treated along the sub-word-level routine.

Other studies took a cognitive neuropsychological approach. Some cases were treated along the sub-word-level routine, others along the lexical one. Neither treatment showed a homogeneous effect across the studies.

Hillis and Caramazza (1994; see also Hillis, 1993) treated two deep dysgraphic patients (SJD and PM) who presented a predominant writing disorder in verbs. The treatment was focused on restoring the sub-word-level routine. SJD was easily able to recover the phoneme-to-grapheme correspondences and consequently to improve his writing of verbs. On the other hand, PM, who presented a similar disorder and was treated identically, did not show a comparable degree of recovery. This discrepancy led the authors to the discouraging conclusion that the identification of the damaged component causing a neuropsychological disorder does not necessarily provide the key to the treatment of a disorder or to estimate the degree of recovery.

Similar results were obtained by Carlomagno, Iavarone, and Colombo (1994). However, the authors interpreted this variability differently. They suggested that the outcome of a treatment for spelling disorders does not only depend on the pattern of the symptoms observed, but also on a constellation of variables including (1) the theoretical assumptions of the treatment (i.e. remediation of the damaged routine versus compensation by means of exercises along the less impaired one), (2) the residual capacities of the routine to be treated; (3) the degree of recovery expected for each single processing unit and, finally, (4) the integrity of other processing units that are not primarily related to written language, such as phonological processing, phonological short-term memory, etc.

In conclusion of this review, an observation made by Luria et al. (1969) is worth remembering on a possible relation between the mother tongue of patients and any positive effect the treatment of a spelling disorder may have. This seems to be supported by Hatfield and Weddel's (1976) results as in their study the only patient who responded to writing rehabilitation was a woman of Austrian origin, i.e. whose native language has a relatively shallow orthography. In fact, more convincing results were obtained from the rehabilitation of the sub-word-level routine in patients of Italian mother tongue (Carlomagno & Parlato, 1989; Carlomagno et al., 1994; Luzzatti, Vitolo, Frustaci, & Colombo, 1996). Furthermore, in the few cases in which the treatment appeared ineffective, the phonological analysis was particularly damaged. "ZG, for instance, was completely unable to segment consonant clusters, whereas the other two patients were not able to isolate the first phoneme of stimuli dictated by the examiner" (Carlomagno, Faccioli, & Colombo, 1996). If these patients had been treated for more than 24 sessions and if the rehabilitation programme had been focused on the acoustic-to-phonological conversion, the expected improvement might have been obtained.

GENERAL PRINCIPLES FOR A REHABILITATION PLAN

In the previous section the major techniques developed for the treatment of spelling disorders were described and their effectiveness discussed. However, in the majority of these studies the characteristics of the writing disorders were taken only superficially into account when planning treatment. Furthermore, due to the varying degree of regularity intrinsic in the phoneme-to-grapheme correspondence shown by different languages, the efficacy of treatment techniques of spelling disorders seems to differ according to the mother tongue of the subjects involved.

In Italian, as opposed to English and French, the sub-word-level routine permits the majority of words to be written correctly. Rehabilitation of acquired dysgraphia along the sub-word-level routine seems therefore much more relevant in Italian than in languages with less shallow orthography.[1] Does this variability influence the decision of whether or not writing disorders should be treated and if so, along which route?

To answer this question the following issues have to be considered:

1. Isolated damage of some of the sub-word-level processing units does not necessarily require a specific treatment. With the exception of impairment of writing non-words, which is of diagnostic importance but little relevance in everyday life, when the lexical routine is spared, spelling deficits are usually moderate, and resent only in less frequent or new words which require the involvement of the non-lexical route.

2. As opposed to French and English, in Italian, isolated damage of the lexical routine causes only limited impairment to a patient's spelling capacity, since relatively few conditions with non-shallow orthographic correspondence are involved.

---

[1] In a recent study of spelling disorders in Italian aphasic patients, Luzzatti et al. (1998) found that 46% of the patients showed a mixed disorder both for irregular words and for non-words (i.e. for both the lexical and the sub-word-level routine). Thirty-four per cent of the patients showed a prevalent damage to the lexical routine (surface dysgraphia) and 13% to the sub-word-level routine (phonological dysgraphia) respectively.

3. In the case of a mixed deficit, which seems to be the principal condition for which writing rehabilitation is advisable, it must be decided whether to rehabilitate along the lexical or along the sub-word-level routine. The choice will depend on the degree of impairment of the routines, but in Italian the sub-word-level routine, which by its very nature is governed by a system of rules, would seem to be the most susceptible to treatment.

DESCRIPTION OF THE TREATMENT

General principles

A spelling rehabilitation procedure along the sub-word-level routine is described in this section. As has already been discussed previously, an appropriate phonological analysis is required prior to activating the phonological-to-orthographic conversion route. The first step of the programme is therefore focused on the treatment of damage to this processing level. Initially, the therapist and the patient work on oral language only. Phonological analysis is treated by asking the patients to isolate and identify the phonemes making up a word. Actual writing exercises will be introduced only when segmentation is sufficiently accurate. At each treatment level the therapist provides some preliminary examples and helps the patient during the exercises. The help is reduced progressively and each level is treated until the patient performs at least 90% of the exercises correctly and with no delay.

Level 1: One-to-one conversion rules:
Continuant phones

Segmentation of words into syllables and syllables into phones

Patients are trained to analyse phonological strings by means of oral exercises for the segmentation of words into syllables and syllables into phones. First, they are trained to segment bisyllabic words with alternated consonant-vowel structure (CVCV, i.e. the most typical syllabic structure in Italian), into the corresponding two syllables. Once this task has been mastered, the therapist starts using words of three syllables or more. The same task may be carried out using non-words of two to four syllables.

Once the patient is able to perform this task, the therapist explains that a syllable may be further divided into two phones. To facilitate identification, patients are trained to prolong each phone as much as possible. In this first phase of treatment, the CVCV words only contain continuant phones (like *sole*, sun, or *mare*, sea): four fricative ([f], [v], [s], [z]) two liquid ([r], [l]), and two nasal ([m], [n]) phones.

A complete list of items used for this and the following phases of treatment are given in Luzzatti et al. (1996). The items used during the treatment were different from those used for the evaluation of the writing disorder. The material used in this phase also contained legal non-words with CVCV structure.[2]

The complexity of the stimuli is then progressively increased along the following schema:

1. *Length of the stimuli.*
2. Presence of *consonant clusters*.
3. Presence of *doubled consonants*[3].

Dictation

Single phonemes (vowels, continuant-consonants): In this phase the speech therapists trains the actual phoneme-to-grapheme conversion and the subsequent activation of graphomotor patterns. The therapist produces the continuant phonemes on which the patient has already been trained: The patient has to retrieve the name of the corresponding letter and/or write it down.

If the patient is unable to name and/or write single letters, the therapist trains the patient on one letter at a time. The retrieval of the name and graphomotor pattern of a letter is facilitated through use of the patient's residual automatised orthographic knowledge, by reminding him of the name of close relatives, famous cities, or very high frequency common names beginning with the letter at issue (Hillis Trupe, 1986; Carlomagno & Parlato, 1989).

Dictation of words and non-words: In this phase, the patient is finally trained to write words (and non-words). Stimuli are still exclusively made up of

---

[2] Keeping in mind the cognitive models that describe the processing of written language, one could argue that a rehabilitation programme that is aimed at the treatment of the sub-word-level route should use non-lexical material only. This would avoid the risk of processing of the stimuli along the lexical route. However, unlike other treatments, this method does not aim at preventing lexical processing, but at increasing auditory-to-phonological conversion skills. Any associated secondary activation of the lexical route will be welcome and not be considered a limitation of the treatment. The choice between lexical material and non-words is only related to the preference of patients for lexical material, and the larger phonological short-term memory load determined by non-words in patients who usually have severe impairment of this function.

[3] In this frame, the peculiar aspect of doubled consonants in Italian must be remembered. While doubled consonants in English, German, and French only convey phonological information about the length of the previous vowel, in Italian, they usually correspond to an actually doubled phoneme. Specifically, training is therefore necessary for the identification and transcription of doubled consonants.

continuant phonemes, i.e. they can be analysed using the prolongation technique. Furthermore, as we already saw, all the continuant phonemes used have regular transcription with a one-to-one sound-to-letter correspondence. As patients are already able to identify and adequately segment a string of phonemes, to convert the 14 treated phonemes (5 vowels and 9 consonants) into the corresponding letters, and to activate the corresponding graphomotor patterns, these different activities are now integrated, by asking the patient to write words and non-words under dictation. Initially, the therapist only gives bisyllabic words (and non-words) with a CV structure. Words with three or four syllables and words with consonant clusters and doubled consonants are introduced later.

Level 2: One-to-one conversion rules: Plosive phones

Segmentation of words into syllables and phones

Once a patient has acquired the ability to write words that are made up of vowels and continuant consonants, the therapist trains the acoustic-to-phonological conversion of plosive phones. As in level 1, the patient has to isolate the single phones of a word spoken aloud by the therapist. However, due to the non-continuant aspect of the plosive consonants, patients are not able to use the prolongation technique to isolate the different sounds. The plosive consonants trained at this level are those with a one-to-one phoneme-to-grapheme correspondence ([p], [b], [t], [d]). In practice, the therapist introduces a CV syllable containing a plosive onset (e.g., [to]) and demonstrates the presence of the plosive phoneme and of the vowel. He or she also easily demonstrates the difference between plosive and continuant phonemes through the comparison of the syllables [to] and [lo].

Once the patient has learned to isolate and to identify the four plosive phonemes, the therapist introduces new consonant clusters containing plosive consonants (e.g. *pasta*; *filtro*, filter).

Dictation of plosive phonemes

In this phase the therapist trains the patient on phoneme-to-grapheme conversion and activation of graphomotor patterns for the four plosive consonants treated. The rehabilitation programme follows the procedure described for continuant syllables.

The patient is then trained to write words and non-words composed of the phonemes (and corresponding graphemes) treated up to now. Since the patient is already able to identity and segment phonological strings containing the trained phonemes, to convert single phonemes into the corresponding letters, and to produce the appropriate graphomotor pattern, these three levels may be now integrated in a dictation task.

Level 3: Syllabic and one phoneme-to-several letters conversion rules

Phonemes with syllabic transcription are introduced in this phase. These are phonemes with regular orthography, which, however, do not follow one-to-one phoneme-to-grapheme conversion rules. In some cases, the correct transcription of these phonemes (e.g. [k], [g], [tʃ], [dʒ]) requires contemplation of the *syllabic context* in which they appear (the following vowel). In other cases, the orthographic reproduction of the phoneme requires two distinct letters (e.g. [ʎ] = GL and [ɲ] = GN). As a first step the therapist introduces the rules for the transcription of the phonemes [k] and [g]: (1) C and G before the vowels [o], [a], [u]; (2) CH and GH before the vowels [i] and [e]. As a second step he or she introduces the rules for the transcription of the affricate phonemes [tʃ], [dʒ] and the fricative phoneme [ʃ]: (1) CI, GI, SCI before by the vowel [o], [a], [u] (2) C, G, SC before the vowels [i] and [e]. As a third step the therapist introduces the transcription rules for the phonemes [ʎ] and [ɲ]. The final condition determined by the syllabic context is the orthographic reproduction of the sequence [kw] for which the letters QU are used if followed by the vowels [a], [i], [e] (e.g., QUADRO, painting; QUERCIA, oak), and CU if followed by the vowel [o] (e.g., CUORE, heart).

The majority of the phonemes following a one-to-several conversion rule (e.g., [ʃ], [ʎ] and [ɲ] have at least one other, less frequent, possible orthographic realisation. The existence of these exceptions is not considered in this phase of the treatment (see level 4).

Finally, the therapist introduces the affricate phonemes [ts] and [dz] which both correspond to the letter Z, stressing the peculiarity implicit in such sounds, i.e., that during the prolongation exercise the fricative component of the phone may deceive the patient into identifying it as a [s] or a [z] instead of [ts] and [dz].

Level 4: Words with ambiguous (irregular) orthography

Despite the well-known regularity of Italian orthography, there is a certain amount of ambiguity in the reproduction of some phonemes, i.e., in certain cases the phoneme-to-grapheme conversion rules leave more than one solution open, of which, usually, one only is correct[4]. It is possible to choose between these alternatives only through the retrieval of previously acquired graphemic lexical knowledge.

During this phase of the treatment, patients learn to identify the phonological context of possible ambiguities and how to reduce to the minimum the conditions where lexical knowledge is mandatory. If this knowledge is impaired, patients only have to learn the few conditions (ambiguous phonological contexts; loan-words) in which the correct orthography has to be checked in a dictionary.

EVALUATION OF THE SPELLING DEFICITS

A prerequisite for the fine-tuning of a writing rehabilitation programme is the evaluation of the patient's residual written language capacities. Specific testing material, which includes items for different variables that may influence the processing abilities along the lexical, and especially along the sub-word-level routine, was developed to test for spelling disorders (Luzzatti et al., 1998).

The test comprises five sections: (A) regular words with complete one phoneme-to-one letter correspondence; (B) regular words containing letters with one-phoneme-to-several-letter correspondence (e.g., [k], [g], [tʃ], [dʒ]); (C) words with non-univocal (e.g., [ʎ] in [paʎa], straw: PAGLIA and not PALIA; [baʎa], wet nurse: BALIA and not BAGLIA, or [ɲ] in [dʒeɲo], genius: GENIO and not GEGNO; [seɲo], sign: SEGNO and not SENIO); (D)

---

[4] The following is a list of the most typical conditions of orthographic ambiguity:

(1) There are some Italian words in which the syllable [ʃe] is reproduced by means of the sequence SCIE instead of the more regular solution SCE (e.g., the correct spelling of the word [ʃentsa], science is SCIENZA and not SCENZA). This also occurs for the syllables [tʃe] and [dʒe] that in some cases must be reproduced by the sequence CIE and GIE instead of CE and GE (e.g. the correct spelling of the words [tʃelo], sky and [idʒene], hygiene is CIELO and IGIENE and not CELO and IGENE). (2) The phonemes [kw] followed by the vowel [o] are reproduced in some cases by the sequence QUO instead of the more regular sequence CUO (e.g., LIQUORE, liquor, QUOCO, cook, QUOTA, rate). (3) The phonemes, [lj], and [nj] of central and southern Italian pronunciation are homophones in northern Italy to the phoneme [ʎ] and respectively [ɲ]; for instance, the transcription of the word [baʎa], wet nurse, and of the word [geraɲo], geranium is unpredictable (BALIA and not BAGLIA; GERANIO, and not GERAGNO). (4) In almost all Italian pronunciation, the plosive consonant [b] followed by the liquid consonants [l] and [r] and by the semiconsonant [j] is homophone to its doubled pair. This homophony makes the transcription of words like [libro], book (LIBRO and not LIBBRO), [febre], fever (FEBBRE and not FEBRE), [biblico] biblical (BIBLICO and not *BIBBLICO) and [publico], public (PUBBLICO and not PUBLICO) ambiguous.

Finally, fully irregular (with respect to the major rules of the Italian orthography) is the transcription of loan words from French and English (e.g. blue-jeans, night-club, or chalet).

loan words which are by now part of the Italian lexicon (e.g. blue-jeans, night-club); (E) non-words with one-sound-to-one letter correspondence (see Table 2).

In order to evaluate different sources of complexity, section A of the test is composed of different subsets of items which permit comparison of (1) words containing only continuant consonants (fricative, liquid, or nasal) with words which also contain non-continuant (plosive) consonants (2) words made up of consonant-vowel syllables with words also containing clusters or doubled consonants; bisyllabic words with polysyllabic words. For a complete list of the items used see Luzzatti et al., 1998. Due to the small number of items, the loan-word section (D) was not considered in the present study.

TREATMENT OF DYSGRAPHIC PATIENTS

The efficacy of the treatment described above was tested in severe dysgraphic patients. Selection principles were an interval of more than 3 years from aphasia onset and previous completion of a spoken language rehabilitation programme. Patients were informed of the experimental nature of the treatment and gave formal consent to participate in the study. A more extensive description of the cases and of the treatment has been given in a previous paper (Luzzatti et al., 1996). The purpose of the study was two-fold: To test the possibility of treating the sub-word-level routine in patients with a severe writing disorder and to test if treating the spelling deficits would improve the remaining linguistic capacities.

Case 1 (patient RO)

RO was a 48-year-old male, who for 4 years after suffering a left hemisphere cerebral abscess (in November, 1987), presented with a severe language disorder. The patient had 8 years of schooling and was an employee in the administration department of a trade company.

A first language evaluation (Italian version of the Aachen Aphasia Test (AAT) Huber, Poek, & Willmes 1984; Luzzatti, Willmes, & De Bleser, 1996) undertaken about 4 months after the onset of the disease revealed a severe nonfluent aphasia with speech apraxia. Speech production was reduced to a few recurring utterances in spontaneous output as well as in repetition, reading, and naming tasks. Oral and written comprehension were also severely impaired. The patient underwent language rehabilitation at the Rho-Passirana Rehabilitation Unit, initially for his comprehension disorder and his speech apraxia, and subsequently for his lexical and morpho-syntactic deficits. The evolution of his language disorders is documented by serial tests with the AAT.

Three years after the onset of the disease the patient still had a severe nonfluent language deficit. Speech output was severely agrammatic with two to

TABLE 2
Subtests of the writing task (Luzzatti et al., 1998)

	Examples	Continuance	Clusters	Doubled c.	Length (sy)	n
(A) Regular words (1): One-phoneme-to-one-letter correspondence (n = 80)						
1	sole	yes	no	no	2	10
2	minerale	yes	no	no	3/4	10
3	senso	yes	yes	no	2	10
4	ferro	yes	no	yes	2	10
5	capo	no	no	no	2	10
6	prato	no	yes	no	2	10
7	letto	no	no	yes	2	10
8	sponda	no	yes × 2	no	2	10

	Examples	Rule	n
(B) Regular words (2): Syllabic and one-to-several conversion rules (n = 15)			
9	gola/ghiro/adagio	[k], [g], [tʃ], [dʒ], [ʃ]	15

	Examples	Ambiguity	n
(C) Words with irregular (non-univocal) transcription (n = 55)			
10	scena/scienza	[tʃ], [ʃ]: ±I	10
11	biglia/balia	[ʎ]: GLI/LI	10
12	segno/genio	[ɲ]: GN/NI	10
13	libro/febbre	BR/BBR	10
14	cuore/quota	[kw]: CU/QU	15

	Examples	n
(D) Loan words (n = 8)		
15	blue-jeans, night-club	8

	Examples	Continuance	Doubled consonant	Syllables	n
(E) Non-words: One phoneme-to-one-letter correspondence (n = 25)					
1	nise	yes	no	2	5
2	vimàne/ramàsola	yes	no	3/4	5
3	seffa	yes	yes	2	5
4	tido	no	no	2	5
5	nitta	no	yes	2	5

three word sentences and omission of function words. The patient used only few verbs and those only in non-finite form (infinitives and past participles). The language examination showed a mild-to-moderate confrontation naming and comprehension disorder, a moderate disorder on the Token Test and the repetition task, and a moderate-to-severe disorder of written language (mild-to-moderate reading disorder, whereas writing was still nil). A comparison to the previous profile by means of the Psychometrical Single Cases Analysis (Willmes, 1985) showed a significant improvement on all tasks. The disorder was classifiable as Broca's aphasia with agrammatism, anomia, agraphia, and dyslexia. The patient's reading deficits presented the features of a phonological dyslexia, with a mild deficit in reading concrete nouns (72%), a moderate impairment in reading abstract nouns (54%), a severe impairment in reading function words (25%) and non-words (14%), and only mild deficit in reading three-syllabic words with unpredictable stress (GONDOLA ['gondola] vs. MENTOLO [men'tolo]) (78%).

The patient was treated for a further 6-month period. A control examination showed a mild, non-significant improvement on the Token Test, whereas the performance on the remaining subtests of the AAT were unchanged. RO's spelling abilities were also examined with the writing test described above. He scored nil on all writing and spelling tasks, including regular high frequency bisyllabic words. Writing of single letters was moderately impaired (60% correct responses). Table 3 shows some examples of errors produced.

Due to the long rehabilitation period and the stabilisation of the language disorder, language rehabilitation was concluded.

Nine months after RO's last evaluation, the present programme for the treatment of writing deficits was realised; due to his major spelling disorders the patient was selected to test its efficacy.

TABLE 3
Examples of RO's errors in the writing task (Feb 92)

Stimuli	Responses	Stimuli	Responses
FILO (thread)	F LO	LUTTO (mourning)	L O
SEMAFORO (traffic l.)	S F O	FRASE (sentence)	SE
VISONE (mink)	V S E	FORMA (form)	F O A
SOMARO (donkey)	S O RO	FUSTO (stem)	F T O
TOPO (mouse)	T O	STRADA (street)	ST A
BUCO (hole)	B O	MACELLO (slaughter house)	M LO
DITO (finger)	T O	SOCIETÀ (society)	S T A
VALLE (valley)	V LE	LIBRO (book)	L O
MUFFA (mould)	M FO		

When writing, RO left free spaces between letters to signal the presence of phones he could not identify and/or convert, or of letters he could not write.

Before starting the treatment, RO's spelling abilities were tested again, using the same writing test. His performance was still nil, and showed the same type of deficits described during the previous evaluation. The treatment schedule was three to four sessions per week. The individual phases of the treatment are described in the following section. As already explained the criteria for proceeding from one treatment phase to the next was the achievement of at least 90% scoring on the tasks of the previous treatment phase.

Description of the treatment

RO's writing rehabilitation began in March 1992, starting from the phonological decomposition of words and non-words into syllables and, successively, of syllables into phones. While RO was able to segment words and non-words of variable length in syllables easily, it took him longer to achieve the prolongation and isolation of continuant phones.

Stimuli were progressively bisyllabic CVCV words (and non-words), words (and non-words) with three to four syllables, and words (and non-words) containing consonant clusters. It was this last phase of the treatment which was most problematic for the patient, since he had extreme difficulty in isolating the consonants of a cluster. Finally, the therapist introduced words and non-words containing doubled consonants.

Once RO was able to analyse correctly a string of continuant phonemes, the therapist gave him the first writing exercise, i.e. dictation of single continuant phonemes (or of the corresponding letters). The task appeared to be very easy for RO who was able to transcribe over 90% of the phonemes and letters.

His ability to write simple words composed of continuant phonemes was more impaired, but it improved progressively during the following weeks, until he could write approximately 80% of bisyllabic CVCV words.

RO's writing abilities were tested again, 6 months later, in September 1992. Table 4 summarises the results obtained. He was able to write 80% of the bisyllabic CVCV words, whereas his performance on words of three to four syllables was clearly more impaired (20% correct responses). Bisyllabic words containing consonant clusters and doubled consonants were also more impaired (35%), whereas writing words containing plosive consonants was still close to nil.

The therapist continued the treatment for another month, still using words and non-words containing continuant phonemes, only. The rate of difficulty was increased by one variable at a time, first CV items of three to four syllables, and later stimuli containing consonant clusters and doubled consonants.

On the next evaluation administered in November 1992 (Table 4), RO, showed a clear improvement in writing stimuli composed of continuant phonemes only: He was able to write about (80%) of words and approximately 50% of non-words correctly.

TABLE 4
RO's performances (%) on the 1st to 6th writing evaluation

n	Type of item	Feb:92	Sept:92	Nov:92	Feb:93	Jul:93	Jan:95
10	Sole	0	80	100	100	100	100
10	Lavoro	0	20	90	80	70	80
20	Forma/valle	0	35	70	90	95	100
10	Dito	0	0	10	60	100	80
20	Prato/tappo	0	25	25	45	90	95
10	Strada	0	0	10	10	90	80
15	One-to-several	0	0	0	27	73	67
55	Irregular	0	0	0	25	25	50
25	Non-words	0	0	44	72	72	60
175	total	0	13	29	50	77	72

The scores correspond to different parts of the task: *sole*, regular, bisyllabic words, composed of continuant phonemes only, with no consonant cluster or geminated phonemes; *lavoro*, idem for words of 3–4 syllables; *forma/valle*, idem, bisyllabic words with consonant cluster geminated phones; dito, like *sole*, but containing plosive phonemes; *prato/tappo*, like *forma/valle*, but containing plosive phonemes; *strada*, bisyllabic words containing complex consonant clusters; *one-to-several*, regular words, but syllabic conversion rules (for the transcription of the phonemes [k], [g], [tʃ], [dʒ], [ʃ]; *irregular*, words with unpredictable transcription; *non-words*, bisyllabic non-words. The table does not include the results for writing of loan-words.

In the light of these results, it was possible to start on exercises with plosive consonants [t], [d], p], [b]. As with the previous treatment, the therapist gave RO bisyllabic words and non-words to segment. After about 3 weeks RO was able to segment the stimulus words into syllables and isolate the plosive phoneme from the subsequent vowel.

The following step focused on the phoneme-to-grapheme conversion of plosive phonemes. The task was so easy for the patient that he was able to start on bisyllabic words and non-words during the first session.

Three months later, in February 1993, the patient's writing abilities were tested again. The figures given in Table 4 indicate that RO's performance was almost normal for the majority of the regular items with one phoneme-to-one letter correspondence (either continuant or plosive). His spelling performance on words containing multiple consonant clusters was however still impaired (10% correct). Table 5 shows some examples of the errors produced.

One month later, the therapist started treatment of the syllabic and one phoneme-to-several letters conversion rules. She first demonstrated by means of examples (words containing the phonemes [ʃ], [ʎ], [ɲ], etc.) the existence of phonemes, transcription of which requires more than one letter and of phones that underlie syllabic conversion rules. To exemplify the task, the therapist introduced a table summarising the syllabic conversion rules. Even though not

TABLE 5
Examples of RO's errors to the writing task (Feb 93)

Stimuli	Responses	Stimuli	Responses
STRADA (street)	STADA	CROSTA (crust)	CROSDA
FRONTE (front)	FROTTE	FILTRO (filter)	FILTO
NASTRO (ribbon)	NASTO	FRUSTA (whip)	FRUTTA
STAMPA (print)	STAPA		

completely unexpected, this level of treatment proved quite difficult for the patient. After approximately 2 months RO was able to use the table spontaneously, and approximately 1 month later he was able to use the syllabic conversion rules without the table.

A control evaluation carried out in July 1993 (see Table 4), showed that RO made appropriate use of the one-to-one as well as of the syllabic phoneme-to-grapheme conversion rules. When writing regular words, RO made only 9 errors out of 95 items. He had also improved his writing of irregular words, reaching 53% of correct responses. When writing irregular (ambiguous) words such as *ragno*, spider, *vaniglia*, vanilla, RO almost always made surface errors (RANIO, VANILIA).

On a final assessment (see Table 4 and Figure 2) 18 months after the end of the treatment, RO still showed only a mild impairment of the ability to write irregular (unpredictable) words and to write non-words.

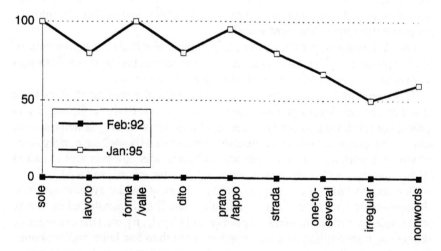

Figure 2. Score profile of RO's performance on the 1st and 6th writing evaluation (for details see Table 4).

Discussion

The improvement obtained by RO leaves no doubt as to the efficacy of a spelling rehabilitation programme along the sub-word-level routine. As expected, the effect of the writing treatment was mirrored in the reading performance (see Table 4), with a clear improvement in reading function words, abstract nouns and non-words (from 45% to 70%, 21% to 42%, and 50% to 87%, respectively; χ^2: words = 10.37, p < .005; non-words = 4.21, p < .05). With regard to the remaining linguistic abilities, RO's spontaneous speech was substantially unchanged, but the AAT profile showed a significant improvement both in the overall level of the profile and the naming task (from the 62nd to the 82nd percentile).

Case 2 (patient DR)

DR, is a 33-year-old dental technician. Ten years prior to our study he had suffered a cerebral haemorrhage caused by the rupture of an aneurysm of the left internal carotid artery (March 1984). The patient underwent neurosurgical treatment and after surgery he developed left hemiparesis and severe aphasia. The patient was first given the Italian version of the AAT in June 1984 which demonstrated a severe language disorder with the features of a global aphasia. He was treated for approximately 3 years for his language deficits. When the treatment was concluded in 1987 the patient presented a severe Broca's aphasia with agrammatism, severe verbal inertia, and dysgraphia.

DR's performance on an AAT given in March 1992 was unchanged from the previous evaluation 8 years before.

Reading aloud was moderately impaired with the features of a phonological dyslexia (see Table 6): DR's response to lexical stimuli was less impaired than to non-words (74/91 [81%] and 12/28 [43%], respectively; χ^2 = 13.83; p < .001). From a qualitative point of view, the majority of the errors made on non-words was devoicing of voiced phonemes: a phenomenon that did not emerge when the stimuli were words.

DR's writing deficit was moderate to severe (see Table 7: 22 correct responses out of 80 regular words, but only 6 out of 55 words with ambiguous orthography; χ^2 = 4.46; p < .05). Altogether he was able to write 32/150 words and 3/25 non-words (χ^2 = 0.65, n.s.). The predominant substitutions made when writing regular words were devoicing of voiced consonants (n = 28), loss of the nasal feature of nasal consonants (e.g., M → B) (n = 18), substitutions of vowels (n = 17), and doubling of single or dedoubling of doubled consonants (n = 15). Furthermore, the patient showed severe inability in writing words containing sounds that require syllabic transcription. Writing of words with ambiguous orthography and of loan-words was severely

TABLE 6
RO's reading performance at beginning and end of treatment

| | n | February 1992 | | July 1993 | |
		R+	%	R+	%
Concrete nouns	29	21	72	23	79
"Irregular" stress	18	14	78	16	88
Abstract nouns	24	13	54	21	87
Function words	20	5	25	14	70
Legal non-words	28	4	14	12	42
Total	119	57	48	86	72

R+ = number of hits. Comparison between words and non-words (1st exam): $\chi^2 = 14.74$; $p < .001$. Comparison between 1st and 2nd exam: words $\chi^2 = 10.37$; $p < .005$; non-words: $\chi^2 = 4.21$; $p < .05$.

impaired. Overall DR showed mixed impairment involving both his lexical and sub-word-level routines, with a better performance, however, on regular words with one phoneme-to-one letter correspondence. Furthermore, he transcribed voiced consonants with the corresponding non-voiced letters, both in words and non-words. The same phenomenon also recurred in repetition and reading aloud of legal non-words, but not of words (e.g., repetition of words = 143/150 vs. repetition of non-words = 19/55, respectively; $\chi^2 = 8.95$, $p < .01$).

DR's phonological short-term memory was severely impaired with a clear length effect (two-syllables word span = 2.4; five-syllables word span = 1.3) but not similarity effect (span for similar letters = 3.1; for dissimilar letters = 3.1).

The stability of the residual writing deficit and DR's interest in obtaining treatment for his spelling disorder made him a good candidate for the rehabilitation programme along the sub-word-level route. For technical reasons it was not possible to start the treatment before April 1993.

Prior to the rehabilitation programme DR was given a control examination for his language deficits and writing disorder, to verify if any variations had occurred since the previous year. As expected, his performance was unchanged (see Table 7). A qualitative analysis of the errors confirmed a prevalence of voicing/devoicing errors (59 out of 147 possible substitutions) and a loss of distinction between single and double consonants. DR also made frequent vowel substitutions ($n = 42$), mostly I → E ($n = 41$) and 15 out of 70 nasal consonants were transcribed with the corresponding non-nasal minimal pair (e.g., M → B). He also made 13 syllabic conversion errors and five out of 55 possible surface errors. The treatment was given in three to four sessions per week.

TABLE 7
DR's performances (%) on the 1st to 6th writing evaluation (for details see Table 4)

n	Type of item	Mar:92	Apr:93	Jun:93	Oct:93	Jan:94	May:94
10	Sole	20	40	40	80	100	100
10	Lavoro	0	0	20	50	90	100
20	Forma/valle	30	20	65	80	100	100
10	Dito	30	50	30	40	100	90
20	Prato/tappo	40	45	50	65	85	95
10	Strada	40	50	60	70	100	100
15	One-to-several	27	13	20	13	40	93
55	Irregular	11	15	24	31	42	67
25	Non-words	12	8	24	44	88	92
175	Total	21	27	34	47	73	87

Description of the treatment

Since DR was able to segment with ease words and non-words composed of continuant phones into syllables, it was possible to start the treatment immediately with exercises on the prolongation and isolation of these phonemes. The major impairment which emerged during this phase of the treatment was the discrimination between voiced and voiceless consonants and between the vowels [i] and [e]. This disorder only appeared during the segmentation exercises, i.e. DR could repeat the target word correctly, but he substituted the consonants [f] for [v] (and vice versa) and the vowels [i] for [e] (and vice versa), when he had to isolate the phonemes of a word. As already observed, the same substitutions were also made in repetition and reading aloud of non-words and were consistent with the similar phenomenon already described in the writing task (involving both words and non-words).

In order to clarify this phenomenon, DR was given a further spelling task of bi- and trisyllabic non-words (e.g., *velofo*, *balota*, etc.). In this task the patient committed 20 voicing/devoicing errors of 66 voiceless/voiced consonants (30.3%). Repetition of the same items was impaired with prevalent devoicing of voiced consonants. Table 8 summarises DR's performances on the different tasks (repetition, reading aloud, and writing of non-words). Devoicing errors were not made when repeating words and emerged only occasionally when reading aloud the same lexical items.

The observed devoicing errors could originate at different processing levels, either of input or of output. The absence of devoicing substitutions in the word repetition task is in line with damage of the sub-word-level routine. However, the different degree of impairment of words and non-words could also be an artifact arising from a mild input deficit of the voiced/voiceless discrimination: This disorder could be more overt when using non-lexical material, since

TABLE 8
Errors produced by dr when processing non-words (supplementary task):
Performances are compared to those obtained with the lexical items
of the standard writing task

	Repetition errors	Reading aloud errors	Spelling errors
Extra non-words ($n = 40$)			
Voiced/voiceless substitution	20	17	20
Loss of nasality	0	1	1
Vocalic substitutions (I ↔ E)	0	12	12
± double consonants	0	20	20
Other errors	8	8	8
Words ($n = 154$)			
Voiced/voiceless substitution	0	14	60
Loss of nasality	0	6	15
Vocalic substitutions (I ↔ E)	1	6	34
± double consonants	0	4	30
Other errors	2	6	51

non-words do not take advantage of lexical feedback. DR's ability to discrimi-
nate among phonemic pairs was tested by asking him to judge if pairs of syllables were the same (e.g. [pa]—[pa]) or different (e.g. [pa]—[ta]). His
performance on this task was only mildly impaired, but when he repeated the
task, using pairs of syllables that could differ in the ± voice (e.g., [pa]—[ba.]),
DR judged 10 pairs of different syllables out of 30 as being the same. This result
confirmed the suspicion that the source of devoicing errors made by DR in the
spelling task and when dealing with non-lexical material in reading aloud and
repetition tasks, is related to a disorder of the voiced/voiceless discrimination
faculty.

To verify this hypothesis, DR was asked to submit to two further tasks.

*Auditory lexical decision of words and non-words in minimal pair for the
voiced/voiceless aspect.*   A total of 50 words containing a voiced consonant
were selected. A non-word was obtained from each of the 50 words by substi-
tuting the voiced consonant with a voiceless minimal pair (e.g. vela (sail)/fela,
topo (mouse)/tobo, clima (clima)/glima). The 50 words + 50 non-word were
then presented in the spoken modality and the patient was asked to decide
whether each letter string was a word or a non-word. In the case of "deafness"
for the voiced/voiceless aspect the patient should not have been able to discrim-
inate non-words from their lexical minimal pairs. DR however, was able to
perform the lexical decision task almost flawlessly making only one error out of
100 items.

Repetition of words that are in minimal pair with other words for the voiced/ voiceless feature.   A total of 68 bi- and trisyllabic words were used: Each word was in minimal pair relation for the voiced/voiceless feature with another word. The target consonant could be at the beginning or in the middle of the word (e.g. *fino*, until/*vino*, wine; *topo*, mouse/*dopo*, after; *vento*, wind/*vendo*, I sell; *pentola*, pot/*pendola*, pendulum clock). Each of the 68 words were spoken aloud by the examiner and DR had to repeat them. He made only eight errors out of the 68 items, but they all concerned the voiced/voiceless feature. A comparison of the results obtained from this and the previous investigation suggests that the presence of a lexical pair for the voiced/voiceless dimension increases the probability of a voicing/devoicing error, but that these errors do not arise at an early perceptual level. Furthermore, given the normal performance in the lexical decision task, the mild impairment observed in repetition seems to arise at some level of phonological output processing.

Present processing models do not appear to give a satisfactory explanation for isolated disorders of the voiced/voiceless dimension along the sub-word-level routine only. However, the results could be predicted in a linguistic frame, if it is considered that a sub-word-level processing of both the input and output modality may underlie a principle of minimal distance, and that the more superficial distinctive features may be more fragile both at the input as well as at the output level.

Given these premises, even in absence of a clear localisation of the mechanism that determined the errors along the voiced/voiceless parameter, we planned a training of DR's auditory analysis. A feedback on the voiced/voiceless aspect of phonemes could be obtained by asking the patient to verify the vibration of the vocal cords with his fingers. Since the disorder was most evident on non-words, the treatment was performed using non-lexical material. After seven sessions the therapist increased the complexity of the stimuli, using non-words of three to four syllables. After a further 10 sessions DR was easily able to process words and non-words made of continuant phonemes, including consonant clusters.

The treatment continued with the analysis of words and non-words containing doubled consonants. DR had much difficulty with this phase, due to his extreme uncertainty in identifying doubled consonants. This deficit was in clear contradiction to his flawless repetition of the phonological string containing the doubled or the simple consonants. This disorder reflected the pattern of impairment observed in the writing task, where DR misspelled 42 consonants along the simple/doubled dimension.

At the end of June 1993, 2 months after the beginning of the treatment, DR took the writing task again, to verify if this phase of the therapy had improved his spelling abilities, even though he had been given no specific treatment for the written modality. In fact, his spelling of words containing clusters and

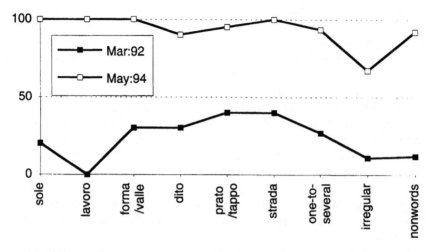

Figure 3.   Profile of DR's performance on the 1st and 6th writing evaluation (for details see Table 4).

doubled consonants improved from 20% to 65% (see Table 7), but altogether he could still write only 34% of the items.

The treatment continued with the discrimination and production of simple and doubled consonants. Given a bisyllabic word or non-word, DR had first to decide whether the stimulus contained a doubled consonant, after which he had to produce the opposite element of the pair.

In the middle of July the therapist started the actual dictation of words and non-words composed of continuant phonemes following regular one-to-one phoneme-to-grapheme conversion rules. Since DR was already able to write the corresponding letters, the therapist started immediately with bi- and trisyllabic CVCV stimuli and consonant clusters.

In October DR's writing abilities were examined once again to verify the effect of the treatment (see Table 7). There was a clear improvement on the words containing the treated consonants (regular one-to-one conversion, parts 1–3).

In the following phase the therapist introduced the phonological analysis of words containing plosive phonemes. As expected DR showed a severe impairment in discriminating voiced from voiceless consonants ([p]—[b], [t]—[d], [k]—[g]). Here too, he repeated the lexical stimuli correctly, but made many devoicing errors on non-words.

Approximately 3 weeks later the therapist started with the actual writing exercises.

In January 1994 a further examination was made of DR's writing abilities (Table 7). There were almost no errors in writing regular words (76/80 correct).

The therapist was therefore able to pass to the third phase of the treatment, i.e., the transcription of phonemes with one phoneme-to-several letters correspondence ([ʃ], [ʎ], [ɲ]) or following syllabic conversion rules ([k], [g], [tʃ], [dʒ]). Since the beginning of the treatment, DR, was aware of his inability to transcribe these phonemes. Such awareness made the comprehension of the task quite easy. The patient learned rapidly the conversion rules.

A further evaluation of DR's writing abilities was made in April 1994, at the end of the treatment. Figure 3 compares the last profile to that obtained on the first evaluation. The patient reached an almost normal performance even on words containing consonants that require the use of syllabic conversion rules. There was still misspelling in the subset of words with non-univocal spelling, but these were almost exclusively surface dysgraphic errors.

A final assessment of DR's writing abilities made in October 1994, 6 months after the end of the treatment, showed that the effect of rehabilitation was stable.

Discussion

Overall, the treatment of DR's spelling disorders took approximately 12 months. The patient had had a severe oral and written language disorder for more than 8 years. His writing deficit originated from damage to both spelling routines. The sub-word-level routine was impaired on two levels: the phonological analysis of the stimuli and the syllabic conversion rules. In spite of the length of time which had elapsed since onset of the disease, DR's spelling ability along the sub-word-level routine was restored practically to normal levels after treatment. The modification of the writing profile showed a progressive recovery that was specific to the different phases of the treatment. The remaining linguistic abilities were substantially unchanged. A qualitative analysis of the errors made by DR during treatment showed that improvements can be directly attributed to the type of therapy given in each phase (Figure 4).

GENERAL DISCUSSION

A cognitive approach to the rehabilitation of writing impairments requires some major decisions. First it is necessary to decide whether to treat the lexical or the sub-word-level routine. This query must however be considered in a more general frame, i.e. if a treatment should be focused on the impaired processing unit or on the maximal enhancement of the spared—or less impaired—processes. With regard to treatment of a spelling impairment, the drawback to lexical treatment is its limited degree of generalisation to non-treated lexical material, while treatment along the sub-word-level routine has little effect on languages such as French or English which have irregular

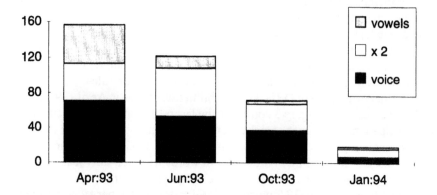

Figure 4. Longitudinal qualitative analysis of DR's spelling errors (vowels = vowel substitutions; x2 = omission of one of the two elements in doubled consonants or, vice versa, doubling of simple consonants; voice = voiced versus voiceless substitutions and vice versa). A comparison of the rates of errors across testing sessions shows a progressive reduction of the number of voiced/voiceless and vocalic substitutions and of the errors along the simple/doubled consonant dimension.

orthography, although a higher rate of efficacy can be expected in languages like Italian, where orthography is more regular and predictable.

This paper described a procedure for the treatment of spelling disorders along the sub-word-level routine. As already suggested by Luria et al. (1969) and by Hatfield and Weddel (1976), particular emphasis was given to the treatment of the unit that permits phonological analysis of the auditory string to be written.

The treatment was tested on two patients with severe writing disorders of 5–8 years duration. Both patients benefited highly from the treatment. Different levels of impairment were documented in the two cases. In RO the treatment focused particularly on an acoustic-to-phonological conversion impairment: once a good level of segmentation had been obtained, he was able to make the conversion into the corresponding orthographic string easily. The results confirm the relevance of the segmentation phase when writing along the sub-word-level route. DR presented a phonological analysis deficit, involving particularly the voiced/voiceless aspect and the discrimination of simple from doubled consonants, as well as a severe impairment of the use of syllabic conversion rules. An examination given 6–18 months after the end of the treatment showed in both patients that the spelling performance had been stabilised. The mild deterioration shown by RO in the ability to write non-words seems to indicate an indirect effect of the treatment on the lexical routine and an initial detachment of the patient from the sub-word-level spelling routine.

REFERENCES

Aliminosa, D., McCloskey, M., Goodman-Schulman, R., & Sokol, S.M. (1993). Remediation of acquired dysgraphia as a technique for testing interpretations of deficits. *Aphasiology, 7,* 55–69.

Behrmann, M. (1987). The rites of righting writing: Homophone remediation in acquired dysgraphia. *Cognitive Neuropsychology, 4,* 365–384.

Carlomagno, S., Faccioli, F., & Colombo, A. (1996). Il trattamento della scrittura per via lessicale. In: S. Carlomagno & C. Luzzatti (Eds.), *La riabilitazione dei disturbi di scrittura nei pazienti afasici.* (pp. 41–78). Milan: Masson.

Carlomagno, S., Iavarone, A., & Colombo, A. (1994). Cognitive approaches to writing rehabilitation: From single case to group studies. In G. Humphreys & J. Riddoch (Eds.), *Cognitive neuropsychology and cognitive rehabilitation.* Hove, UK: Lawrence Erlbaum Associates Ltd.

Carlomagno, S., & Parlato, V. (1989). Writing rehabilitation in brain damaged adult patients: A cognitive approach. In: X. Seron & G. Deloche (Eds.), *Cognitive approaches in neuropsychological rehabilitation.* Hillsdale, N.J.: Erlbaum.

De Bleser, R., & Luzzatti, C. (1989). Models of reading and writing and their disorders in classical German aphasiology. *Cognitive Neuropsychology, 6,* 501–513.

Deloche, G., Dordain, M., & Kremin, H. (1993). Rehabilitation of confrontation naming in aphasia: Relations between oral and written modalities. *Aphasiology, 7,* 201–213.

Deloche, G., Ferrand, I., Metz-Lutz, M.N. (1992). Confrontation naming rehabilitation in aphasia: A computerized written technique. *Neuropsychological Rehabilitation, 2,* 117–124.

Ferrand, I., & Deloche, G. (1991). Thérapie éxperimentale de l'écriture dans un cas d'atteinte de la voie phonologique avec préservation de la production des monosyllabiques. Réunion de la Société de Neuropsychologie de Langue Française, Paris.

Hatfield, M.F. (1983). Aspect of acquired dysgraphia and implication for re-education. In C. Code, & D.J. Mueller (Eds)., *Aphasia therapy.* London: Arnold.

Hatfield, M.F., & Weddell, R. (1976). Re-training in writing in severe aphasia. In R. Hoops & Y. Lebrun (Eds.), *Recovery in aphasics* (pp. 65–78) Amsterdam: Swets & Zeitlinger.

Hillis, A.E. (1993). The role of models of language processing in rehabilitation of language impairments. *Aphasiology, 7,* 5–27.

Hillis Trupe, A.E. (1986). Effectiveness of retrining phoneme to grapheme conversion. In R.H. Brookshire (Ed.), *Clinical aphasiology conference proceeding.* Minneapolis: BRK Publishers.

Hillis, A.E., & Caramazza, A. (1994). Theories of lexical processing and rehabilitation of lexical deficits. In G. Humphrey & J. Riddoch (Eds.), *Cognitive neuropsychology and cognitive rehabilitation.* Hove, UK: Lawrence Erlbaum Associates Ltd.

Huber, W., Poeck, K., & Willmes, K. (1984). The Aachen Aphasia Test. *Advances in Neurology, 42,* 291–303.

Luria, A.R., Naydin, V.L., Tsvetkova, L.S., & Vinarskaya, E.N. (1969). Restoration of higher cortical function following local brain damage. In P.J. Vinken & G.W. Bruyn (Eds.), *Handbook of clinical neurology.* (Vol. 3) (pp. 368–433). Amsterdam: Elsevier.

Luzzatti, C., Laiacona, M., Allamano, N., De Tanti, A., & Inzaghi, M.G. (1998). Writing disorders in Italian aphasic patients: A multiple single-case study of dysgraphia in a language with shallow orthography. *Brain, 121,* 1721–1734.

Luzzatti, C., Vitolo, F., Frustaci, M., & Colombo, C. (1996). Il trattamento della scrittura per via segmentale. In: S. Carlomagno & C. Luzzatti (Eds.), La riabilitazione dei disturbi di scrittura nei pazienti afasici. (pp. 79–119). Milan: Masson.

Luzzatti, C., Willmes, K., & De Bleser, R. (1996). *Aachener Aphasie Test (AAT): Versione Italiana* (Seconda Edizione). Firenze: Organizzazioni Speciali.

Patterson, K. (1986). Lexical but nonsemantic spelling. *Cognitive Neuropsychology, 3,* 341–367.

Pizzamiglio, L., & Roberts, M.M. (1967). Writing in aphasia: A learning study. *Cortex, 3,* 250–257.

Schwartz, L., Nemeroff, S., & Reiss, M. (1974). An investigation of writing therapy for adult aphasic: The world level. *Cortex, 10,* 279–293.

Seron, X., Deloche, G., Moulard, G., & Rousselle, M. (1980). A computer based therapy for the treatment of aphasic subjects with writing disorders. *Journal of Speech and Hearing Disorders, 45,* 45–58.

Wernicke, C. (1885–1886). Die Neueren Arbeiten über Aphasie. *Fortschritte der Medizin, 3,* 824–830; *4,* 371–377; *4,* 463–482.

Willmes, K. (1985). An approach to analysing a single subject's scores obtained in a standardized test with application to the Aachen Aphasia Test (AAT). *Journal of Clinical and Experimental Neuropsychology, 7,* 331–352.

Zesiger, P., & de Partz, M.P. (1991). Rééducation cognitives des troubles de l'orthographie et/ou de l'écriture. In M.P. de Partz & M. Leclercq (Eds.), *La rééducation neuropsychologique de l'adulte.* Paris: Editions de la Société Neuropsychologique de Langue Française.

Manuscript received October 1999

NEUROPSYCHOLOGICAL REHABILITATION, 2000, *10* (3), 279–309

Agrammatism: Deficit or compensation? Consequences for aphasia therapy

Luise Springer and Walter Huber

University Hospital, University of Technology (RWTH), Aachen, Germany

Klaus-J. Schlenck and Claudia Schlenck

Fachklinik Enzensberg/Füssen, Germany

During the natural course of aphasia, agrammatism occurs as a symptom complex of either the acute or the chronic phase. Distinguishing these two clinical forms, we discuss its underlying nature in term of deficit and compensation. Furthermore, variations due to adaptation and/or restriction in information processing capacities are considered.

In recent years, we developed a new approach to the treatment of severe agrammatism, which is called Reduced Syntax Therapy (REST, Schlenck, Schlenck, & Springer, 1995). This approach comprises three major features: (1) activation of functional level information, (2) mapping of thematic roles onto simplified syntactic structures, and (3) leaving aside morphosyntactic markings. From a linguistic point of view, only basic processes of constituent structure formation are considered, which are in part also present in elliptic speech of normal speakers. The patients are instructed to expand one-word utterances into two- and three-constituent utterances in several steps, while ignoring function words and inflectional endings.

The efficacy of REST was studied in 11 patients with severe chronic agrammatism due to extensive left hemisphere lesions. In 9 patients significant expansion of simple phrase structures could be achieved whereas increase in closed class elements (function words and inflectional endings) remained small and limited to few patients. Therefore, we concluded that REST most likely enhances elementary proto-language functions of labelling and sequencing in the unimpaired right hemisphere, which may become the starting point for a gradual and laborious learning of simple syntax and grammar.

Requests for reprints should be sent to Luise Springer, Lehranstalt für Logopädie, Universitätsklinikum der RWTH, Pauwelsstraße 30, D-52074 Aachen, Germany. Telephone: ++49-(0)241-80 89966, fax: ++49-(0)241-8888 503.

E-mail: lspringer@post.klinikum.rwth-aachen.de

We would like to thank two anonymous reviewers and Klaus Willmes for many helpful suggestions.

© 2000 Psychology Press Ltd
http://www.tandf.co.uk/journals/pp/09602011.html

INTRODUCTION

Since Hughlings Jackson (1879) it has been stressed several times that aphasic symptoms can reflect either the underlying deficit or the attempt to compensate this deficit. The symptom complex of agrammatisms is a good example for this line of reasoning. On the surface, the main features of severe agrammatism are the following (cf. e.g., Caplan, 1987; Kerschensteiner et al., 1978):

1. Incomplete sentence structures consisting of individual content words which are linearly grouped together on semantic grounds rather than prosody or morphology.
2. Reduced repertoire of content words exhibiting little lexical variability, mainly restricted to concrete nouns with high frequency.
3. Absence of morphology that is governed by syntactic agreement demands such as personal endings on verbs or case markings on nouns and adjectives.
4. Highly limited repertoire of so-called function words consisting at most of co-ordinating conjunctions or adverbs (such as German "und", "dann"), modifying particles (such as German "schon") or prepositions which carry content (e.g., German "in", "zu").

Under the deficit hypothesis, these symptoms are always related to the normal language system. They reflect directly an impairment of morphosyntactic knowledge and/or a specific restriction of grammatical processing capacities (Caramazza & Zurif, 1976; Schwartz, Linebarger, & Saffran, 1985). Alternatively to a morphosyntactic deficit, some authors postulated an impairment of lexical knowledge and/or processing (cf. the discussion by Linebarger, 1995). There are, however, several clinical findings which can hardly be covered by the deficit approach and therefore require alternative explanations.

In the majority of patients, agrammatic symptoms become apparent during the chronic rather than the acute phase of recovery, i.e. not earlier than 6 months post-onset (Willmes & Poeck, 1993). In some cases, patients suffer from complete loss of speech for several years before they start to develop the typical concatenations of one-word utterances into short phrases with morphosyntactic marking still missing. Under the view of the deficit hypothesis, the late occurrence can be explained if there was initially a severe disorder of motor speech planning (speech apraxia) overriding the morphosyntactic impairment (Huber, Poeck, & Weniger, 1997). Of course, these cases must be distinguished from a combination of severe speech apraxia and global aphasia which initially are likewise characterised by no speech output, but in addition show severe impairment of comprehension.

Other patients with late occurrence of agrammatism went through an acute phase in which they showed positive symptoms of global aphasia in their spontaneous speech (Stachowiak et al., 1977). Their attempts to speak resulted in speech automatisms, single neologisms, perseverations, and stereotypical phrases, which they uttered in most part against their communicative intention. At the same time reading and writing were as a rule completely lost and language comprehension was limited to single highly familiar words and phrases. The patients relied on extralinguistic cues and situational guessing. Obviously, the central language system must have been extensively damaged in these patients. Along the lines of the deficit hypothesis, one would have to postulate that the late and gradual development of elementary phrase structures and morphosyntactic skills follows the regularities of the normal system despite such a severe impairment. It seems more plausible to assume that compensatory language learning becomes operative in these patients.

Another feature which cannot be explained in a straightforward fashion under a strong deficit hypothesis is the varying performance of sentence production depending on task demands and communicative situations. The varying performance reported for comprehension and judgement tasks led to ongoing controversies on the underlying mechanisms of agrammatism (Whitaker, 1997) and on the possibility of computational trade-off effects (e.g., Frazier & Friederici, 1991; Haarmann, Just, & Carpenter, 1997). Discrepancies in degree and kind of agrammatic disturbance are also common across expressive tasks. For example, in picture description the sentence patterns produced may show more constituents and more morphosyntactic marking than in spontaneous language (cf. Heeschen, 1985; Hofstede & Kolk, 1994b). Such discrepancies require a processing account of the deficit hypothesis. Due to the limited processing capacities of agrammatic patients (e.g., Kolk, 1993), message formulation has to be as simple as possible in spontaneous speech. Most of the capacity is already needed for the inner control of conversational interaction including propositional planning. Therefore patients rely in their spontaneous speech on telegraphic style intermingled with automatised formulations consisting of overlearned phrases and linguistic stereotypes. Under the processing account, the agrammatic symptoms themselves are seen as a compensatory response rather than reflecting a deficit in knowledge. For example, Kolk and Heeschen (1990) postulate agrammatism to be a preventive or corrective adaptation to an underlying delay of message-driven syntactic computation and lexical access.

It has also been claimed that these patients rely on simple and automatised expressions as a form of conversational adaptation (Kolk & Heeschen, 1990). In more formal situations such as being interviewed by a therapist the patients try to produce sentences as complete as possible even if long pauses for sentence planning are necessary. In contrast, in a more informal situation such as chatting with other patients single-word utterances and stereotypical phrases are predominantly used (cf. also Springer, Miller, & Bürk, 1998). Again, the variation cannot be explained by just assuming a central deficit of morphosyntactic knowledge. The agrammatic symptoms do not allow a direct interpretation as if they would reflect an impairment of normal functions. They rather reflect the general adaptation of an impaired system to varying cognitive demands and situations during the process of functional reorganisation with respect to underlying brain pathology.

Functional reorganisation

Two major modes of functional brain reorganisation can be postulated for the development of agrammatism (Huber, 1996). First, the damaged functions of the dominant hemisphere are restituted and substituted within the language network of the dominant left hemisphere. Obviously this requires lesions affecting only part of the left perisylvian areas. One can expect this mode of functional reorganisation to take place during the first months post-onset. Second, right hemisphere compensation must occur in those patients who suffered from extensive left hemisphere lesions and who start to develop agrammatic output late, i.e. beyond the period of so-called spontaneous recovery (Willmes & Poeck, 1984).

In a recent PET (positron emission tomography)-activation study right-hemisphere compensation was even demonstrated in patients with lesions limited to posterior areas of the left middle cerebral artery (MCA) distribution territory after complete recovery from Wernicke's aphasia several months and even years post-onset (Weiller et al., 1995). A similar right hemisphere uptake is even more likely in patients with a large left hemisphere lesion. On the other hand functional recovery within the damaged left hemisphere was reported for patients who showed good and rather fast language improvement during the first 6–12 months post-onset (Heiss et al., 1993, Zahn et al., 1999). Similar options of brain recovery can be expected for acute and chronic agrammatism which so far is not studied by functional brain imaging. Depending on the individual case, the left hemisphere damage may initially result in loss of syntactic knowledge or in limitation of rapid access requiring either right hemi-sphere compensation or left hemisphere restitution and substitution, respectively.

There is indirect evidence from correlating CT (computed tomography)-lesions and aphasic syndromes in stroke patients (Willmes & Poeck, 1993). Checking our databank we investigated to what proportion Broca's aphasia is the result of only anterior or of large lesions of the MCA territory. According to the classification routine of the Aachen Aphasia Test (AAT), agrammatism is a cardinal symptom of Broca's aphasia (Huber, Poeck, & Willmes, 1985). There-fore, the view of agrammatism being a compensatory response of the nondominant hemisphere can only be justified if Broca's aphasia is indeed correlated with large perisylvian rather than anterior lesions. The results of the *post hoc* investigation of a total of 187 consecutive AAT examinations are shown in Table 1. In all patients the aetiology was vascular and the duration of aphasia was at least 1 month.

Among single AAT examinations Broca's aphasia was found in only 2% of the cases examined before, but in 25% beyond 6 months post-onset. When multiple AAT examinations before and after 6 months were studied, it became apparent that 24% of all cases demonstrated a change in syndrome from global to Broca's aphasia. Only 8% were already found to have Broca's aphasia at first examination. Obviously, Broca's aphasia is more likely to occur late than early during the course of recovery.

A total of 41 cases with Broca's aphasia occurring later than 6 months post-onset were found after collapsing single and multiple AAT examinations. The distribution of size of lesion was as follows (cf. Table 1): 13 cases with

TABLE 1

Occurrence of aphasic syndromes and CT lesions in 187 consecutive patients with left hemisphere stroke and a minimum duration of 1 month

CT lesion MCA territory		Distribution of standard syndromes Single examinations							
		< 6 months				> 6 months			
Subtotal/total	Cases (%)	G	W	B	Other	G	W	B	Other
Large 42/77	55	7	0	0	1	27	1	5	1
Anterior 11/28	39	4	0	0	1	1	1	3	1
Posterior 27/50	54	3	9	0	10	0	2	0	3
Subcortical 19/32	59	3	0	2	8	1	0	5	0
99/187	53	17	9	2	20	29	4	13	5
		35%	19%	4%	42%	57%	8%	25%	10%

CT lesion MCA territory		Change of standard syndromes Multiple examination (</> 6 months)				
Subtotal/total	Cases (%)	G→G	G→B | x	B→B | x	W → W | x	Other
Large 35/77	45	25	7	1	1	1
Anterior 17/28	61	4	10	2	0	1
Posterior 23/50	46	2	2	1	15	3
Subcortical 13/32	41	6	2	3	0	2
88/187	47	37	21	7	16	7
		42%	24%	8%	18%	8%

G, global; B, Broca; W, Wernicke aphasia; x, non-classifiable or anomic aphasia.
Source: Aachen aphasia databank (1983–1988)

large perisylvian lesions, 15 cases with anterior lesions, and 10 with subcortical lesions. The presence of large perisylvian lesions is directly compatible with the assumption of a complete impairment of left perisylvian language functions and consequently with a compensation via language of the nondominant right hemisphere. In part, this may also hold for subcortical and anterior lesions, given recent findings on chronic hypoperfusion in the affected hemisphere of stroke patients (Heiss et al., 1993; Rodriguez et al., 1992; Weiller et al., 1990).

Since Kinsbourne (1971) it was repeatedly suggested that right hemisphere functions are involved in the recovery from aphasia after left hemisphere damage (Basso, Gardelli, Grassi, & Mariotti, 1989; Czopf, 1972; Fazzini, Bachman, & Albert, 1986; Geschwind, 1985; Karbe et al., 1998; Knopman et al., 1984; Lee et al., 1984; Levine & Mohr, 1979; Meyer et al., 1980). However, no specific reference was made to agrammatism as being a compensatory symptom of the nondominant hemisphere. Recently, right hemisphere symptoms of aphasia were thoroughly discussed by Code (1997), focusing on speech automatism, but again not considering agrammatism.

Differences between acute and chronic agrammatism

Our main claim is that agrammatism is different both in linguistic structure and in underlying mechanisms of phrase structure generation depending on the time of occurrence during the course of aphasia. In the acute phase up to approximately 1 month post-onset, the full picture of agrammatism is rarely found (in less than 10% of the clinical population of all aphasic patients). The condition of acute agrammatism requires small cortical or subcortical lesions within the anterior distribution territory of the middle cerebral artery. In the chronic phase, agrammatism is a developing symptom complex in patients with large left hemisphere lesions who initially presented with global aphasia. This change from global aphasia to Broca's aphasia with agrammatism is quite frequent (in about 30% of the aphasic population). In our clinical experience, there is no complete recovery from chronic agrammatism although improvement is possible under the impact of continuous aphasia therapy. The prognosis of acute agrammatism is much more favourable and it may even improve without professional therapy. Spontaneous recovery from acute Broca's aphasia with agrammatism into anomic aphasia, residual, or no aphasia was reported in 60% of patients (Willmes & Poeck, 1984).

The difference in prognosis, size of lesion as well as time of occurrence makes it plausible to assume different types of functional reorganisation which result in different patterns of agrammatic symptoms. The development of chronic agrammatism must involve compensatory right hemisphere functions after a complete loss of the left perisylvian language system. In contrast, acute agrammatism most likely reflects a temporary deficit of morphosyntactic knowledge and/or processing which is caused by partial damage to the anterior and/or central left perisylvian language zone. (The first few days after a cerebrovascular accident must, of course, be excluded from this consideration as all language functions are usually temporarily blocked in most cases; Biniek, 1993.)

The linguistic potential of the nondominant right hemisphere is a matter of ongoing debate (e.g., Bogen, 1997; Richards & Chiarello, 1997). Indeed, it is hard to conceive how morphosyntactic abilities can evolve from right hemisphere functions at all. The notion of a bilaterally represented "proto-language" may offer a basis for explaining the chronic type of agrammatism. One might argue that the bilateral brain has available elementary linguistic capacities of labelling and sequencing which root early in the history of the human evolution (Corballis, 1992; Rizzolatti & Arbib, 1998). The capacities of protolanguage are operative in the child's development up to the age of 2 years before the acquisition of the linguistic specificities and complexities of the adult target language sets in. Specific language acquisition seems to be exclu-sively based on left hemisphere lateralisation which eventually enables the child to process language in highly automatised and rapid fashion.

It would seem that protolanguage capacities of the right hemisphere remain available even after complete language lateralisation. So-called Pidgin languages which arise among second language learners who do not obtain a formal training are characterised by protolanguage patterns (Bickerton, 1990; Pinker, 1994). We propose that similar protolanguage mechanisms become operative in chronic agrammatism. This occurs late during the course of aphasia as large left hemisphere damage seems to have inhibitory effects on activation and development of right hemisphere functions as long as 12 months post-onset (diaschisis effects, e.g., Cappa et al., 1997). On the other hand, in acute agrammatism with good recovery due to small left hemisphere damage with no lasting transcallosal diaschisis, protolanguage mechanisms of the nondominant hemisphere might be a temporary starting condition before the functional recovery of the left hemisphere takes place.

In our clinical experience three types of recovery from agrammatism must be distinguished:

1. Acute agrammatism with good recovery.
2. Chronic agrammatism with poor recovery.
3. Chronic agrammatism with good recovery.

The time course of recovery in acute and chronic agrammatism is strikingly different. In acute agrammatism, recovery is substantial and often complete. It is reached within the first year post-onset whereas in chronic agrammatism, recovery is not always the case. If it occurs, small linguistic changes are observed over several years. The improvements tend to be limited to simple, but complete sentence structures with occasional morphosyntactic errors. Sentence subordination develops very late and only in some patients. In recovered chronic agrammatism, sentence production as a rule requires conscious planning and effortful formulation. When rapid formulation is required conversational adaptation to "telegraphic style" will be seen.

Therapy of agrammatism

Many efficacy studies have shown that agrammatic patients improve significantly under symptom-specific therapy when compared to untreated patients (Basso, Capitani, & Vignolo, 1979; Byng & Lesser, 1993; Poeck, Huber, & Willmes, 1989; Shewan & Kertesz, 1984; Wertz et al., 1986). However, the improvement shown in spontaneous speech is of special interest. Most patients show significant practice effects during therapy in various types of linguistic tasks that require syntactic knowledge such as picture description, sentence arrangement, and retelling stories (e.g., Doyle, Goldstein, & Bourgeois, 1987; Thompson, Thompson, 1998; Shapiro, & Roberts, 1993; Springer, Willmes & Haag, 1993; Van de Sandt-Koenderman & Bonta, 1998; Weniger, Springer & Poeck, 1987; Wiegel-Crump, 1976). In free conversation patients often fall back to the level of one-word utterances in their spontaneous speech. Therefore, when chronic agrammatic speech, although difficult to improve, is still the main concern in therapy for the patients and their relatives.

The chances to achieve transfer into spontaneous language may, of course, depend on the treatment method. The starting point of therapy planning is to specify the deficit in a model of normal language processing. According to the sentence production model of Garrett (1984), two types of treatment must be distinguished, namely, focusing either on the positional or on the functional level of normal sentence processing (for an alternative network approach cf. Schlenck et al., 1995).

Under the positional level approach it is assumed that surface structures are specifically affected in agrammatism. Therefore, linguistic parameters such as word order, syntactic functors (realised by closed class words) as well as morphosyntactic marking are the objective of therapy. These units and regularities are introduced along hierarchies of complexity and practised across major linguistic modalities. A typical example of this approach is the Helm Elicited Language Program for Syntax Stimulation (HELPSS) developed by Helm-Estabrooks, Fitzpatrick, and Barresi (1981) and Helm-Estabrooks and Ramsberger (1986). This programme uses a story completion format to elicit sentence structures of increasing syntactic complexity. Another example is the language oriented therapy (LOT) by Shewan and Bandur (1986), in which task hierarchies are introduced separately for several input and output modalities.

In the German literature, a didactic treatment of agrammatism was frequently discussed (Huber, 1991; Springer, 1994), which bears similarity to second language teaching. This approach puts emphasis on completeness of phrase structures, presence of morphology, and correctness of word order. The latter aspect is rather important as the word order of German is relatively free with only the finite verb being specifically fixed. For example, in declarative sentences, the finite verb has to be in second position of main clauses, but in last position of subordinate clauses. As a rule, the different morphosyntactic aspects (e.g., word order, verb inflection, etc.) are trained separately. However, when integration is required the processing and control capacities of the patients often get overloaded and they fall back to agrammatic sentence production.

Under the functional level approach, the treatment is focused on predicate-arguments structures or on thematic roles of verbs with increasing number of arguments. An example of this approach is the sentence generation training proposed by Thompson (1998).

Several variants of treatment were developed under the hypothesis of a mapping deficit, i.e. the projection of functional onto positional level information (and vice versa) is assumed to be specifically impaired in agrammatism whereas information on either level remains relatively accessible (Byng, 1988; Jones, 1986; Le Dorze, Jacob, & Coderre, 1991; Schwartz, Saffran, Fink, Myers, & Martin, 1994). The impaired mapping processes are treated primarily in metalinguistic tasks. The patients learn to identify thematic roles irrespective of word order. Subsequently, sentence production is expected to be likewise improved even without explicit training. Such a positive transfer was, however, not always found (Nickels, Byng, & Black, 1991).

Under either approach—functional or positional—direct practice effects seem to be easily obtained. Practice effects appear to be more extensive after training on the functional level than on the positional level. It is not clear, however, to what extent this is simply a consequence of differences in underlying mechanisms of agrammatism being present in the patients. But a transfer into spontaneous language is again difficult to achieve and is rarely investigated. In our view, this is mainly due to aphasic limitations of processing capacity. In the therapy session, patients are usually confronted with one problem at a time. There is enough freedom to activate all language resources still available and there is no communicative pressure put on the patient. However, in free conversation, patients are often confronted with all their linguistic, cognitive, and emotional problems simultaneously. This requires language processing routines completely different from the ones they supposedly learned in therapy. Therefore, large differences in the linguistic patterns of agrammatic speech are observed as a result of variation in task demands and situational context.

The basic rationale of both the functional and the positional level approach to the treatment of agrammatism can be viewed as follows. First, the aphasic symptoms are taken to reflect linguistic deficits which can be localised in a model of normal sentence formulation. Second, the treatment tries to repair linguistic breakdown. The nature of the impairment may differ in being either a loss of linguistic knowledge or an insufficient access to preserved linguistic knowledge. Only in the latter case, systematic deblocking techniques may prove to be successful (cf. Weigl & Bierwisch 1970). This is also true of facilitation techniques that try to activate highly familiar and overlearned phrases in a holistic fashion (Huber, Springer, & Willmes, 1993).

A totally different rationale considers the compensatory potentials of the bilateral brain. The best known example is the melodic intonation therapy (MIT; Sparks, Helm, & Albert, 1974) which tries to make use of right hemisphere prosodic functions for the facilitation of speech. This is meant to be particularly successful in Broca's aphasia.

The so-called preventive method as devised by Beyn and Shokhor Trotskaya (1966) also makes use of compensatory capacities of the brain. Agrammatism is viewed as disintegration of the predicative system. The basic therapy concept is to avoid the development of a telegraphic style by excluding the use of denoting nouns that establish reference to living and non-living objects of the mental world. In order to prevent telegraphic enumerations of nouns, the therapist tries to stimulate only emotional and interpersonal expressions which typically consist of interjections, and adverbial and predicative phrases. During the acute phase, the patients are encouraged to utter such fragments of highly familiar phrases. Later on, these fragments are expanded into more complete sentence structures which carry propositional rather than emotional and interpersonal content. At this stage the preventive method becomes very similar to methods of the positional level approach. Thus, the preventive approach combines deficit and compensation oriented methods of intervention.

In recent years, we developed a treatment method, the so-called Reduced Syntax Therapy (REST; Schlenck et al., 1995) which deliberately encourages rather than prevents the production of telegraphic style. Originally, REST was developed for the treatment of chronic agrammatism. The basic rationale is compensatory, i.e. REST tries to optimise the reduced language capacities of the nondominant hemisphere.

REDUCED SYNTAX THERAPY (REST)

Goals

The first goal is to enable the patient to generate reduced sentence structures as fluently as possible. These structures have to fulfil the following linguistic constraints. First, the starting point of each utterance is a main verb and its obligatory complements (verb constraint). Second, the verb phrase has to be non-finite, i.e. there are no inflectional endings for person or tense and there are no auxiliary verbs (non-finiteness constraint). Third, the position of obligatory complements has to be in line with the basic word order of the target language, e.g. in German being a subject–object–verb (SOV) language the order has to be complement before verb (word order constraint). Fourth, syntactic morphology is neglected, i.e. the training is focused on main categories (verb, noun, adjective, predicating preposition), functors like determiners and pronouns are excluded as well as verb agreement and case marking (morphology constraint).

What is our theoretical justification for focusing on reduced sentence structures of this kind? Severe agrammatism is primarily seen as a compensatory response of intact right hemisphere functions to a complete loss of the syntactic capacities of the left hemisphere. Therefore the REST approach aims first at stimulating and expanding basic strategies of content word activation and concatenation, i.e. of protolanguage processing. From this starting point basic syntactic parameters of the target language are introduced reflecting in part the structure of elliptic utterances found in normal colloquial speech. Thereby the REST approach diminishes the amount of capacities required for producing syntactically complete and morphologically spelled out utterances. The patient is likely to gain free capacities for other aspects of the production process, like message planning, word activation and motor speech planning. Thus, the utterances are produced faster, and remain still comprehensible, despite their reduced sentence structures, just like contextual ellipsis or so-called telegraphic style in normal conversation (Clark & Clark, 1977; Klein, 1981). Typically, these elliptic structures are lacking finiteness (Kolk & Heeschen, 1990; 1992), e.g., either the verb appears in a non-finite form or it is omitted.

In comparison to mapping therapy (Schwartz et al., 1994), the focus of REST lies on expanding syntactic frames rather than improving the processing of thematic roles. But it is a secondary aim of REST to practice variable thematic roles by changing the strict subcategorisation frame of the verbs. In contrast to the sentence generation programme of Thompson (1998), REST systematically leaves out morphosyntactic structures, thus focusing on base structures alone.

Treatment methodology

Applying the REST approach, we follow the five levels shown in Table 2 for both German and English. Each level is practised until mastery is reached and transfer into spontaneous language is observed. In severe chronic agrammatism the ceiling performance is usually reached in level 2 although treatment can continue to level 5, requiring repeated periods of intensive therapy. In acute agrammatism and mild forms of chronic agrammatism training to level 3 often facilitates immediate complex syntactic processing. The treatment methods should then be changed to a didactic treatment of those

TABLE 2
Reduced Syntax Therapy (REST)
with phrase structures exemplified for German and English

Level 1	2-word utterances: VP with direct object	
● Theme	WHAT/HOW DOING	
● Structure	N - V	V - N
	A - V	V - A
● Examples	*Kaffee trinken*	drinking coffee
	schnell laufen	running fast
Level 2	2^{+1}-word utterances: VP with prepositional phrase	
● Theme	WHERE/WHERE TO - WHAT DOING/DONE	
● Structure	PP - V	V - PP
● Examples	*nach Wien gefahren*	gone to Vienna
Level 3	3-word utterances: VP plus subject	
● Theme	WHO - WHAT DOING/DONE	
● Structure	N - N - V	N - V - N
● Examples	*Katie Bein gebrochen*	Katy broken leg
Level 4	3/4-word utterances: VP plus S-adverb	
● Theme	WHEN - (WHO) - WHAT DOING/DONE	
● Structure	A - (N) - N - V	(N) - V - N - A
● Examples	*gestern Brief geschrieben*	written letter yesterday
Level 5	3/4-word utterances: VP plus subject	
● Theme	(WHO) - WHOM - WHAT DOING/DONE	
● Structure	(N) - N - N - V	(N) - V - N - N
● Examples	*(Lisa) Leo Brief geschrieben*	(Lisa) written letter to Leo

morphosyntactic features which are still disturbed. The standard practice task requires the patient to convey the propositional core of events by means of multiple word utterances. This is elicited by non-imitative techniques such as picture description, story completion, and telegram formulation. The task is always embedded in a communicative context introduced by the therapist.

Level 1. Initially, only two-word utterances are practised which always consist of a non-finite verb and a noun functioning as a direct object (cf. German, *Kaffee trinken, Auto waschen, Zeitung lesen, Zähne putzen,* or English *drink(ing) coffee, wash(ing) car, read(ing) paper, brush(ing) teeth*). The verb phrases to be constructed should be highly familiar in everyday language usage and it should be easy to create a mental image of their meanings as they refer to typical activities of everyday life. In an inflecting SOV language like German, the patient is encouraged to produce the verb always in the final position of each utterance and to use only infinite forms neglecting the personal endings (which are fully productive in German). Furthermore, the patient is explicitly encouraged to leave out all "little words" (e.g., article and possessive pronouns which require case assignment in German). The general linguistic idea is to keep out all morphosyntactic variation, but to allow for variation in lexical morphology when pragmatically required. Such lexical variation may occur with respect to number (singular versus plural of the noun) and tense (infinitive/gerundive versus past participle of the verb representing present and past tense, respectively). Typical examples for German are *Hände waschen, Brief geschrieben, Blumen bekommen* (cf. English *washing hands, written letter, got flowers*). Depending on the reference situation, lexical variation may be spontaneously performed by the patient or can be easily stimulated and corrected by the therapist.

When applying REST, the position of the verb has to be always in accordance with the basic word order of the target language. In a subject–verb–object (SVO) Language like English verb–noun (V-N) structures would be practised. Furthermore, it is important to start with morphologically unmarked verb phrases that are frequently found in the surface structure of this language (e.g., in English *shake hands* or *wash dishes*, etc.) In other words, highly familiar, lexicalised sentence fragments are introduced first and taken as a structural model for generally reduced sentence formulations. In normal language, these structures can be naturally found in elliptic answers and in informal speech using telegraphic style.

All sentence fragments to be practised are strings which consist only of the major categories V and N (or V and A [= adjective/adverb]), even if they would require additional function words in elliptic utterances of normal speech such as *wash hands* instead of *wash your hands*. The general rationale is to enable the patient just to produce strict subcategorisation frames, i.e. only the verb and its obligatory complement.

The two-word structures (N-V in German or V-N in English) are systematically practised in tasks that allow the patient to produce elliptic answers to cueing questions of the therapist. The linguistic context may vary, for example:

1. Naming of multiple choice sets of pictures with minimal semantic contrast in agent, object, or activity.
2. Completion of brief and long stories with and without parallel depiction.

Irrespective of the context, the therapist always uses the same type of question for cueing which is orally put forward in morphosyntactically complete forms, e.g.

- Therapist: *Was macht/machen X? Was hat X gemacht?* (*X is doing what? X has done what?*)

The therapist refers in either lexicalised or pronominalised form to a specific agent (X) shown on the pictures or given in the story. But, in level 1 and 2, X must not be realised by the patient. Therefore, the spoken cues are supported by written and graphic cues which model for the patient the structure of the elliptic answer:

- Written cue: WAS MACHEN? or WAS GEMACHT? (DOING WHAT? or DONE WHAT?)

The graphic cues introduce minimal metalinguistic information marking both word category (noun, verb) and word order. The interaction between therapist and patient is illustrated by the following example as transcribed from video recordings:

- Stimulating context: 3 picture cards showing the same man eating a Wurstbrot, eating spaghetti, or eating soup.
- Therapist introducing the "telegram strategy":
  How would you describe this picture to another person?
  You need to say only two words! I will give you an example: *This man here, he is doing what?* (pointing to the depicted activity and the written cue) . . . eat(ing) bread (original German, *Brot essen*)
- Starting practice
  Th.   Here (pointing to the next picture) *he is doing what?*
  P.   Noodle (original German, *Nudel*)
  Th.   Right. We have here noodles. But you did not tell me *what he is doing.*
  P.   uh . . . uh
  Th.   Is he buying, eating, cooking noodles? . . . *He is doing what?*
  P.   Noodles . . . uh . . . ea-ting (original German, *Nudeln e-ssen*)
  Th.   Say it again as a whole phrase. *He is doing what?*
  P.   Eating noodles (original German, *Nudeln essen*)
  Th.   Very good. And here (pointing to the next picture) *He is doing what?*
  P.   Eating soup (original German, *Suppe essen*)
- Expanding practice
  Th.   Now I am going to turn over all the cards. Everything is in the past.
  He has eaten (original German, *er hat gegessen*)
  He has done what? (pointing to the backside of the last card)
  Can you remember. *He has done what?*
  P.   Eating soup (original German, *Suppe essen*)
  Th.   It should be in the past. How would you change the word "eating"?

P.   Ea—-ting (verbal searching) (original German, *e—-essen*)
      (indicating "no" by turning her head)
Th.   Has ea- (original German, *Suppe ge-* . . .). . . .
P.   Eaten (original German, *gegessen*)
Th.   Say it again as a whole phrase. *He has done what?*
P.   Eaten soup (original German, *Suppe gegessen*)
Th.   (turning the card back to the picture) That's right.
      (pointing to the next card) *Here, he has done what?*
P.   Eaten noodles (original German, *Nudeln gegessen*)
Th.   (turning the card back to the picture) That's right. . .
      Your memory is very good.
P.   (laughs)

This example demonstrates how the strict categorisation frame of the verb "eat" can be established by semantic variation of the object noun. Furthermore, the additional activation of lexical morphology (number and tense) is exemplified.

It is important to keep the exercises linguistically variable, in order to avoid pure learning of stereotypical language patterns. Therefore, the verb and noun slots are variably filled while keeping either one constant. Still in level 1 of REST, the structure of the verb phrase (VP) should be changed according to the strict subcategorisation parameters of the target language. In German we introduce intransitive verbs together with morphologically unmarked adverbs, e.g., *gut schlafen, lange bleiben, viel arbeiten* (cf. *sleeping well, staying long, working hard*). These intransitive predicates can be stipulated by two-step questions of the type, *Was macht X?...Wie?* (cf. *X is doing what?...How?*).

Another expansion of level 1 are verbs containing a prefix or particle, e.g., *Mantel anziehen.* In SVO languages such particles are as a rule positioned after the verb (cf. *put on coat*). The REST approach systematically avoids structures in which the particle is separated from the verb, i.e. there are no structures being trained like *ziehen Mantel an* or *put coat on.* Thereby, the syntactic processing demands are kept low.

Level 2.   On this level of REST therapy, prepositional phrases are introduced which express spatial relationships (location and direction), e.g., *im Bett liegen, zum Bahnhof gehen, nach Köln fahren* (cf. *lying in bed, going to (the) station, driving to Cologne*). It might appear inappropriate to use prepositions at all in a reduced syntax approach, since prepositions are often considered to be functions words like articles and pronouns. However, in logical semantics they are treated like predicates, and it was empirically found that they are relatively better preserved in agrammatism when they carry meaning of their own (Friederici, 1985). This is clearly the case for spatial prepositions.

In severe agrammatism, level 2 often cannot be initiated because the prepositions can neither be retrieved nor semantically differentiated. Therefore they have to be trained separately before one proceeds into REST. Even if such a separate training fails, the verb phrases of level 2 should be practised without prepositions, thereby not giving up the aim of expressing variable thematic roles by reduced phrase structures.

The REST-structures are again stipulated by questions of the format, *Was macht/machen X? (X is/are doing what?)*. If the patient's response contains only the verb, the missing locational or directional complement is stimulated in a second step by introducing the corresponding interrogative pronouns, *Wo/Wohin? (Where/Where to?)* The comprehension of these pronouns is supported by simple pictograms and by symbolic gesturing. The symbol "point" stands for *Wo*, an "arrow" for *Wohin* N. In languages which do not have adverbial pronouns, classifying expressions can be used instead, e.g., *(in what) manner?, (at what) place?, (in what) direction?*

The training material of level 1 and 2 comprises a list of 100 phrases which should be mastered with a probability of at least 80% across the various task contexts. In order to reinforce the transfer into spontaneous language, the oral and written cues are also used by the therapist when she or he is engaged with the patient in free conversation. The training is carried on until the patient shows spontaneous usage in approximately 50% of occasions in free conversation.

Level 3.   The VP structures of level 1 and 2 are now expanded by a subject noun, being always animate, thereby reinforcing a general linguistic strategy which takes the subject of a sentence as agent (Jarvella & Sinnot, 1972). Correspondingly, the subject noun is stipulated by the interrogative pronoun, *Wer? (Who?)*. If the patient responds only with a subject noun the missing verb phrase is stimulated as in levels 1 and 2.

The REST structures being practised in level 3 consist of three constituents: subject–complement–nonfinite verb, e.g., *Frau Zeitung lesen, Kinder schnell laufen, Mann zum Krankenhaus gehen (cf. lady reading paper, children running fast, man going to hospital, etc.)*. These structures are rarely found in elliptic utterances of normal speakers. They are truly "agrammatic", in the sense of missing function words (auxiliaries and articles). Why do we nevertheless introduce and practice them in level 3? Obviously subject–verb agreement, one of the most demanding morphosyntactic operations is not required, just as case assignment was not required in level 1 and 2. From a functional perspective, however, these structures nevertheless allow the speaker to convey thematic relations and are consequently comprehensible for the communicative partner.

After introducing the subject, the verb is again systematically contrasted between present and past tense by using the infinitive form versus the past participle. When practising past tense, an additional semantic contrast has to be observed. REST structures like *Mädchen Brief geschrieben* (cf. *girl written (a) letter*) denote in their dominant meaning an activity of the past. In contrast, structures like *Mädchen Brief bekommen* (cf. *girl got letter*) denote an event. These contrasts are, of course, a consequence of the different semantic aspects of the verb and their corresponding thematic roles. With verbs denoting an event, a different semantic format for the stipulating question has to be used, namely *Was ist passiert? (What happened?)*.

For practising the REST structures of level 3, we use telegram-tasks, as illustrated by the following example (translated from the original German):

Th.   Imagine there was an accident and you want to send a telegram, but you do not have the money to pay for a long message. You can only choose three words. *What has happened?* Listen to the story.
      On a skiing holiday, your friend Monica has broken her leg and her mother must be informed as soon as possible. You have only enough money for three words. What three words would you use? . . . I am at the post office. Could you tell me the three words.

P.   . . . leg . . .

Th.   I will write down the word "leg". You have enough money left for two more words:

P.   Phone . . .

Th.   Imagine you will get a telegram like this: "leg . . . phone".
      Would you understand the message?

P.   No . . . Monica. . .

Th.   Yes, it is important to start with *Who* (pointing to written and pictorial cue) and, *What happened?* . . .

P.   Broken leg. . .

Th.   That's it. Please say all three words again.

P.   Monica broken leg (original German, *Monika Bein gebrochen*)

The target structures of level 3 can be varied in several ways. The subject can be combined with verb phrases containing intransitive verbs (e.g., *president spoken on TV*), predicating adjectives (e.g., *granny sad*) or predicating nouns (e.g., *father carpenter*). The subject itself can be varied in number, using either lexicalised plural forms (e.g., children) or explicit expressions by means of numerals (e.g., *three*) or noun conjunctions (e.g., *girl and boy*).

Level 4 and 5.   On level 4, free adverbial expressions are introduced primarily for temporal and local modification. They are again stipulated by an interrogative pronoun (English, *When* and *Where* (German, *Wann* and *Wo*). In a step-wise fashion, these free adverbials are combined with all REST structures practised earlier in level 1 to 3. Examples are: *yesterday got flowers, next year going to Europe, tonight president speaking on TV*.

On level 5, one finally proceeds to verbs with the most complex subcategorisation frames. These are transitive verbs being complemented by both a direct and an indirect object. The corresponding thematic roles are always inanimate object and animate experiencer as in *taken (away) bag (from) granny* (cf. German, *Oma Tasche weggenommen*).

When these verb phrases are structurally mastered, irrespective of morphology, they can be expanded by adding subject nouns and/or free adverbials. An example for the most complex REST structure stripped from all morphology would be:

- English: WHEN   WHO   DONE WHAT   WHOM   WHERE
  yesterday . . . thief . . . taken (away) bag . . . (from) granny . . . (at) station
- German: WANN   WER   WEM   WAS GEMACHT   WO
  gestern . . . Dieb . . . Oma . . . Tasche (weg) genommen . . . (am) Bahnhof

When reaching structures of this complexity it is important to keep constant the word order of the core SVO/SOV-structure. The free adverbials are placed in pre- or post-position. In many patients with severe chronic agrammatism, structures which have to be filled by as few as three words cannot be achieved due to limitations in verbal working memory. In these patients individual adaptation is necessary. The therapist can choose among the following options: leaving aside prepositions, treating free adverbials as separate one- or two-word utterances, or separating subjects from the verb phrase prosodically. This would change the given example into a sequence of one- and two-word utterances, which follow the temporal and spatial order of events:

- English: *yesterday . . granny . . station . . . . thief . . taken bag.*
- German: *gestern . . Oma . . Bahnhof . . . . Dieb . . Tasche genommen.*

With level 5 the final level of REST-therapy is reached. By means of morphologically reduced phrase structures most thematic roles for formulating messages can be expressed and differentiated. From level 4 onward, the REST-structures are always practised as parts of discourse. Appropriate tasks are story completion, story retelling, linguistic role playing, etc.

On all levels, it is necessary to support the formulation of REST structures by pictorial material, especially when new structures are introduced. The selection of the linguistic material should be adapted to the personal interests, linguistic skills, and communicative needs of the patients as long as the overall principles are observed, namely systematic expansion of sentence fragments. A rich source is the Photo Series of Everyday Life Activities (ELA; Stark, 1992).

This series contains lists of 1 to 4-place verbs, each of which is illustrated on several different photos varying the referents for their thematic roles.

Therapy study

We applied REST to the treatment of 11 patients with severe, chronic agrammatism (Schlenck et al., 1995). All patients had received extensive treatment within the traditional symptom-specific approach, i.e. the practised structures always had to be morphologically fully spelled out. Under impact of this approach, significant improvements were obtained in variable language functions as measured by the Aachen Aphasia Test (AAT; Huber et al., 1985), but none of the patients showed any change in the severe agrammatism of their spontaneous language. As REST specifically aims at improving the spontaneous formulation of messages, we wanted to find out to what extent these patients would improve the phrase structures of their spontaneous language after a period of intensive treatment applying the REST approach.

Table 3 shows the sample characteristics. Six of the treated patients were male, five were female. All patients were right-handed. The median age was 46 years. The aetiology was vascular in all cases with extensive infarcts of the left perisylvian lesion. In all patients the aphasia was chronic with a median duration of 40 months, in no case was the duration less than 1 year, i.e., all patients were clearly beyond spontaneous recovery. According to the Aachen Aphasia Test (AAT), in eight patients the impaired language was classified as Broca's, in two as global, and in one as non-classifiable aphasia.

TABLE 3
Sample characteristics

Patient	Aetiology	Duration (months)	Age (years)	Sex	Syndrome AAT - Allocation
1. H.V.	Vascular	17	43	M	Broca
2. H.T.	Vascular	25	37	M	Broca
3. U.D.	Vascular	40	31	F	Non-classifiable
4. W.M.	Vascular	11	73	M	Broca
5. A.K.	Vascular	132	60	F	Broca
6. M.H.	Vascular	61	56	M	Broca
7. W.H.	Vascular	64	58	M	Broca
8. M.B.	Vascular	122	46	F	Broca
9. M.W.	Vascular	11	34	F	Global
10. W.B.	Vascular	51	47	F	Broca
11. M.S.	Vascular	21	32	M	Global
Median		40	46		
Range		11–132	31–73		

All 11 patients were severely agrammatic. In the AAT the syntactic structure of their spontaneous speech was rated as 1 on a scale from 0 to 5, i.e. their utterances consisted only of one or sometimes two words. This was the case even though all patients had received intensive speech therapy including syntax exercises over a long period. With respect to the AAT-subtest scores, the group was fairly heterogeneous. The percentile ranks for Language Comprehension (md 56, range 13–95) and for Confrontation Naming (md 51, range 22–79) differed widely. Most of the patients had a reduced verbal short-term memory which in part caused their low performance in Repetition (md 39, range 32–71) and on the Token Test (md 39, range 7–86).

Each patient received a total of 30 full hour treatments according to the principles of reduced syntax therapy. Five came as outpatients three times per week over a period of 12 weeks including pre- and post-treatment assessment. The other six were treated on specialised aphasia wards at two different institutions.

As a means of controlling the effect of therapy, we analysed the spontaneous speech as routinely assessed by the AAT before and after the period of treatment. Each semi-standardised interview lasted between 10 and 15 minutes. The audiotaped interviews were orthographically transcribed and segmented into utterances corresponding to thought-units or propositions based on semantic, prosodic, and/or morphosyntactic criteria (cf. Huber et al., 1985). As we wanted to assess the morphosyntactic structure of only those utterances conveying new information, all utterances containing automatised and stereotypical elements were excluded from the analysis of the phrase structure. The median number and the range of phrases obtained across the 11 patients was comparable in pre- and post-treatment interviews (md 49, 23–85 vs md 52 37–85).

The phrase structure analysis was based on surface structure information alone. The following morphosyntactic variables were determined:

- Word category distinguishing between verb, noun, adjective (open class) and subtypes of function words such as articles, prepositions, pronouns and conjunctions (closed class).
- Syntactic constituency being either a simple or complex verb, noun phrase, adverbial phrase, or prepositional phrase.
- Morphological markings, namely case, gender and number of noun phrases and prepositional phrases as well as finite and non-finite forms of main verbs, modal verbs, and auxiliaries.
- Order and number of constituents.

What were our expectations? Assuming that chronic agrammatism resulted from complete loss of morphosyntactic knowledge as acquired by the dominant left hemisphere, it is unlikely that language-specific parameters of syntax and morphology can be stipulated by the REST approach. Therefore, we did not expect more function words and inflectional endings to become apparent after the treatment. Rather the number and variability of constituents per utterance should be increased due to intact protolanguage capacities which would be enhanced by the REST approach.

Alternatively, one might assume that morphosyntactic knowledge of the target language is available even in chronic agrammatism. This could be either due to ongoing functional reorganisation in the dominant hemisphere or to premorbid bilateral representation in both hemispheres. Under such assumptions, the REST approach could have an initiating effect leading to an evolvement of morphosyntactic processing abilities. Depending on the underlying brain mechanism, this can be the result of either disinhibition or reorganisation.

The quantitative result of our treatment study demonstrated significant expansion of clause structures in most patients as shown in Table 4. We distinguished utterances with one, two, and three or more constituents before and after treatment. Nine of the 11 patients showed significant changes in their syntactic structure; they produced significantly more two- and three-constituent-utterances and significantly less one-constituent-utterances. As REST focuses specifically on verbs, we also assessed changes in their relative occurrence (see Table 5). Five of the 8 patients with expanded clause structures

TABLE 4
Spontaneous speech: Relative distribution of clause structures
with 1, 2, and 3 constituents in pre- and post-treatment assessment

Patient number	Pre-treatment			Post-treatment			Percentage of 2/3-const. pre vs post	Fisher's exact test p-value[1]
	1 const. Total (%)	2 const. Total (%)	3 const. Total (%)	1 const. Total (%)	2 const. Total (%)	3 const. Total (%)		
1	47 (70)	14 (21)	6 (9)	35 (45)	37 (47)	6 (8)	30 55	.0018*
2	66 (78)	13 (15)	6 (7)	33 (39)	31 (36)	21 (25)	22 61	.0001*
3	44 (91)	4 (9)	0 (0)	43 (63)	25 (35)	1 (2)	9 37	.0002*
4	30 (81)	3 (8)	4 (11)	21 (49)	13 (31)	9 (20)	19 51	.0026*
5	41 (71)	15 (26)	2 (3)	8 (22)	16 (43)	13 (35)	29 78	.0001*
6	21 (91)	2 (9)	0 (0)	25 (48)	25 (48)	2 (4)	9 52	.0003*
7	40 (82)	5 (10)	4 (8)	33 (46)	22 (31)	16 (23)	18 54	.0001*
8	35 (85)	5 (12)	1 (3)	24 (65)	9 (24)	4 (11)	15 35	.0323*
9	65 (96)	3 (4)	0 (0)	45 (56)	21 (26)	14 (18)	4 44	.0001*
10	44 (68)	17 (26)	4 (6)	36 (77)	11 (23)	0 (0)	32 23	.2075
11	39 (96)	2 (4)	0 (0)	42 (93)	3 (7)	0 (0)	4 7	.5446

[1] for the pre-post treatment proportion of clauses with 1 versus 2/3 constituents, one tailed.
* significant.

TABLE 5
Spontaneous speech: Relative distribution of verbs in clauses

| Patient number | Pre-treatment | | | Post-treatment | | | Percentage of phrases with verbs pre vs post | Fisher's exact test p-value[1] |
	No verb Total (%)	Infinite verb Total (%)	Finite verb Total (%)	No verb Total (%)	Infinite verb Total (%)	Finite verb Total (%)		
1	52 (78)	11 (16)	4 (6)	36 (46)	35 (46)	7 (9)	22 54	.0001*
2	58 (68)	25 (30)	2 (2)	53 (62)	27 (32)	5 (6)	32 38	.2597
3	41 (85)	7 (15)	0 (0)	48 (70)	19 (27)	2 (3)	15 30	.0376*
4	29 (78)	4 (11)	4 (11)	31 (72)	8 (19)	4 (9)	22 28	.3503
5	45 (78)	13 (22)	0 (0)	20 (54)	14 (38)	3 (8)	22 60	.0150*
6	17 (74)	5 (22)	1 (4)	6 (12)	45 (86)	1 (2)	26 88	.0001*
7	35 (72)	10 (20)	4 (8)	38 (54)	14 (20)	19 (26)	28 46	.0364*
8	38 (93)	3 (7)	0 (0)	29 (78)	8 (22)	0 (0)	07 22	.0680
9	56 (82)	12 (18)	0 (0)	59 (74)	18 (22)	3 (4)	18 26	.2197
10	51 (78)	9 (14)	5 (8)	42 (89)	5 (11)	0 (0)	22 11	.1021
11	39 (39)	2 (5)	0 (0)	42 (93)	3 (07)	0 (0)	05 07	.5446

[1] for the pre-post treatment proportion of clauses with and without verbs, one tailed.
* significant.

indeed produced more verbs. However, only in patient 7 was substantial morphological marking of verbs observed.

Other aspects of the possible improvement in morphosyntactic skills although not explicitly treated by REST are changes in the distribution of open and closed class elements (see Table 6) and of unspecified and specified nouns (see Table 7). Four patients showed significant increase of closed class items in their spontaneous speech. Patient 7 even approximated the normal range of 50–70% closed class elements in normal spontaneous speech of German as assessed by the AAT interview (Biniek, 1993). Finally, 3 of the 11 patients demonstrated an increase in using specified noun phrases (see Table 7).

After discharge from our therapy programme, 4 patients received no further aphasia therapy. After 10–18 months their spontaneous language was analysed again. The follow-up results are given in Table 8. In patients 1, 6, and 9, who achieved significant increases in constituent numbers (see Table 4), the improvement remained stable (except for variation in proportion of multiple constituent utterances in patient 9). But in patient 7, who was the best responder to REST, the number of one-constituent utterances increased again, although not hitting the initial values. This patient was the only one among the 4 follow-up patients who did not live in a family, but unfortunately became socially isolated in a nursing home. During the treatment he achieved substantial improvement 64 months after spontaneous left hemispheric haemorrhage and subsequent complete destruction of the basal ganglia.

TABLE 6
Spontaneous speech: Distribution of open versus closed class elements

| Patient number | Pre-treatment | | | | Post-treatment | | | | Fisher's exact test p-value[1] |
| | Word class | | | | Word class | | | | |
	Open (%)		Closed (%)		Open (%)		Closed (%)		
1	90	(68)	43	(32)	157	(69)	69	(31)	.4048
2	88	(65)	48	(35)	108	(58)	79	(42)	.1255
3	51	(89)	6	(11)	74	(70)	31	(30)	.0041*
4	51	(93)	4	(7)	62	(79)	16	(37)	.0287*
5	77	(85)	14	(15)	60	(55)	29	(45)	.0055*
6	25	(89)	3	(11)	69	(87)	11	(13)	.4825
7	55	(63)	2	(27)	101	(49)	107	(51)	.0001*
8	49	(74)	17	(26)	45	(75)	15	(25)	.5433
9	68	(64)	39	(36)	72	(70)	31	(30)	.2034
10	66	(89)	8	(11)	46	(81)	11	(19)	.1321
11	40	(85)	7	(15)	39	(76)	12	(24)	.2053

[1] one tailed test for the pre-post treatment proportion of closed class elements. * significant.

TABLE 7
Spontaneous speech: Distribution of unspecified and specified nouns

| Patient number | Pre-treatment | | | | Post-treatment | | | | Fisher's exact test p-value[1] |
	N (%)		[(Det)(A) N] (%)		N (%)		[(Det)(A) N] (%)		
1	43	(67)	21	(33)	82	(69)	36	(31)	.4370
2	49	(64)	27	(36)	55	(60)	37	(40)	.3219
3	27	(90)	3	(10)	16	(57)	12	(43)	.0047*
4	24	(92)	2	(8)	34	(71)	14	(29)	.0279*
5	47	(77)	14	(23)	28	(52)	26	(48)	.0041*
6	16	(100)	0	(0)	12	(94)	1	(6)	.4483
7	20	(79)	7	(26)	34	(56)	27	(44)	.0806
8	32	(78)	13	(29)	30	(86)	5	(14)	.0989
9	46	(81)	3	(6)	38	(95)	2	(5)	.5963
10	46	(94)	11	(19)	32	(91)	3	(9)	.1367
11	49	(94)	2	(6)	27	(93)	2	(7)	.6682

Det, determiner; A, adjective. [1] one tailed test for the pre-post treatment proportion of specified nouns. * significant.

TABLE 8

Distribution of clause structures in spontaneous speech post-treatment and follow-up 10–18 months later

Patient number	Pre-treatment			Post-treatment			Percentage of 2/3-const.	Fisher's exact test
	1 const. Total (%)	2 const. Total (%)	3 const. Total (%)	1 const. Total (%)	2 const. Total (%)	3 const. Total (%)	pre vs. post	p-value[1]
1	34 (45)	37 (47)	6 (8)	34 (42)	36 (44)	11 (14)	(55) (58)	.4175
6	25 (58)	25 (48)	2 (4)	28 (45)	31 (50)	3 (5)	(52) (55)	.4512
7	33 (46)	22 (31)	16 (23)	14 (72)	57 (18)	8 (10)	(54) (28)	.0011*
9	45 (56)	21 (18)	14 (18)	37 (48)	42 (42)	9 (10)	(44) (52)	.1712

[1] for the pre-post treatment proportion of clauses with 1 versus 2/3 constituents, one tailed.
* significant.

DISCUSSION

The aim of REST is not to engage patients in relearning normal syntactic patterns but to use simplified sentence formulation routines. Starting with the predicate and its basic thematic relations, the intended message is transformed into reduced syntactic structures which resemble elliptic utterances of normal speech. Morphosyntactic elements are largely ignored. In this respect, REST is clearly not a positional level approach. On the other hand, it does not focus on thematic roles alone, but starts from basic verb subcategorisation frames which carry variable thematic roles. Furthermore, REST aims at compensation of limited processing resources. In acute agrammatism, this may facilitate a restoration of normal syntactic processing. In chronic agrammatism, this may optimise the reduced language capacities being left and in some cases even stipulate long-lasting relearning of complex syntax and morphology.

The efficacy of the REST approach was examined in a group of 11 patients with chronic agrammatism. After intensive treatment, in 8 of these patients the spontaneous language showed significantly more constituents per utterance, more non-finite verbs, and in 4 cases even more morphosyntactic elements. From preliminary follow-up data in 4 of the patients one can conclude that the improvements obtained from a relatively short training period may be long lasting. Even if the linguistic outcome appears to be limited, it is important to note that transfer into spontaneous language was achieved. This improvement took place despite the fact that the mean duration of aphasia was over 3 years during which several attempts were made to stimulate the relearning of grammatically correct sentences. None of these earlier attempts had led to a stable transfer into spontaneous speech.

From the very beginning of therapy all patients except one accepted the REST approach quite well. However, it was easy to convince the one exception of the value of REST, although not his caretakers since they demanded grammatically correct sentences to be the goal. At the end of treatment, all caretakers reported more initiative in communication and fluency on the side of the patients despite ongoing agrammatism. Therefore, the verbal interactions between aphasic and non-aphasic partners was felt to require less effort.

What are the possible neurolinguistic factors explaining the favourable outcome of REST in chronic agrammatism? The fact that we did not observe a substantial increase of morphosyntactic elements in the majority of the patients is in agreement with the protolanguage hypothesis. Apparently, REST enhances the linear chaining of major lexical categories. This is a capacitiy which can be ascribed to the undamaged non-dominant hemisphere. However, one has to consider the rather short although intensive period of therapy. We can certainly not exclude the possibility that some morphosyntactic relearning can be achieved in chronic agrammatism over longer periods of several months if not years. Even more so if one thinks about the time consuming efforts non brain damaged adults are confronted with when they learn a foreign language. Such morphosyntactic relearning was indeed found in 4 of the 11 patients. After treatment, their spontaneous language was characterised by fragments of morphologically spelled out sentences intermingled with reduced phrase structures as reinforced by REST. This is illustrated by the following example taken from patient 7:

Th: *Sie haben doch schon mal von Rom erzählt?*
      (Didn't you tell me about Rome once before?)
P: (referring to the Trevi fountain where tourists traditionally throw in money)
      äh...reingucken...äh...Wasser...und dreht sich um...Geld Geld hinten und tropft ähm...Geld hinten werfen...Glück
      (uh...looking in...uh....water...and turns [oneself] around...money money back and is dripping uhm...throwing money back...fortune).

Such fragments of grammatical sentences indicate the beginning of more extensive morphosyntactic relearning. This is definitely different from first language acquisition. In aphasia, we never observed systematic restructuring with partial overgeneralisations which is characteristic for the development of syntax in children. Yet, after several years, agrammatic patients may present with well-recovered syntax and grammar, although there are still occasional relapses to agrammatic phrases. Recursive sentence structure with multiple embeddings generally remains scarce.

Under the perspective of strategies learned by the patients, the REST approach must also be discussed within the framework of adaptation theory—and especially the ellipsis-hypotheses—as developed by Kolk and Heeschen (1992). These authors claim that agrammatic aphasics suffer from an underlying computational deficit causing difficulties of processing language in real time. Agrammatic patients would respond to their computational deficit by using elliptical structures as found in certain registers of everyday language. Following strategies of elliptic speech, agrammatic patients are assumed to avoid the computational demands of morphosyntactic processing, e.g., inflectional marking of the verb according to tense, aspect, and agreement with the subject in number and person. By reducing computational load for sentence planning, agrammatic patients can better hold their place within conversation and increase their conversational speed.

According to our clinical experience, training of REST structures may be useful even in those patients who have recovered well from agrammatism, but show a trade-off effect. These patients produce morphosyntactically nearly complete sentences at the cost of a laborious and slow mode of expression. REST enables these patients to use elliptical speech as a strategic choice. Indeed, there are experimental studies demonstrating that some agrammatic patients naturally change speech styles according to task demands or communicative context (Heeschen, 1985; Hofstede & Kolk, 1994a; Kolk & Heeschen, 1990; Yiu & Worral, 1996). Recently, Kolk (1998) has suggested that "a positive effect on communicative efficacy can be obtained by means of a therapy that teaches the patient to adopt a syntactically simpler style of speech".

It is an implicit assumption of adaptation theory that the underlying morphosyntactic knowledge is either fully available or at least better preserved than is superficially apparent in spontaneous speech. Consequently, the proponents of adaptation theory argue that the elliptical structures used by aphasics will conform to the grammatical rules of elliptical utterances in normal language. These assumptions are highly controversial for two reasons. First, restrictions to mainly open class elements observed in agrammatic speech are not a general feature of normal elliptic speech. Second, agrammatism results from extensive left hemisphere damage and frequently occurs late during recovery and is a long lasting disability. Therefore, the notion of preserved implicit morphosyntactic knowledge despite agrammatism requires clinical specification. In chronic patients, such knowledge might be in part relearned during the course of aphasia, but seems only to be available under controlled processing conditions, e.g., in restricted metalinguistic tasks without time constraints. However, when fluent communication is required, these patients recovering from chronic agrammatism have no other choice than resorting to agrammatic speech again. The goal of REST in these patients is to make their agrammatic utterances more fluent and semantically more comprehensible by expanding the underlying verb–argument structures. Thus, the REST approach aims at allocating reduced syntactic planning devices to limited processing recourse.

There are, undoubtedly, patients with chronic agrammatisms who show severe loss of grammatical knowledge under all on-line and off-line processing conditions. The agrammatic utterances of these patients deviate from normal elliptic speech with respect to both morphology and word order. Here the adaptation theory definitely offers no explanation. Nevertheless, it is worth while to apply REST in the therapy of these patients as soon as isolated lexical activation of verbs is possible. In many cases, progress in therapy is limited to learning only the most simple REST structures of levels 1 and 2. Even for those simple structures, fluent and automatic production is not easily achieved.

In our clinical experience, a free stylistic variation, as postulated by adaptation theory, between relatively fluent telegraphic style and grammatically fully spelled out sentence formulations is occasionally seen during rapid recovery in the acute and post-acute stages. Initially these patients show elliptic speech with frequent interruptions thereby trying to avoid morphosyntactic errors or to deal with word finding difficulties. In these patients the REST approach may provide adaptation strategies that help to minimise predominantly lexical, phonological, or speech apractic difficulties. Furthermore, the restitution of temporarily blocked morphosyntactic planning may be enhanced. Therefore, REST is not a preventive approach as it encourages rather than prevents patients from producing sentences in telegraphic style. This enables patients to communicate more fluently and with less effort and supports recovery during the post-acute period. However, Beyn and Shokhor-Trotskaya (1966) held an opposing view, stating that only systematic blocking of telegraphic speech will enable patients to recover normal syntax. It would be most interesting to compare these two opposing views in a controlled therapy study.

In sum, the REST approach fits some assumptions of adaptation theory. REST tries to motivate and stimulate patients to choose a "simpler language" in conversation. Future neurolinguistic research has to specify what this "simpler language" relies on. Even after extensive left hemisphere damage, the ability to produce normal elliptic speech might remain relatively undisturbed with the advantage of demanding less computational capacity than morphosyntactically complete speech. Alternatively, agrammatic language as evolving during the natural course of aphasia reflects bilateral protolanguage capacities which can be facilitated in the intact nondominant hemisphere. In fact, these two hypotheses could even be seen as compatible: The remaining ability to construct the skeleton of elliptical utterances and to gradually spell them out morphologically could be a bilateral "protolanguage" function. In either case the REST approach would fit and expand the capacities which are still available in conditions of aphasia.

REFERENCES

Basso, A., Capitani, E., & Vignolo, L.A. (1979). Influence of rehabilitation on language skills in aphasic patients: A controlled study. *Archives of Neurology, 36*, 190–196.

Basso, A., Gardelli, M., Grassi, M.P., & Mariotti, M. (1989). The role of the right hemisphere in recovery from aphasia: Two case studies. *Cortex, 25*, 555–566.

Beyn, E.S., & Shokhor-Trotskaya, M.K. (1966). The preventive method of speech rehabilitation in aphasia. *Cortex, 2,* 96–108.

Bickerton, D. (1990). *Language and species.* Chicago: University of Chicago Press.

Biniek, R. (1993). *Akute Aphasie.* Stuttgart: Thieme.

Bogen, J.E. (1997). Does cognition in the disconnected right hemisphere require right hemisphere possession of language? *Brain and Language, 57,* 12–21.

Byng, S. (1988). Sentence processing deficits: Theory and therapy. *Cognitive Neuropsychology, 5,* 629–676.

Byng, S. & Lesser, R. (1993). A review of therapy at the level of the sentence in aphasia. In M. Paradis (Ed.), *Foundation of aphasia rehabilitation* (pp. 319–362). Oxford: Pergamon Press.

Caplan, D. (1987). *Neurolinguistics and linguistic aphasiology: An introduction.* Cambridge: Cambridge University Press.

Cappa, S.F., Perani, D., Grassi, F., Bressi, S., Alberoni, M., Franceschi, M., Bettinardi, V., Todde, S., & Fazio, F. (1997). A PET follow-up study of recovery after stroke in acute aphasics. *Brain and Language, 56,* 55–67.

Caramazza, A., & Zurif, E. (1976). Dissociation of algorithmic and heuristic processes in language comprehension. *Brain and Language, 3,* 572–582.

Clark, H.H., & Clark, E.V. (1977). *Psychology and language.* New York: Harcourt Brace Jovanovich.

Code, C. (1997). Can the right hemisphere speak? *Brain and Language, 57,* 38–59.

Corballis, M.C. (1992). On the evolution of language and generativity. *Cognition, 44,* 197–226.

Czopf, J. (1972). Über die Rolle der nicht dominanten Hemisphäre in der Restitution der Sprache der Aphasischen. *Archiv für Psychiatrie und Nervenkrankheiten, 216,* 162–171.

Doyle, P., Goldstein, H., & Bourgeois, M. (1987). Experimental analysis of syntax training in Broca's aphasia: A generalization and social validation study. *Journal of Speech and Hearing Disorders, 52,* 143–155.

Fazzini, E., Bachmann, D., & Albert, M.L. (1986). Recovery of function in aphasia. *Journal of Neurolinguistics, 2,* 22–46.

Frazier, L., & Friederici, A. (1991). On deriving properties of agrammatic comprehension: Syntactic structures and task demands. *Brain and Language, 40,* 51–66.

Friederici, A.D. (1985). Levels of processing and vocabulary types: Evidence from online comprehension in normals and agrammatics. *Cognition, 19,* 249–258.

Garrett, M. F. (1984). The organization of processing structure for language production: Applications to aphasic speech. In D. Caplan, A.R. Lecours, & A. Smith (Eds.), *Biological perspectives on language* (pp. 172–193). Cambridge, MA: MIT Press.

Geschwind, N. (1985). Mechanisms of change after brain lesions. *Annals of New York. Academy of Science, 457,* 1–11.

Haarmann, H.J., Just, M.A., & Carpenter, P.A. (1997). Aphasic sentence comprehension as a resource deficit. A computational approach. *Brain and Language, 59,* 76–120.

Heeschen, C. (1985). Agrammatism versus paragrammatism: A fictitious opposition. In M.-L. Kean (Ed.), *Agrammatism* (pp. 207–248.) New York: Academic Press.

Helm-Estabrooks, N., Fitzpatrick, P.M.J. & Barresi, B. (1981). Response of an agrammatic patient to a syntax stimulation program for aphasia. *Journal of Speech and Hearing Disorders, 46,* 422–427.

Helm-Estabrooks, M., & Ramsberger, G. (1986). Treatment of agrammatism in long term Broca's aphasia. *British Journal of Disorders of Communication, 21,* 39–45.

Heiss, W.-D., Kessler, J., Karbe, H., Fink, G.R., & Pawlik, G. (1993). Cerebral glucose metabolism as a predictor of recovery from aphasia in ischemic stroke. *Archives of Neurology, 50,* 958–964.

Hofstede, B.T.M., & Kolk, H.H.J. (1994a). The choice for ellipsis: A case study of stylistic shifts in an agrammatic speaker. *Brain and Language, 47,* 507–509.

Hofstede, B.T.M., & Kolk, H.H.J. (1994b). The effects of task variation on the production of grammatical morphology in Broca's aphasia: A multiple case study. *Brain and Language, 46,* 278–328.

Huber, W. (1991). Ansätze in der Aphasietherapie. *Neurolinguistik. 5,* 71–92.

Huber, W. (1996). Defizit und Kompensation bei Aphasie. In Deutsche Gesellschaft für Sprachheilpädagogik (Ed.), *Interdisziplinäre Zusammenarbeit: Illusion oder Vision? Herausforderung und Chance in der Rehabilitation Sprachbehinderter. XXII. Arbeits- und Fortbildungstagung, Münster 26–28. September 1996* (pp. 701–716). Hamm: Gebrüder Wilke Buch- und Offsetdruck.

Huber, W., Lüer, G., & Lass, U. (1988). Sentence-processing strategies of Broca's aphasics and normal speakers as reflected by gaze movements. In G. Denes, PC. Semenza, & P. Bisiacchi (Eds.), *Perspectives on cognitive neuropsychology* (pp 135–160) Hove, UK: Erlbaum.

Huber, W., Poeck, K., & Willmes, K. (1985). The Aachen Aphasia Test. In F.C. Rose (Ed.), *Progress in aphasiology* (pp. 291–303). New York: Raven.

Huber, W., Springer, L., & Willmes, K. (1993). Approaches to aphasia therapy in Aachen. In: A.L. Holland, & M.M. Forbes (Eds.), *Aphasia treatment—world perspectives* (pp. 55–86). San Diego CA: Singular Publishing Groups Inc.

Huber, W., Poeck, K., & Weniger, D. (1997). Aphasie. In W. Hartje & K. Poeck (Eds.), *Klinische Neuropsychologie* (pp. 80–143). Stuttgart: Thieme.

Jackson, J.H. (1879). On the affections of speech from disease of the brain. *Brain, 1,* 304–330.

Jarvella, R.J., & Sinnott, J. (1972). Contextual constraints on noun distributions to some English verbs by children and adults. *Journal of Verbal Learning and Verbal Behavior, 11,* 47–53.

Jones, E. (1986). Building the foundations for sentence production in a non-fluent aphasic. *British Journal of Disorders of Communication, 221,* 63–82.

Karbe, H., Thiel, A., Weber-Luxenburger, G., Herholz, K., Kessler, J., & Heiss, W.-D. (1998). Brain plasticity in poststroke aphasia: What is the contribution of the right hemisphere? *Brain and Language, 64,* 215–230.

Kerschensteiner, M., Poeck, K., Huber, W., Stachowiak, F.-J., & Weniger, D. (1978). Die Broca-Aphasie. Klinisches Bild und Überlegungen zur neurolinguistischen Struktur. *Journal of Neurology, 217,* 223–242.

Kinsbourne, M. (1971). The minor cerebral hemisphere. *Archives of Neurology, 25,* 302–306.

Klein, W. (1981). Some rules of regular ellipsis in German. In W. Klein & W.J.M. Levelt (Ed.), Crossing the boundaries in linguistics. Studies presented to M. Bierwisch. Dordrecht: Reidel.

Klein, W. (1993). Ellipse. In J. Jacobs, A. von Stechow, W. Sternefeld, & T. Venneman (Eds.), *Syntax. ein internationales Handbuch zeitgenössischer Forschung* [An international handbook of contempory research]. New York: de Gruyter.

Knopman, D.S., Rubens, A.B., Selnes, O.A., Klassen, A.C., & Meyer, M.W. (1984). Mechanisms of recovery from aphasia: Evidence from serial xenon 133 cerebral blood flow studies. *Annals of Neurology, 15,* 530–535.

Kolk, H.H.J. (1993). A time-based approach to agrammatic production. *Brain and Language, 50,* 282–303.

Kolk, H. (1998). The malleability of agrammatic symptoms and its implications for therapy. In E. Visch-Brink & R. Bastiaanse (Eds.), *Linguistic levels in aphasiology* (pp.193–209). London: Singular Publishing Group.

Kolk, H.H.J, & Heeschen, C. (1990). Adaptation and impairment symptoms in Broca's aphasia. *Aphasiology, 4,* 221–232.

Kolk, H.H.J., & Heeschen, C. (1992). Agrammatism, paragrammatism and the management of language. *Language and Cognitive Processes, 7 (2),* 89–129.

Le Dorze, G., Jacob, A., & Coderre, L. (1991). Aphasia rehabilitation with a case of agrammatism: A partial replication. *Aphasiology, 5,* 63–85.

Lee, H., Nakada, T., Deal, J.L., Lin, S., & Kwee, I.L. (1984). Transfer of language dominance. *Annals of Neurology, 15,* 304–307.

Levine, D.N., & Mohr, J.P. (1979). Language after bilateral cerebral infarctions: Role of the minor hemisphere in speech. *Neurology, 29,* 927–938.

Linebarger, M.C. (1995). Agrammatism as evidence about grammar. *Brain and Language, 50,* 52–91.

Meyer, J.S., Sakai, F., Yamaguchi, F., Yamamoto, M., & Shaw, T. (1980). Regional changes in cerebral blood flow during standard behavioral activation in patients with disorders of speech and mentation compared to normal volunteers. *Brain and Language, 28,* 597–613.

Nickels, L., Byng, S., & Black, M. (1991). Sentence processing deficits: a replication of therapy. *British Journal of Disorders of Communication, 26,* 175–199.

Pinker, S. (1994). *The language instinct.* London: The Penguin Press.

Poeck, K., Huber, H., & Willmes, K. (1989). Outcome of intensive language treatment in aphasia. *Journal of Speech and Hearing Disorders, 54,* 471–479.

Richards, L., & Chiarello, C. (1997). Activation without selection: Parallel right hemisphere roles in language and intentional movement? *Brain and Language, 57,* 151–178.

Rizzolatti, G., & Arbib, M.A. (1998). Language within our grasp. *Trends in Neuroscience, 21,* 188–194.

Rodriguez, G., Nobili, F., De Carli, F., Francione, S., Marenco, S., Celestino, M.A., Hassan, K., & Rosadini, G. (1992). Regional blood flow in chronic stroke patients. *Stroke, 24,* 94–99.

Schlenck, K.J., Schlenck, C., & Springer, L. (1995). *Die Behandlung des schweren Agrammatismus - Reduzierte-Syntax-Therapie (REST).* Stuttgart: Thieme.

Schwartz, M.F., Saffran, E., Fink, R.B., Myers, J., & Martin, M. (1994). Mapping therapy: A treatment programme for agrammatism. *Aphasiology, 8,* 19–54.

Schwartz, M.R., Linebarger, M.C., & Saffran, E.M. (1985). The status of the syntactic deficit theory of agrammatism. In M.L. Kean (Ed.), *Agrammatism.* New York: Academic Press.

Shewan, C.M., & Bandur, D.L. (1986). *Treatment of aphasia: a language-oriented approach.* San Diego: College-Hill Press.

Shewan, C.M., Kertesz, A. (1984). Effects of speech and language treatment on recovery from aphasia. *Brain and Language 23,* 272–299.

Sparks, R., Helm, N., & Albert, M. (1974). Aphasia rehabilitation resulting from Melodic Intonation Therapy. *Cortex, 10,* 303–316.

Springer, L. (1994). Methoden zur Behandlung des Agrammatismus. In I.M. Ohlendorf, T.A. Pollow, W. Widdich, & D.B. Linke (Eds.), *Sprache und Gehirn—Grundlagenforschung für die Aphasietherapie* (pp. 147–166). Freiburg: Hochschulverlag.

Springer, L., Miller, N., & Bürk, F. (1998). A cross-language analysis of conversation in a trilingual speaker with aphasia. *Journal of Neurolinguistics, 11,* 223–241.

Springer, L., Willmes, K., & Haag, E. (1993) Training the use of wh-questions and prepositions in dialogues: A comparison of two different approaches in aphasia therapy. *Aphasiology, 7,* 251–270.

Stachowiak, F.-J., Huber, W., Kerschensteiner, M., Poeck, K., & Weniger, D. (1977). Die globale Aphasie. Klinisches Bild und Überlegungen zur neurolinguistischen Struktur. *Journal of Neurology, 214,* 75–87.

Stark, J. (1992). *Everyday life activities (ELA) photo series.* Wien: Bosmüller.

Thompson, C.K. (1998). Treating sentence production in agrammatic aphasia. In N. Helm-Estabrooks & A.L. Holland (Eds.), *Approaches to the treatment of aphasia* (pp. 113–146). San Diego: Singular Publishing Group.

Thompson, C.K., Shapiro, L.P., & Roberts, M. (1993). Treatment of sentence production deficits in aphasia: A linguistic-specific approach to wh-interrogative training and generalization. *Aphasiology, 7,* 111–133.

Van de Sandt-Koenderman, W.M.E., & Bonta, E. (1998). Agrammatism: Theory and therapy. In E. Visch-Brink & R. Bastiaanse (Eds.), *Linguistic levels in aphasiology* (pp. 211–229). London: Singular Publishing Group.

Weigl, E., & Bierwisch, M. (1970). Neuropsychology and linguistics: Topics of common research. *Foundations of Language, 6,* 1–18.

Weiller, C., Isensee, C., Rijntjes, M., Huber, W., Müller, S., Bier, D., Dutschka, K., Woods, R.P., Noth, J., & Diener, H. (1995). Recovery from Wernicke's aphasia: A positron emission study. *Annals of Neurology, 37,* 723–732.

Weiller, C., Ringelstein, E.B., Reiche, W., Thron, A., & Buell, U. (1990). The large striato-capsular infarct. A clinical and pathophysiological entity. *Archives of Neurology, 47,* 1085–1091.

Weniger, D., Springer, L., & Poeck, K. (1987). The efficacy of deficit-specific therapy materials. *Aphasiology, 3,* 215–223.

Wertz, R.T., Weiss, D.G., Atem, J.L., Brookshire, R.H., Garcia-Bunuel, L., Holland, A.L., Kurtzke, J.F., LaPointe, L.L., Milianti, F.J., Brannegan, R., Greenbaum, H., Marshall, R.C., Vogel, D., Carter, J., Barnes, N.S., & Goodman, R. (1986). Comparison of clinic, home, and deferred language treatment for aphasia. Veterans Administration cooperative study. *Archives of Neurology, 43,* 653–658.

Whitaker, H.A. (Ed.) (1997). *Agrammatism.* San Diego: Singular Publishing Group.

Wiegel-Crump, C.A. (1976). Agrammatism and aphasia. In Y. Lebrun & R. Hoops (Eds.), *Recovery in aphasics.* (pp. 243–253). Amsterdam: Swets & Zeitlinger.

Willmes, K., & Poeck, K. (1984). Ergebnisse einer multizentrischen Untersuchung über die Spontanprognose von Aphasien vaskulärer Ätiologie. *Nervenarzt, 55,* 62–71.

Willmes, K., & Poeck, K. (1993). To what extent can aphasic syndromes be localized? *Brain, 116,* 1527–1540.

Yiu, E.M.L., & Worrall, L. (1996). Limitations of models of sentence production: Evidence from cantonese data of normal and aphasic speakers. In B. Dodd, R. Campbell & L. Worrall (Eds.), *Evaluating theories of language* (pp. 184–193). London: Whurr.

Zahn, R., Huber, W., Eberich, S., Nemeny, S., Specht, K. Kring, T., Willmes, K., Reith, W., Thron, A., Schwarz, M. (1999). Semantic processing of auditory words in acute recovery from transcortical sensory aphasia and in normal subjects: A functional magnetic resonance imaging study. (submitted for publication).

Manuscript received October 1999

NEUROPSYCHOLOGICAL REHABILITATION, 2000, *10* (3), 311–336

Cognitive treatments of sentence processing disorders: What have we learned?

Charlotte C. Mitchum[1], Margaret L. Greenwald[2], and Rita Sloan Berndt[1]

[1]*University of Maryland School of Medicine, Baltimore, MD, USA and*
[2]*Wayne State University School of Medicine, Detroit, MI, USA*

Several cognitive neuropsychological studies describing treatments of sentence processing disorders have been reported in recent years. We review the outcome of 10 studies that describe treatment outcomes for 17 aphasic patients. Although the studies used different approaches to intervention, they shared the goal of improving reversible sentence comprehension, and they targeted a hypothesised deficit of "thematic mapping". Several trends in treatment outcomes were observed. In most cases, there was strong evidence that the treatments induced a change in the pattern of sentence processing. Moreover, the outcomes indicated that impaired reversible sentence comprehension can arise from a range of impairments, only some of which directly implicate structural and/or lexical deficits assumed to be the source of poor thematic mapping abilities. Patterns of post-therapy generalisation within and across processing modalities appeared to be related, among other things, to the therapy approach and to the selection of treatment materials. These findings are discussed with regard to the theoretical implications of sentence processing treatment data.

Recent attempts to advance the understanding of the processes involved in cognitively-inspired experimental therapies have identified a pressing need to specify how the therapy alters cognitive function. Some researchers even suggest that such specification is crucial to the development of a "theory of therapy", which they argue is the critical next step in the development of rational aphasia treatments (Byng & Black, 1995; Caramazza & Hillis, 1993).

Requests for reprints should be sent to Charlotte C. Mitchum, Department of Neurology, University of Maryland School of Medicine, 22 South Greene Street, Baltimore, MD 21201, USA. Telephone: (410) 706-7158, Fax: (410) 706-0324, Email: cmitchum@umaryland.edu

Preparation of this manuscript was supported by a grant from the National Institute on Deafness and Other Communication Disorders (R01-DC00262) to the University of Maryland School of Medicine.

© 2000 Psychology Press Ltd
http://www.tandf.co.uk/journals/pp/0960201 1.html

Toward this goal, Byng and Black (1995) examined the details of therapy tasks and patient/tester interactions in three studies that focused on the same theoretical locus of language deficit. They concluded their review by identifying a number of variables that need to be controlled across future therapy studies in order to facilitate comparative evaluation of different therapies.

The appraisal of the current state of therapy studies we offer here is similarly motivated to determine what, if anything, these experimental therapies have contributed to clinical and theoretical interpretation of language disorders. Like Byng and Black (1995), we find it useful to focus on a set of therapy studies that claim to target a single hypothetical locus of deficit. Our goal is to identify consistencies among patients' responses to therapy despite the differences in detail across studies. We argue here that treatment outcomes can be highly informative, not only about the effects of various interventions, but also about the underlying source(s) of patients' deficits, and about the validity of the model used to guide the intervention. In our view, it is premature to attempt to propose a theory of therapy, especially in light of the limited details presented in the models of language processing that are available. Our hope at this point is to begin to unravel the complex results that have emerged from these therapy studies, and thus to begin to understand what we can learn from them.

In the discussion that follows we focus on treatments designed to improve aphasic sentence processing. There are now enough published studies available, roughly grounded in the same theoretical model, that we can begin to draw some general conclusions about the utility of attempting intervention targeted at sentence processing impairments. We begin with a review of assumptions regarding normal sentence processing, then consider how the normal theory is used to interpret aphasic sentence processing. We discuss several different approaches to sentence processing therapy that are guided (more or less) by the mapping deficit hypothesis of aphasic sentence processing. The discussion is focused primarily on the patterns of outcome that have emerged from the treatment studies reviewed.

NORMAL AND APHASIC SENTENCE PROCESSING

The theoretical constructs that have guided cognitive treatments of sentence processing disorders constitute only a sketch of the components implicated in normal sentence processing. Much of the terminology now generally used to describe these treatments was developed specifically to describe normal sentence *production* (e.g., Garrett, 1980; Levelt, 1989). These production models postulate independent levels of representation that need to be computed—from the development of a "message" to be conveyed to the articulation of the words chosen to convey it. Much aphasia research, and many of the sentence processing treatment studies, have focused on the "grammatical encoding" aspects of production models, setting aside concerns about how the "message" is formulated to begin with, and about how the motor speech system ultimately realises the selected words. Grammatical encoding in production models involves two separate representational levels: The "Functional level" represents, in abstract form, semantic and thematic elements of the words that will ultimately comprise the sentence (e.g., Bock & Levelt, 1994; Garrett, 1988). The "Positional level" specifies the syntactic and phonological features of sentence elements. Many of the sentence production impairments that have been described in aphasia are attributed to problems of grammatical encoding involving one or both of these levels of representation, or in the translation between them (see Berndt, in press, for review).

These same representational levels are sometimes used to describe aspects of sentence comprehension (Mitchum & Berndt, in press). For comprehension, the phonological and syntactic (positional) representation is computed first (from the auditory signal) and translated to the semantic/thematic meaning representation (at the functional level). Although this borrowing of terminology from production models simplifies description and comparison across tasks, it must be emphasised that the requirements of production and comprehension are very different. Production starts with some concept to be expressed, and the goal is an ordered string of articulated morphemes. Comprehension begins with an ordered (fleeting) auditory signal, and the goal is a concept of what was meant. Despite these differences in the processes close to "input" and "output" in the two tasks, there is a widespread assumption that the types of information required at the functional and positional levels, and perhaps the procedures for "mapping" between them, are similar for production and comprehension.

Many aphasic patients have great difficulty understanding and producing sentences, and the patterns of impaired sentence processing are varied. Of particular interest for cognitive neuropsychological study of aphasia is the particular inability to comprehend "semantically reversible" sentences; that is, a sentence in which either noun could serve as the thematic agent (e.g., the girl is kissing the boy). In some cases of aphasia, this type of sentence poses a much greater challenge for comprehension and/or production than so-called "non-reversible sentences" in which only one noun could logically take the role of agent (e.g., the boy is kicking the ball.). This pattern of sentence comprehension in aphasia (often described as "asyntactic") has been the focus of much interest in the study of aphasic language. The issue of debate centres on why a patient fails to comprehend reversible, but not non-reversible, sentences. While a number of theoretical descriptions of the observed pattern have been offered (Grodzinsky, 1986; Pulvermuller, 1995), none has been able to account for all of the observed patient data (Berndt, 1998; Berndt, Mitchum, & Haendiges, 1996; Berndt, Mitchum, & Wayland, 1997c).

Despite the lack of agreement regarding its cause, the pattern of sentence comprehension impairment described above is generally viewed as an indication that content word meaning is used as a basis for sentence interpretation. While this strategy is adequate for semantically non-reversible sentences (i.e., in the example above, only boys, and not balls, can kick), the interpretation of semantically-reversible sentences requires syntactic analysis in addition to knowledge of word meaning. Thus, the selective failure to interpret semantically-reversible sentences often is attributed to an inability to construct a full syntactic (i.e., positional level) representation (e.g., Grodzinsky, 1986; Pulvermuller, 1995). However, the same patients frequently are able to make accurate judgements of sentence grammaticality (Linebarger, Schwartz, & Saffran, 1983) suggesting that the syntactic representation itself is intact.

The mapping deficit hypothesis

The finding of spared grammaticality judgements in patients with poor understanding of reversible sentences has been taken as evidence that the problem does not arise from degraded syntactic representations, but from an inability to map between the intact syntactic and thematic representations (Saffran & Schwartz, 1988; Schwartz, Linebarger, Saffran, & Pate, 1987). The problem reflects an essential inability to appreciate thematic roles of sentence elements on the basis of sentence surface structure, and the problem is evident in both sentence production (Saffran, Schwartz, & Marin, 1980) and comprehension (Schwartz, Saffran, & Marin, 1980). There are two variants of the so-called "mapping deficit hypothesis" that address different facets of patient performance data. The "lexical" variant attributes the impairment to a loss of lexically-specified mapping information contained in the sentence verb. This information dictates how a verb's thematic roles are expressed syntactically, and thus yields information about "who is doing something, and to whom it is being done". Patients with this form of mapping impairment demonstrate errors on even the simplest reversible active sentences. The "procedural" mapping hypothesis explains the pattern of sentence processing failure that is evident only in sentences with a shift of arguments from their canonical positions (e.g., passive voice structures). This form of mapping deficit directs attention to the procedures that assign (or link) thematic roles (agent, theme, goal) to their relevant noun phrases on the basis of their syntactic functions (subject, direct object) (Saffran & Schwartz, 1988; Schwartz et al., 1987).

The problem of performance variability

Although the construct of a mapping deficit offers clear predictions for patient performance, it also acknowledges a role for inferential processes that operate in conjunction with residual mapping skills. The consequence of impaired lexical mapping rules and/or procedures can be an exaggerated reliance on the available information, including lexical and pragmatic knowledge. The use of heuristics can result in wide variability in test performance among aphasic patients with the same hypothesised source of impaired sentence processing, and may influence the pattern of performance obtained from an individual patient subjected to repeated testing (Badecker, Nathan, & Caramazza, 1991; Berndt et al., 1996).

Patients' ability to comprehend and produce reversible sentences can fail for a variety of reasons. Patterns of sentence comprehension can be affected by secondary (non-syntactic) influences such as response to changes in the task (Cupples & Inglis, 1993), manipulation of sentence length (Mitchum, Haendiges, & Berndt, 1995) and lexical/semantic content of the sentence verbs (Berndt & Mitchum, 1997; Jones, 1984). Studies of agrammatic sentence production have yielded similar patterns of variable performance (Saffran, Berndt, & Schwartz, 1989). Even patients selected for study on the basis of impaired lexical retrieval of verbs (i.e., a very specific, potentially causal symptom of disordered production) reveal considerable heterogeneity in the nature of the sentence structures they produce (Berndt, Haendiges, Mitchum, & Sandson, 1997a).

Theoretical interpretation of sentence processing disorders observed in aphasic patients must assume that different processing impairments can underlie superficially similar symptoms. The challenge is to unravel the symptoms of impaired sentence processing in such a way as to determine which are the result of non-linguistic and/or strategic influences, and which stem from a dysfunction of primary cognitive and/or linguistic operations.

EXPERIMENTAL TREATMENTS OF A MAPPING DEFICIT IN COMPREHENSION

If heterogeneity among patients poses a challenge to the theoretical interpretation of patients' language impairments, it comes as no surprise that the same problem undermines the development of appropriate interventions for the same impairment. Individual variation among patients is particularly evident in any attempt to replicate a successful therapy. Without exception, attempts at exact replication have resulted in a different outcome from what was reported in the original study. In some cases, individual differences among the patients dictated a modification of the original therapy technique (Byng, 1988; LeDorze, Jacob & Coderre, 1991; Mitchum et al., 1995). However, even when patients with the same (hypothesised) locus of impairment are given *exactly* the same therapy, the reported outcomes are quite variable (Schwartz et al., 1994; Berndt & Mitchum, 1997; Haendiges, Berndt, & Mitchum, 1996).

The problems that undermine replication of therapy are the same methodological complications that challenge theoreticians. No two patients are alike in every pertinent way. Furthermore, in studies that address the mapping deficit hypothesis, there is little diagnostic guidance for interpreting the nature and variety of cognitive impairments that give rise to the general symptom of asyntactic sentence processing. Clearly, abnormal performance on tests that presume to assess, for example, interpretation of semantically-reversible sentences, could arise from any combination of underlying essential deficits. Test results are valuable for identifying a deficit, and proper use of testing can eliminate or verify a variety of possible explanations of performance. However, traditional diagnostic tests (used clinically and for language research) provide only incomplete measures of language processing.

Therapy studies offer the unique opportunity to manipulate patients' strategies and/or alter their cognitive processing in such a way as to enlighten the original interpretation of the language impairment. For example, in all mapping therapy studies, the decision to include a patient for treatment was based on the results of a cognitive neuropsychological profile of the patient's sentence processing abilities. In many cases, patients' responses to therapy inspired a *re*-interpretation of the language impairment that originally motivated the study. For some patients, the inability to deal with the treatment materials was attributed to impaired execution of a particular linguistic function. For other patients, the complications involved non-linguistic cognitive deficits, which often were related to the task demands. Although these deficits were not necessarily a primary factor underlying the thematic mapping deficit, their presence clearly influenced the outcome of the therapy study. In every case, the response to thematic mapping therapy offered considerable insight regarding the specific nature of the patient's symptom of impaired sentence processing.

Thematic mapping treatments and their outcomes

Responses to thematic mapping treatment have varied widely. Extensive outcome data are available for at least 17 aphasic patients who have undergone some form of thematic mapping therapy (see Table 1). For each participant, a thematic mapping deficit was diagnosed and assumed to underlie poor sentence comprehension. Although the approach to therapy varied across studies, all interventions shared the goal of improved reversible sentence comprehension.[1]

There are several different approaches to sentence comprehension therapy that focus on the sentence verb. The "Sentence Query" approach first trains the patient to identify the verb in written sentences, and then to respond to a series of queries regarding thematic roles of the sentence nouns (e.g., "who" is kicking) (Jones, 1986; Schwartz et al., 1994). Responses to the "wh"-queries require circling or underlining the appropriate phrase in the written sentence that answers the role-based query. The crucial aspect of this therapy is that everything is expressly based on the meaning of the verb. Byng and colleagues

---

[1] We do not extensively review the details of the treatment studies discussed here. All patients included in this review are described in published studies. For details of the materials and methods used in each approach, the reader is referred to the original publication(s).

TABLE 1
Sentence comprehension therapy outcomes

	Patient	Study
No measured limitation in post-therapy sentence comprehension		
	BRB	Byng (1988)
	FO	Schwartz et al. (1994)
	EW	Schwartz et al. (1994)
Persistent mapping deficits involving processing of sentence structure or content		
	BB	Jones (1986)
	GG	Schwartz et al. (1994)
	IC	Schwartz et al. (1994)
	GR	Schwartz et al. (1994)
	FM	Berndt & Mitchum (1997)
	PB	Marshall et al. (1997)
	AER	Nickels et al. (1991); Byng et al., (1994)
Persistent mapping deficits involving problems other than (or in addition to) processing of sentence structure or content		
Poor event interpretation	LC	Byng et al. (1994)
	MM	Marshall et al. (1993)
Poor auditory-verbal retention	EM	Byng et al. (1994)
	ML	Mitchum et al. (1995)
Adoption of strategy	EA	Haendiges et al. (1996)
	JH	Schwartz et al. (1994)
	JG	Byng (1988)

have described "Sentence Ordering Therapy", which is also verb-centred (Byng, 1988; Byng, Nickels, & Black, 1994; Nickels, Byng, & Black, 1991). In this approach to mapping therapy, patients are instructed to identify the agent and theme in action pictures. Each sentence is represented by a sentence anagram of the content words and a syntactic frame. The content words are individually inserted into an appropriate position in a (written) grammatical frame in order to create a written sentence that matches the meaning of a pictured event. Another therapy described by Byng (1988) similarly focused on word order in reversible sentences, but used prepositions instead of verbs.

A series of reversible sentence comprehension studies that did not highlight the role of the verb in sentences used an active/passive sentence feedback procedure (A/P feedback) (Berndt & Mitchum, 1997; Haendiges et al., 1996; Mitchum et al., 1995). Like other mapping therapy approaches, this procedure attempted to link sentence structure with sentence meaning. Patients were asked to indicate when a spoken sentence and picture shared the same meaning, and they were told whether or not they were correct. There was no emphasis on the verb. However, the alternating use of active and passive sentences, in conjunction with a specific system of sentence repetition and feedback about responses, was designed to raise patients' awareness of how different sentence structures map to sentence meaning.

As noted above, the mapping deficit hypothesis is concerned strictly with the mapping between syntactic structure (Positional level) and a semantic/thematic interpretation (Functional level), both of which are assumed to be largely intact. Our analysis of the mapping therapy studies accounts for patients' therapy responses as either supporting the diagnosis of a thematic mapping deficit, or as revealing some other processing impairment (either in addition to, or instead of, a mapping deficit). Although the analyses performed for individual patients differ across studies, we were able to extract essential information regarding the therapy approach and general outcome from the published studies.

Seventeen patients have participated in the mapping therapy studies reviewed here (see Table 1). For many participants, mapping therapy resulted in greatly improved sentence processing. Only three, however, were shown to demonstrate excellent performance in all post-therapy measures. For other participants, the therapy often was successful, but persistent limitations were discovered nevertheless during post-testing. It must be stressed that the identification of limited generalisation of treatment effects does not necessarily indicate a poor response to therapy. In some cases, the limitations emerged only because the study included an extensive range of pre- and post-therapy tests. In Table 1 we have identified mapping therapy studies on the basis of whether or not the post therapy sentence processing impairments indicated a persistent mapping deficit, or revealed some other problem not specific to mapping that undermined the therapy outcome.

Persistent mapping deficits involving the processing of sentence structure or content.   For seven participants, the outcome of therapy indicated a persistent problem that we interpret as continued difficulty in mapping syntactic functions onto their thematic roles. BB and GG were unable to extend what they learned about mapping for one sentence structure (active voice) to other, more complex sentence structures (e.g., passives, multi-clause sentences). Neither patient was able to transfer spontaneously what was learned for comprehension of canonical sentences to the interpretation of non-canonical structures. For patient BB, comprehension of passive sentences was eventually improved by explicit training. Thus, while the evidence is sparse, it would appear that spontaneous generalisation across surface structures may be rare despite generally successful outcome for treated structures. To the extent that the relationships among different linguistic surface structures can be identified, the likelihood of generalisation may be able to be maximised (Thompson, Shapiro, & Roberts, 1993).

Five additional patients continued to exhibit problems that appeared to be related to sentence content rather than sentence structure. Schwartz et al. (1994) attributed the poor response to therapy of patients IC and GR to severely compromised lexical/semantic knowledge. Clearly, an ability to interpret at least the meaning of nouns, and some understanding of verbs, are required for sentence comprehension. In the absence of this ability, mapping therapy may be doomed to failure. Poor lexical access to verbs may undermine the ability to exploit lexically-represented mapping rules (i.e., mapping rules stored in the verb representation and closely linked to verb meaning) (Saffran et al., 1980). The outcome of mapping therapy is likely to be affected by the extent to which poor access to verbs impedes access to the lexical mapping rules of a particular verb (Marshall, Chiat, & Pring, 1997).

Several patients have shown a post-therapy pattern of generalisation that affects only a subclass of verbs (FM, PB and AER). For two patients, generalisation of the mapping skills learned in therapy tasks was limited in untreated materials to verbs that obeyed the same mapping rules as treated verbs (AER and PB). FM responded differently to sentences based on the semantic entailments of sentence verbs that define the extent to which the verb assigns a clear agent. These results indicate that some patients' responses to therapy may be sensitive to the thematic organisation of verbs. Findings of verb-specific learning and generalisation in treatment studies suggest that such data might contribute information about how verbs are best grouped thematically and semantically. To the extent that such mapping constraints define a coherent subclass of verbs, treatment studies will need to control the types of verbs employed in the selection of treatment materials, and in assessment of generalisation.

Persistent mapping deficits involving problems other than (or in addition to) processing sentence structure or content. In addition to these residual impairments apparently involving representations of sentence structure and content, some patients' responses to mapping therapy have indicated other, untreated deficits that were not identified prior to the initiation of treatment. LC and MM demonstrated poor interpretation of the pictures used to evaluate sentence comprehension. For LC the impairment was detected *during* therapy when it became evident that the planned treatment (a replication attempt) would not be possible due to her inability to extract relevant information from the picture stimuli. The same deficit was identified for patient MM *prior* to mapping therapy. In her case, the ability to derive linguistically-relevant information from the depicted event became the goal of therapy.

Poor retention of the verbal code for auditory sentences undermined the outcome for patient EM. Byng et al. (1994) attributed this patient's limited response to mapping therapy to an inability to retain the sentence while constructing a representation from the picture. For this patient, successful mapping therapy would (presumably) require some adjustment of the therapy task to eliminate the demands of simultaneous auditory/visual input. The limited auditory–verbal span of ML (Mitchum et al., 1995) was not character-ised as a problem in simultaneous processing of the visual/verbal stimuli. Rather, his poor retention of spoken sentences was evident only for sentences of a length that exceeded the limits of his auditory/verbal span.

Several patients developed strategies that permitted successful learning of the therapy task, but nevertheless undermined the ability to acquire (or access) the skills that serve thematic mapping in general (EA, JH and JG) This type of task adaptation may be quite prevalent, but it is difficult to detect unless treat-ment and/or post-therapy testing is controlled to prevent the appearance of good comprehension through the application of consistent response strategies. For example, testing with a variety of non-treatment materials, and the use of tasks with slightly different demands than the therapy task can reveal the use of strategies. When the use of strategies is suspected (or predicted), it is useful to incorporate probes during therapy that will alert the tester as soon as possible to their emergence. The detection of superficial strategies used by patients in tests of sentence comprehension should yield some insight into underlying bases of patterns taken to reflect impaired thematic mapping.

Generalisation patterns

One of the most informative aspects of interpreting the results of treatment studies involves assessment of the extent to which changes that occur as a result of treatment extend beyond the specific tasks and materials used in the treat-ment. Successful generalisation of treatment effects can indicate commonali-ties across sentence structures or can delimit the locus of treatment effects (Byng et al., 1994; Haendiges et al., 1996). Failures of generalisation can simi-larly be useful in attempting to understand the nature of treatment effects. Despite wide variation among patients, thematic mapping therapy studies have yielded some consistent trends in generalisation results.

Generalisation to comprehension of untreated sentences.   Sixteen patients who have participated in cognitive neuropsychological treatment studies of sentence processing are listed in Table 2.[2] Of these, 11 responded to mapping therapy with generalisation to comprehension of *canonical* sentences that were not included in therapy. The poor response of the five remaining patients may be accounted for by the apparent nature of these patients' mapping deficits. As discussed above (see Table 1), IC and GR were reported to show poor lexical semantic processing, while LC and MM showed sentence processing patterns (post-therapy) indicative of poor event perception. EM's sentence processing was also characterised by poor event perception, complicated by limited

---

[2]FO (Schwartz et al., 1994) was not included in this discussion since his comprehension was intact prior to therapy: The goal of therapy for FO was to improve sentence production.

TABLE 2
Generalisation of sentence comprehension to reversible sentences with untrained
lexical content

Patient	Study	Generalisation by sentence type	
		Active	Passive
Verb-centred and sentence ordering therapies			
JG	Byng (1988)	Yes	No*
EM	Byng et al. (1994)	No	No*
LC	Byng et al. (1994)	No	No*
AER	Byng et al. (1994), Nickels et al. (1991)	Yes	No*
BB	Jones (1986)	Yes	Yes
EW	Schwartz et al. (1994)	Yes	Yes
GG	Schwartz et al. (1994)	Yes	No
GR	Schwartz et al. (1994)	No	No
JH	Schwartz et al. (1994)	Yes	No
IC	Schwartz et al. (1994)	No	No
PB	Marshall et al. (1997)	Yes	No*
Active feedback therapies			
ML	Mitchum et al. (1995)	Yes	Yes
EA	Haendiges et al. (1996)	Yes	Yes
FM	Berndt & Mitchum (1997)	Yes	Yes
Other therapies			
BRB	Byng (1988)	Yes	Yes*
MM	Marshall et al. (1993)	No	No*

*In these studies, generalisation to passive sentence comprehension was tested before and after therapy, but would not necessarily be anticipated since passive sentences were not used in training (but see BRB).

retention of the auditory verbal code. She was unable to retain the spoken sentence while also trying to extract information from the stimulus picture. Although these deficits are not specific to thematic mapping, it is useful to recognise that they nevertheless undermined generalisation to new sentences with the same structure as the treatment materials.

When generalization to *non-canonical* sentences is examined, the pattern changes quite dramatically. In contrast to the excellent generalisation to untrained active sentences, the generalisation to untrained passive sentences was poor. Although many of the therapy studies reported here included passive sentence structures in the therapy materials, only some of the patients showed improved comprehension of this non-canonical structure. One of these was patient BB (Jones, 1986), who required extensive training specifically with passive sentences in order to eventually demonstrate this improved performance. Of the five patients treated for a mapping deficit by Schwartz et al. (1994), only one (EW) responded well to the introduction of passive sentences (i.e., their "type C" training structures), and he was the only one who showed similar improvement in the post-therapy assessment. One reason for this patient's improvement may be that he was unencumbered by any positional-level (surface structure) processing difficulty. He was remarkably able to apply spontaneously what he had learned about thematic mapping to a variety of sentence types on the basis of a few structural exemplars given during training (an outcome reminiscent of patient BRB, reported by Byng, 1988).

Generalisation to untrained passive sentences was observed for the three patients who took part in the treatment that used an A/P (Active/Passive) feedback approach to therapy. This result is in striking contrast to the limited generalisation to passive sentences observed among most of the other patients. We attribute this finding to differences in the nature of the therapy approaches. The verb-centred training tasks used in most mapping therapies (Byng et al., 1994; Jones, 1986; Marshall et al., 1997; Marshall, Pring, & Chiat, 1993; Nickels et al., 1991; Schwartz et al., 1994) arguably are directed at activation of lexical mapping rules. Attention is directed to identification of the meaning of the verb by demonstration and discussion of how verb meaning dictates thematic role assignment. Until the patient becomes very comfortable identifying "what" is being done, and "who" is doing it, the training task (written sentences or anagrams) includes only active sentence structures. The subsequent introduction of non-canonical sentences is not an easy transition for all patients, even those who were responsive to the same training task with canonical sentences (see Jones, 1986; Schwartz et al., 1994). In contrast, the A/P feedback therapy included both active and passive sentences from the onset of therapy. The therapy focused on the structural distinctions between active and passive sentences and, at the same time, linked sentence structure to sentence meaning. This approach may have engaged the structural analysis of sentences in a manner qualitatively different from the verb-centred therapies and, consequently, may have translated more effectively to comprehension of (untrained) passive sentences.

Generalisation from comprehension to production.   One of the most surprising outcomes of comprehension treatment has been the reported effect it has had on patients' sentence *production*. Even patients who did not show improved comprehension of untreated active sentences are described as showing gains on measures of sentence production (Byng et al., 1994; Marshall et al., 1993; Schwartz et al., 1994;). This is a potentially important result, since it could indicate that production and comprehension normally share processing components. That is, if treatment were focused *only* on comprehension, with no involvement of sentence production, spontaneous changes in production following comprehension treatment would suggest a functional link between the two processing systems.

There is reason to believe, however, that the treatment data do not clearly indicate a common functional source of thematic mapping. The extent of reported generalisation appears to be dictated by the nature of the therapy task. Only one patient who participated in verb-centred therapy failed to show generalised improvement in (active) sentence production. In fact, this patient (IC) showed no generalisation at all, and her poor performance was attributed to a serious deficit of lexical–semantic processing. All other patients were reported to have improved in production. In contrast, the three patients who participated in the A/P feedback therapy did not show improved sentence production. We account for this disparity in outcomes on the basis of two factors. First, the claim of improved production of active sentences is based on improvement in patients' production of a main verb, along with increased numbers of verb arguments. While this constitutes clear improvement of sentence production, it is not evidence that the processing mechanism that had been the target of treatment—thematic mapping—improved in production. That is, if only canonical sentences are examined for production (or comprehension), it is difficult to rule out the possibility that patients are mapping thematic agent to logical subject simply by default. While verb-centred therapies appear to convince patients of the importance of including a verb when producing sentences, the increased use of verbs and verb arguments must be closely examined for evidence of newly gained knowledge of thematic mapping rules. For example, tasks that verify the intended target (e.g., picture description) yield a stronger basis for measurement of thematic role expression than do spontaneous or narrative speech. If thematic mapping rules were carried over to production of passive sentences, the result would provide much stronger evidence that mapping skills were being exploited in production.[3]

A second difference between the verb-centred therapies and the A/P feedback therapy is related to the directional aspects of processing. The patient's ability to apply what is learned about thematic mapping *from* the comprehension training task (involving only "input") *to* the production of sentences (i.e., "output") relies on the assumption that production and comprehension exploit the same thematic mapping resource. That is, while differences in processing demands are assumed to place some directional constraints on the flow of information within a sentence processing model, it is generally assumed that the processing "goal" of mapping between sentence meaning and sentence structure is relevant to both comprehension and production. In the theoretical analysis of most mapping therapy studies, it is assumed that the mechanism of thematic mapping for semantically reversible sentences is the

---

[3]The suggestion that verb-centered therapies may not necessarily reflect improved thematic mapping in sentence production does not diminish the important changes that are established by this therapy approach. Clearly, the functional benefits of an improved ability to speak in sentences following many years of reliance on holophrastic communication is a significant outcome of therapy. Our only concern is the theoretical claim that the patterns of generalisation indicate functional identity of thematic mapping mechanisms used in production and comprehension.

same for both comprehension and production, and so directional constraints on therapy are not generally considered. For example, Byng et al. (1994) describe the *comprehension* phase of their mapping therapy in the following way:

> "The component processes of this stage of the therapy seem to require the development of (1) a conceptual representation of an event from a picture; (2) a "labelling" of the component entities of the event at two levels: the first a conceptual specification of the roles of the participants and the action involved in the event, and the second a retrieval of the lexical forms describing the participants and the action; (3) the insertion of the lexical items into the sentence frame; (4) a verification process to check whether the sentence produced makes sense and matches the picture." (p. 324)

This description of processing events is well aligned with models of normal sentence *production*, but not with models of comprehension. The retrieval of linguistically relevant information from the event with subsequent insertion into a grammatical frame to express the event are procedures necessary to prepare for articulation of a sentence. While some aspects of linking the Functional and Positional levels may be involved, the initiation of that link for comprehension comes from an auditory stimulus. Subsequent events include parsing of the sentence into constituent structures, with the nouns then assigned to thematic roles. In this regard, we view the A/P feedback therapy as qualitatively different from verb-centred therapies, and much more aligned with the process of sentence comprehension. Verb-centred therapies, in contrast, seem to exercise skills clearly required for sentence production. It may be significant that the patterns of treatment generalisation support this analysis.

The failure of the patients treated with A/P feedback therapy to show improvement in sentence production, following clear improvement in comprehension, suggests that an explicit treatment of sentence production is needed to affect production. An alternative interpretation, however, is that the A/P feedback therapy did not really result in normal sentence comprehension. In fact, all three patients who received this treatment continued to demonstrate various problems with comprehension of some types of untreated structures. This argument is tempered by data from another patient, AL, (described later) who, despite showing completely normal sentence comprehension, was unable to produce passive voice sentences.

TREATMENTS OF SENTENCE PRODUCTION IMPAIRMENTS

Tasks designed to stimulate verb retrieval can improve the use of verbs in agrammatic speakers (e.g., Fink, Schwartz, Sobel, & Myers, 1998) and even in severely impaired, globally aphasic speakers (Weinrich, Shelton, Cox, &

McCall, 1997). However, the relationship between verb retrieval and sentence production is not simply a matter of verb availability. That is, access to phonological word forms is not likely to be an adequate basis for syntactic expression of thematic roles. Patients who demonstrate intact verb retrieval when given semantic information (such as in action picture naming) can also demonstrate clearly agrammatic sentence production (Maher, Chatterjee, Rothi, & Heilman, 1995). Moreover, patient AL, to be described later, appeared to have preserved access to verbs when producing sentences in the active voice, but failed at the point of verb production when constrained to produce sentences in the passive voice. We take these findings as an indication of the complexity of the relationship between verb retrieval and sentence production.

Verb retrieval and sentence construction therapies

Two therapy studies described by Mitchum and Berndt (1992) and Mitchum, Haendiges and Berndt (1993) were designed as explicit tests of the relationship between single verb retrieval and the use of verbs for sentence production. A striking finding was observed in both studies: Verb retrieval therapy facilitated the retrieval of verbs in picture naming, but had no effect on patients' ability to produce (the same) verbs in sentences. A second therapy was then administered to improve the availability of SVO (subject–verb–object) sentence structure. The critical feature of this treatment (which required patients to produce verbs marked for tense) is that the selection of the sentence structure (i.e., the tense to be used in the verb phrase) was semantically motivated through the use of temporally sequential pictures. Thus, we view the treatment as directed at the translation between Functional and Positional levels within the production model. Following this treatment, the patients were able to produce a wide range of (never-trained) lexical verbs in sentences, including sentences elicited without picture stimuli (see Table 3). Neither study attempted to retrain production of anything other than the simplest SVO active sentence structures, and there was no observed spontaneous generalisation to untrained structures. We interpret these results as an indication that treatment of verb retrieval must involve the placement of verbal elements within a syntactic slot (a "grammatical frame") if improved verb retrieval is to have an effect on *sentence* production. Moreover, because the therapy was carried out verbally for one patient (Mitchum & Berndt, 1992) and in writing for the other patient (Mitchum et al., 1993), it was argued that the effects of therapy successfully isolated the pre-phonological level of functional-to-positional translation. The results also suggest that improved production of various sentence structures may require explicit structural training.

A similar outcome was reported by Reichman-Novak and Rochon (1997), who treated the production impairment of an agrammatic patient using a

TABLE 3
Responses obtained from ML (spoken) and EA (written) before and after grammatical frame therapy. (The task required production of an original sentence that included a target word; no pictures were used.)

	Target	Before therapy	After therapy
ML	Shovel	"The shovel"	"A woman is shoveling the snow"
	Comb	"Comb the suitcase"	"The man is combing the hair"
	Cannon	"We take it to the big cannon"	"The woman will fire the cannon"
	Drill	"Take a drill"	"The mechanic will drill the tires"
EA	Doctor	"The doctor is cough and cold"	"The doctor is helping the man"
	Shovel	"The shovel is a dig"	"The man is loading the shovel"
	Paint	"He is paint"	"The man will paint the house"
	Mop	"She mop and broom"	"The woman will clean the mop"

two-part series of exercises that focused first on verb retrieval, and then on grammatical frame construction. The patient responded well to the verb retrieval therapy, but improved verb production had no effect on his sentence production impairment. A second therapy to improve production of the grammatical frame combined the approaches of Mitchum and Berndt (1992) and Schwartz et al. (1994), but targeted production of passive (rather than active) sentences. The result of this therapy was improved production of passive sentences, but at the cost of deteriorated production of active sentences.

While it is evident that isolated verb retrieval can dissociate from sentential verb retrieval, the nature of this processing relationship requires further exploration. In contrast to the results reviewed above, Marshall, Pring, and Chiat (1998) reported improved sentence production following action naming therapy. However, in addition to the possibility that the source of the naming impairments differed across the patients, the therapy used by Marshall and colleagues was qualitatively different from the other therapies. Marshall's treatment focused on verb meaning, and while no sentence production was practised, there were tasks that paired nouns and verbs based on word meaning. The effect of the therapy was improved production of treated and untreated verbs. Marshall and colleagues offered several possible accounts of the therapy result. They concluded that structural information crucial to syntactic frame construction is contained not only in the lexical verb representations, but also in phonological representations. In this view, knowledge of the number of arguments needed by a verb may be intact, but the lack of prosodic information undermines construction of the surface phrases. Their patient was unable to exploit the structural information until a semantically-based therapy improved access to verbs' phonological forms.

Treatment of a selective impairment of passive voice sentence production

A remarkable pattern of verb retrieval and sentence production observed in an anomic patient further indicates the complex nature of lexical-syntactic inter-actions. Patient AL was a fluent speaker with a moderate disruption of verbal expression, which had been unresponsive to traditional naming therapy (Mitchum, Greenwald, & Berndt, 1997). A cognitive neuropsychological assessment of AL's sentence processing revealed intact comprehension of active and passive reversible sentences. Repetition of sentences was flawless for a variety of canonical and non-canonical structures. He was able to produce active SVO sentences in tasks requiring picture descriptions beginning with the agent noun.[4] However, production of passive sentences (beginning with non-agent nouns), using the same task and materials, was very poor.

The striking disparity in production of active and passive sentences was accompanied by a disparity in verb production; verbs were not produced in attempts to realise the structural form of passive sentences. As shown in Table 4, AL's production of verbs in well-structured active sentences was nearly flawless. When constrained to begin a sentence with the non-agent noun, AL produced responses that were relevant, often grammatically well-formed, and sometimes structurally complex; but in each response he assiduously avoided production of a passive. In early tests, he produced some sentences under the passive constraint that could be interpreted as thematic role reversals (e.g., "the wall is painting the woman"). Since thematic mapping for comprehension was

TABLE 4
Examples of constrained picture descriptions elicited from AL before sentence production therapy

Target picture	Active	Passive
Horse jumps fence	"The horse is jumping"	"The fence ..."
Boy pushes box	"The boy is fixing the boxes"	"The boxes ... three"
Man drinks tea	"The man is drinking from the cup"	"The tea is hot"
Girl rides bike	"The girl is riding the bike"	"The bike is ... not very pretty"
Man cuts rope	"The man is cutting the rope"	"The rope is ... piece meal"
Boy eats apple	"The boy is eating the apple"	"The apple ... is paramount"
Girls kicks boy	"The girl is kicking the boy"	"The boy is perturbed because the girl is kicking the boy"

---

[4]We elicit picture descriptions that constrain production of sentence structures by requiring the patient to use a specific noun in the pre-verbal NP. Active SVO structures are elicited by con-straining the patient to start the sentence with the thematic agent. The same picture is used in a sep-arate block to elicit a passive sentence response by constraining the patient to start the sentence with the non-agent noun.

completely intact, this pattern was interpreted as a production-specific thematic mapping deficit. As noted above, this dissociation of mapping skills in comprehension and production is similar to the pattern observed for two patients (ML and EA) following improvement of their sentence comprehension in an experimental treatment. The same pattern for AL, whose comprehension did not require treatment, supports our assertion that the procedures engaged for mapping in comprehension and production are functionally distinct, can be selectively impaired, and require explicit treatment approaches.

AL took part in two production therapies designed to assess his ability to relearn use of passive sentence structures. First, we wanted to determine whether simple lack of familiarity with passive voice structures, or their lower frequency within the language, might cause AL to avoid their production. The first treatment thus tested the possibility that explicit repetition exercises would "stimulate" the production of passive sentences by inducing facility in production of the morphological elements needed. The therapy task required immediate verbatim repetition of intermixed active and passive sentences spoken aloud by the examiner; there was no link to underlying sentence meaning. The repetition therapy yielded no impressive changes in AL's ability to produce a passive sentence for picture description (.50 pre vs. .63 post; McNemar Test, $z = 1.13, p = .23$).

A second treatment designed for AL relied on his intact ability to read (and to comprehend) active and passive sentences. All therapy materials were written words; no pictures were required. A model sentence was presented in writing along with an anagram sentence that could be ordered to create a sentence with exactly the same meaning as the "model" sentence, but in the alternative sentence voice. The explicit goal of the therapy was to point out to AL that active and passive sentences share the same essential meaning and lexical content, even though they have different surface structures. Therapy was carried out over 12 sessions (see Figure 1 for overview). AL was required to read the model active or passive sentence and order words in sentence anagrams to construct a response in the alternate voice. The initial trials grouped function and content words into phrasal anagrams (noun phrase, verb phrase), which AL easily manipulated into the alternate voice sentence. The introduction of word-by-word anagrams caused AL some difficulty, which he gradually overcame. In trials where AL showed a poor response, cues were provided according to a predetermined hierarchy: (1) look at the model and think of the meaning; (2) start with the verb; (3) "who" is doing the action?; (4) demonstration of word order with attention to verb morphology. After 77 trials over five one-hour sessions, AL was readily able to change the voice of both active and passive sentence targets, using the anagrams. Although he continued to "build" sentences over a series of responses, qualitative changes in his approach indicated that he learned to consider the verb first and construct noun phrases as arguments around the predicate (see Figure 2).

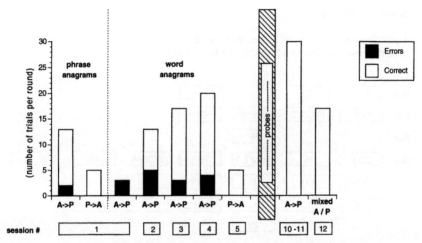

Figure 1. AL's performance in sentence ordering therapy across sessions as a treatment tasks changed. Following probes (see text) sessions 10–12 required a spoken response to a written sentence in the alternate voice.

Although it was apparent that AL had accomplished the goal of therapy, four sessions were devoted to administration of probes designed to determine if he had adopted a superficial strategy for the therapy task (see Figure 1). These probes included: (1) the addition of adjectival modifiers that altered the model/target sentences without changing the sentence voice; (2) the addition of an extraneous verb that required AL to select the appropriate lexical content of the target sentence; and (3) a task unlike the therapy, in which AL heard two sentences of differing voice and was required to judge ("yes" or "no") if the two sentences shared the same meaning. The response to all probes was positive and indicated that AL had accomplished the therapy task by learning to appreciate the shared meaning of active and passive sentences. A further set of therapy trials (sessions 10–12 on Figure 1) followed the probe series. These final sessions used the same model sentences from the prior therapy, but required AL to provide a *spoken* sentence in response to the written model. This was accomplished with relative ease. A post-therapy assessment showed a significant increase in AL's production of passive voice structures in a constrained picture description task (.50 pre vs. .86 post; McNemar Test, $z = 2.82$; $p = .004$). We believe that the critical element in the success of this treatment was the focus on Functional-to-Positional level translation, brought about by the emphasis on linking sentence meaning to specific structures.

The improvement in passive voice production in response to this treatment did not result in any decline in correct production of active voice structures, as had been found by Reichman-Novak and Rochon (1997) with their patient. This difference in outcomes may indicate an important difference between the two therapies. The grammatical frame therapy described by Reichman-Novak

Session # 1; Trial # 1

"Model" Sentence: THE WOMAN IS POURING THE SOUP
"Target" Sentence: THE SOUP IS POURED BY THE WOMAN

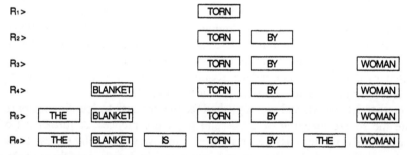

Session #4; Trial #51

"Model" Sentence: THE WOMAN IS TEARING THE BLANKET
"Target" Sentence: THE BLANKET IS TORN BY THE WOMAN

Figure 2. Examples of changes in performance across treatment rounds in passive sentence production therapy used with patient AL.

and Rochon linked the production of passive sentences to the insertion of lexical content into a passive sentence frame, but provided no information about the meaning overlap of active and passive sentences. The patient may have responded to the therapy by essentially replacing actives with passives at a purely structural (positional) level. In contrast, AL's treatment explicitly pointed out that active and passive sentences express the same basic meaning, but that they require construction of different grammatical frames. Perhaps since AL had intact sentence comprehension (and thus could thematically interpret sentence meaning), the effect of demonstrating the optional use of active/passive structures to express the same sentence meaning yielded improved production of passive sentences at no expense to production of active sentences.

There are numerous approaches to therapy for aphasic sentence production disorders (see Byng & Lesser, 1993; Thompson, 1994). However, there have been relatively few cognitively-inspired therapies designed to study the effects of sentence production therapy independently of sentence comprehension. Most therapies that affect sentence production are closely intertwined with tasks involving sentence comprehension. Nevertheless, the studies that have been described explicitly for production seem to yield similar patterns of outcome (Mitchum & Berndt, 1992; Reichman-Novak & Rochon, 1997; Van de Sandt-Kondeman, Bonta, Wielaert & Vishch-Brink, 1997). Common findings suggest that training production of grammatical frames can yield improved production of lexical verbs in sentences, and can do so more effectively than therapy dedicated to improving production of single verbs. However, generalisation of grammatical frame therapy across different morphosyntactic structures may be limited. If construction of specific grammatical structures requires explicit retraining, it would be useful to consider predictions about generalisation derived from linguistic models of sentence production (Thompson, 1992; Thompson, Shapiro, & Roberts, 1993). Further development of production therapies may, like the studies of sentence comprehension therapy, reveal cumulative common results that will provide a basis for beginning to determine how therapy can, and cannot, alter cognitive processing.

DISCUSSION

The results of sentence processing therapy studies that focus on a hypothesised thematic mapping deficit have refined our ability to interpret aphasic sentence processing impairments in a number of ways. A major contribution is the enhanced interpretation of underlying deficits that can give rise to the standard pattern of asyntactic sentence comprehension. Each patient described in the therapy studies reviewed here was selected for therapy using the same criterion: poor comprehension of semantically-reversible sentences. In many cases, the response to thematic mapping therapy resulted in a re-interpretation of the deficit based on the patient's response to therapy, or to post-therapy testing. For some patients, there was evidence of a clear and persistent impairment of components integral to thematic mapping. For others, the persistent impairment implicated difficulties related to less specific elements of the task. This finding serves as a basis for refining the currently inadequate tests that are used to detect asyntactic comprehension.

An account of both the successes and failures of therapy studies can also provide insight regarding the organisation of processing components engaged in a cognitive task. The mapping studies reviewed here indicated that certain components of sentence processing require explicit therapy, whereas others may improve through generalisation. Patients who responded successfully to thematic mapping therapy typically were capable of interpreting sentences structurally similar to those used in training, including sentences with untrained lexical content. However, generalisation to interpretation of untrained sentence structures was limited. It was especially evident that passive voice sentence comprehension rarely improves following successful training with active voice structures. The inclusion of both active and passive sentences from the initiation of therapy was shown to enhance comprehension of both sentence types. Further study of the training requirements for various sentence types may establish a clearer understanding of how different syntactic structures generalise across tasks of sentence comprehension.

Some evidence of cross-structural generalisation is available for sentence *production* from linguistic therapy studies that are not explicitly designed to address deficits of thematic mapping. Treatment generalisation patterns for various sentence structures have resulted from production therapies that use sentence anagrams to demonstrate the movement of linguistic elements from deep to surface structure positions (Springer, Willmes, & Haag, 1993; Thompson et al., 1993). This approach has established some standards for predicting patterns of generalisation in sentence production therapy, and may provide a basis for expanding studies of similar structural generalisation in sentence comprehension therapy.

Thematic mapping therapy studies have also refined our interpretation of the manner in which cognitive functions normally are shared between sentence comprehension and production. Sentence processing therapy studies that centre on verb meaning typically control the nature of the therapy task with attention to requirements of "input" or "output". However, we have argued that even when stages of therapy provide only written materials ("input"), and do not permit practice in sentence production ("output"), the tasks that comprise the therapy may exercise elements of processing in the direction of production. We interpret reports of generalisation from comprehension to production as a consequence of the therapy task. The changed pattern of sentence production may arise subsequent to patients' learning to construct a canonical grammatical frame. Although improved production of two and three argument sentences in response to thematic mapping therapy is clearly a positive result of the therapy, the increased production of verbs and their arguments is not by itself indicative of improved thematic mapping. Further evidence, such as a clear analysis of role expression in targeted sentence production, or generalisation to passive sentence production, would demonstrate recovery of thematic mapping for sentence production.

If it is assumed that production and comprehension share at least some processing components, failure to *produce* passive sentences following thematic mapping therapy might be interpreted as an indication that the therapy did not restore normal sentence *comprehension*. Indeed, even the patients who learned to comprehend passive sentences failed to show improved passive sentence production. However, patient AL (described earlier) spontaneously demonstrated the same pattern prior to therapy: poor production of passive sentences despite good production of active sentences and completely intact sentence comprehension. His sentence processing pattern provides important evidence that the post-intervention results obtained in mapping therapy studies can occur naturally, and without therapy.

The striking pattern of sentence production observed in AL also places some constraints on interpretations of sentence production disorders that hinge on the assumption that the relative availability of lexical verbs influences the production pattern. The association between poor verb retrieval and poor sentence production has long been observed in aphasia (Kohn, Lorch, & Pearson, 1989; Saffran et al., 1980), and access to the lexical representation of a verb has been considered crucial to sentence construction (Berndt, Haendiges, Mitchum, & Sandson, 1997a). However, this claim is tempered by evidence from AL, and from patients who show intact lexical access to verbs, but nevertheless demonstrate poor sentence production (Berndt, Haendiges, & Wozniak, 1997b; Caramazza & Hillis, 1989; Maher et al., 1995; Marshall et al., 1998). There is also considerable evidence that production of non-canonical sentences is relatively more difficult than canonical sentence production even when the verb is provided to patients in a constrained picture description task (Caplan & Hanna, 1998). While the relative accessibility of verbs clearly is a necessary component of sentence production, it is equally evident that verb retrieval is not a sufficient basis for production of all sentence types.

Studies of generalisation in sentence comprehension therapy have revealed patterns of learning that show sensitivity to lexical/semantic and structural properties of verbs that may be related to rules of thematic mapping (Berndt & Mitchum, 1997; Marshall et al., 1997; Shelton, Weinrich, McCall, & Cox, 1996). The potential relevance of these learning patterns to similar verb influences in sentence production has not been elaborated. It is expected, however, that verb-based structural generalisation obtained from therapy studies will contribute to an eventual description of the theoretical underpinnings of verb organisation.

We have suggested several ways in which therapy studies can refine our understanding of the cognitive system. Perhaps the most essential contribution of any therapy study is the ability to offer a window into the dynamic aspects of cognitive processing that reveals patterns of learning and generalisation. Under the right conditions, patterns of response to therapy can be used to guide modeling of the processing relationships among cognitive components. The key to exploiting this opportunity for clinical applications is in knowing what patterns indicate whether or not the changes are taking a favourable direction. The presence of recognisable patterns in response to specific therapies may be used to guide the decision to alter, stop or continue with a specific treatment. It is the identification of these learning patterns, and an understanding of the interventions that induce them, that will eventually lay the groundwork for a theory of rehabilitation (cf. Baddeley, 1993). The studies of mapping therapy reviewed above demonstrate that studies of the cognitive treatment of sentence processing disorders have yielded a set of complex yet interpretable findings, and these findings speak to a remarkably wide range of theoretical and clinical issues. Having learned all of this from a handful of studies over a period of only about 10 years, we suggest that this endeavour is clearly on the right track.

REFERENCES

Baddeley, A. (1993). A theory of rehabilitation without a model of learning is a vehicle without an engine: A comment on Caramazza and Hillis. *Neuropsychological Rehabilitation, 3*, 235–244.

Badecker, W., Nathan, P., & Caramazza, A. (1991). Varieties of sentence comprehension deficits: A case study. *Cortex, 27*, 31–321.

Berndt, R.S. (in press). Producing sentences. In B. Rapp (Ed.), *Handbook of cognitive neuropsychology*. Philadelphia, PA: Psychology Press.

Berndt, R.S. (1998). Sentence processing in aphasia. In M.T. Sarno (Ed.), *Acquired aphasia* (3rd ed.). San Diego, CA: Academic Press.

Berndt, R.S., Haendiges, A.N., Mitchum, C.C., & Sandson, J. (1997a). Verb retrieval in aphasia: 2. Relationship to sentence processing. *Brain and Language, 56*, 107–137.

Berndt, R.S., Haendiges, A.N., & Wozniak, M.A. (1997b). Verb retrieval and sentence processing: Dissociation of an established symptom association. *Cortex, 33*, 99–114.

Berndt, R.S., & Mitchum, C.C. (1997). An experimental treatment of sentence comprehension. In N. Helm-Estabrooks & A. Holland (Eds.) *Approaches to the treatment of aphasia*. San Diego, CA: Singular Publishing Group.

Berndt, R.S., Mitchum, C.C., & Haendiges, A. N. (1996). Comprehension of reversible sentences in "agrammatism": A meta-analysis. *Cognition, 58*, 289–308.

Berndt, R.S., Mitchum, C.C., & Wayland, S. (1997c). Patterns of sentence comprehension in aphasia: A consideration of three hypotheses. *Brain and Language. 60*, 197–221.

Bock, K., & Levelt, W. (1994). Language production and grammatical encoding. In M.A. Fiernsbacher (Ed.) *Handbook of psycholinguistics*. San Diego, CA: Academic Press.

Byng, S. (1988). Sentence processing deficits: Theory and therapy. *Cognitive Neuropsychology, 5*, 629–676.

Byng, S., & Black, M. (1995). What makes a therapy? Some parameters of therapeutic intervention in aphasia. *European Journal of Disorders of Communication, 30*, 303–316.

Byng, S., & Lesser, R. (1993). A review of therapy at the level of the sentence in aphasia. In M. Paradis (Ed.), *Foundations of aphasia rehabilitation*. New York: Pergamon Press.

Byng, S., Nickels, L, & Black, M. (1994). Replicating therapy for mapping deficits in agrammatism: Remapping the deficit? *Aphasiology, 8*, (4), 315–342.

Caplan, D., & Hanna, J.E. (1998). Sentence production by aphasic patients in a constrained task. *Brain and Language, 63*, 184–218.

Caramazza, A., & Hillis, A.E. (1989). The disruption of sentence production: Some dissociations. *Brain and Language, 36*, 625–650.

Caramazza, A., & Hillis, A. (1993). For a theory of remediation of cognitive deficits. *Neuropsychological Rehabilitation, 3*, 217–234.

Cupples, L., & Inglis, A.L. (1993). When task demands induce "asyntactic" comprehension: A study of sentence interpretation in aphasia. *Cognitive Neuropsychology, 10*, 201–234.

Fink, R.B., Schwartz, M.F., Sobel, P.R., & Myers, J.L. (1998). Effects of multilevel training on verb retrieval: Is more always better? *Brain and Language, 60*, 41–44.

Garrett, M.F. (1980). Levels of processing in sentence production. In B. Butterworth (Ed.), *Language production* (Vol. 1). New York: Academic Press.

Garrett, M.F. (1988). Processes in language production. In F.J. Newmeyer (Ed.), *Linguistics: The Cambridge survey: III. Language: Psychological and biological aspects* (pp. 69–96). Cambridge: Cambridge University Press.

Grodzinsky, Y. (1986) Language deficits and the theory of syntax. *Brain and Language, 27*, 135–159.

Haendiges, A.N., Berndt , R.S., & Mitchum, C.C. (1996). Assessing the elements contributing to a "mapping" deficit: A targeted treatment study. *Brain and Language, 52*, 276–302.

Jones, E.V. (1984). Word order processing in aphasia: Effect of verb semantics. In F.C. Rose (Ed.), *Advances in neurology, Vol 42.* (Progress in aphasiology). New York: Raven Press.

Jones, E.V. (1986). Building the foundations for sentence production in a non-fluent aphasic. *British Journal of Disorders of Communication, 21*, 63–82.

Kohn, S.E., Lorch, M.P., & Pearson, D.M. (1989). Verb finding in aphasia. *Cortex, 25*, 57–69.

LeDorze, G., Jacob, A., & Coderre, L. (1991). Aphasia rehabilitation with a case of agrammatism: A partial replication. *Aphasiology, 5*, 63–85.

Levelt, W.J.M. (1989). *Speaking: From intention to articulation.* Cambridge, MA: MIT Press.

Linebarger, M.C., Schwartz, M.F., & Saffran, E.M. (1983). Sensitivity to grammatical structure in so-called agrammatic aphasics. *Cognition, 13*, 361–394.

Maher, L.M., Chatterjee, A., Rothi, L.J., & Heilman, K.M. (1995). Agrammatic sentence production: The use of a temporal-spatial strategy. *Brain and Language, 49*, 105–124.

Marshall, J., Chiat, S., & Pring, T. (1997). An impairment in processing verbs' thematic roles: A therapy study. *Aphasiology, 11*, 855–876.

Marshall, J., Pring, T., & Chiat, S. (1993). Sentence processing therapy: Working at the level of the event. *Aphasiology, 7*, 177–199.

Marshall, J., Pring, T., & Chiat, S. (1998). Verb retrieval and sentence production in aphasia. *Brain and Language, 63*, 159–183.

Mitchum, C.C., & Berndt, R.S. (in press). Cognitive neuropsychological approaches to diagnosing and treating language disorders: Production and comprehension of sentences. In R. Chapey (Ed.), *Language intervention strategies in adult aphasia* (4th edition). Baltimore, MD: Lippincott, Williams & Wilkins.

Mitchum, C.C., & Berndt, R.S. (1992). Verb retrieval and sentence construction: Effects of targeted intervention. In G. Humphreys and J. Riddoch (Eds.), *Cognitive neuropsychology and cognitive rehabilitation.* Hove, UK: Lawrence Erlbaum Associates Ltd.

Mitchum, C.C., Greenwald, M.L., & Berndt, R.S. (1997). Production-specific thematic mapping impairment: A treatment study. *Brain and Language, 60*, 121–123.

Mitchum, C.C., Haendiges, A.N., & Berndt, R.S. (1993). Model-guided treatment to improve written sentence production: A case study. *Aphasiology, 7*, 71–109.

Mitchum, C.C., Haendiges, A.N., & Berndt, R.S. (1995). Treatment of thematic mapping in sentence comprehension: Implications for normal processing. *Cognitive Neuropsychology, 12*, 503–547.

Nickels, L., Byng, S., & Black, M. (1991). Sentence processing deficits: A replication of treatment. *British Journal of Disorders of Communication, 26*, 175–199.

Pulvermuller, R. (1995). Agrammatism: Behavioral description and neurobiological explanation. *Journal of Cognitive Neuroscience, 7*, 165–181.

Reichman-Novak, S., & Rochon, E. (1997). Treatment to improve sentence production: A case study. *Brain and Language, 60*, 102–105.

Saffran, E.M., Berndt, R.S., & Schwartz, M.F. (1989). The quantitative analysis of agrammatic production: Procedure and data. *Brain and Language, 37*, 440–479.

Saffran, E.M., & Schwartz, M.F. (1988). 'Agrammatic' comprehension it's not: Alternatives and implications. *Aphasiology, 2*, 389–394.

Saffran, E.M., Schwartz, M.F., & Marin, O. (1980). The word order problem in agrammatism: Production. *Brain and Language, 10*, 263–280

Schwartz, M. F., Linebarger, M.C., Saffran, E.M., & Pate, D.S. (1987). Syntactic transparency and sentence interpretation in aphasia. *Language and Cognitive Processes, 2*, 85–113.

Schwartz, M.F., Saffran, E.M., Fink, R.B., Myers, J.L., & Martin, N. (1994). Mapping therapy: A treatment programme for agrammatism. *Aphasiology, 8*, 9–54.

Schwartz, M.D., Saffran, E.M., & Marin, O.S. (1980). The word order problem in aphasia: Comprehension. *Brain and Language, 10*, 249–262.

Shelton, J.R., Weinrich, M., McCall, D., & Cox, D.M. (1996). Differentiating globally aphasic patients: Data from in-depth language assessments and production training using C-VIC. *Aphasiology, 10* (4), 319–342.

Springer, L., Willmes, K., & Haag, E. (1993). Training in the use of wh-questions and prepositions in dialogues: A comparison of two different approaches in aphasia therapy. *Aphasiology, 7*, 251–270.

Thompson, C.K. (1992). A neurolinguistic approach to sentence production treatment and generalization research in aphasia. In J. Cooper (Ed.), *Aphasia treatment: Current approaches and research opportunities*. Bethesda, MD: National Institute of Deafness and Other Communication Disorders.

Thompson, C. (1994). Treatment of nonfluent Broca's aphasia. In R. Chapey (Ed.), *Language intervention strategies in adult aphasia*. (3rd Ed). Baltimore: Williams & Wilkins.

Thompson, C.K., Shapiro, L.P., & Roberts, M.M. (1993). Treatment of sentence production deficits in aphasia: A linguistic-specific approach to wh-interrogative training and generalization. *Aphasiology, 7*, 111–133.

Van de Sandt-Kondeman, W.M.E., Bonta, E., Wielaert, S.M., & Vischh-Brink, E.G. (1997). Stimulating sentence production in agrammatic patients: The effect of the Visual Cue Programme on spontaneous speech. *Aphasiology, 11* (8), 735–759

Weinrich, M., Shelton, J.R., Cox, D.M., & McCall, D., (1997). Generalization from single sentence to multisentence production in severely aphasic patients. *Brain and Language, 58*, 327–352.

Manuscript received October 1999

NEUROPSYCHOLOGICAL REHABILITATION, 2000, *10* (3), 337–363

The role of communication models in assessment and therapy of language disorders in aphasic adults

Sergio Carlomagno, Valeria Blasi, Ludovica Labruna, and Anna Santoro

Seconda Università di Napoli, Naples, Italy
and I.R.C.C.S. Santa Lucia, Rome, Italy

This paper addresses the influence of pragmatic theory on management procedures for communicative disorders in adults with aphasia. We illustrate first the ecological construct and the limitations of functional views to pragmatically oriented methods for assessment and therapy of these disorders. Second, we discuss theoretical and practical limits in applying taxonomic model(s) of communicative competence derived from speech-act theory.

However, experimental paradigms for studying language/context interaction in normal adults have been introduced in the study of communicative deficits in aphasic adults. Therefore, we discuss whether concepts from models of language/context interaction might be incorporated into management procedures. To do so, we illustrate how the application of a model of communicating in context, i.e., producing definite reference (Clark & Wilkes-Gibbs, 1986), can result in new assessment methods and treatment paradigms.

INTRODUCTION

This paper is concerned with pragmatically oriented methods to manage communicative disorders in aphasic adults.

The pragmatic approach to aphasia assessment and therapy have initially focused on relationships between patient and environment and on therapeutic

---

Requests for reprints should be sent to Prof. Sergio Carlomagno, Istituto di Scienze Neurologiche, Seconda Università di Napoli, Via Pansini 5, 80131 Napoli, Italy. E-mail: sercarlo@unina.it

Studies on the development of PACE setting have been supported by grants to Sergio Carlomagno from the Ministero Università e Ricerca Scientifica e Technolgica, Italy and the I.R.C.C.S. Santa Lucia, Roma, Italy.

We are also grateful to anonymous reviewers for helpful comments.

© 2000 Psychology Press Ltd
http://www.tandf.co.uk/journals/pp/09602011.html

strategies allowing compensation for defective language processing in daily communicative contexts. Such a "functional" view is incomplete with respect to the concept of pragmatics as the study of relationships between language and context. However, core principles of pragmatic analysis have been introduced into assessment methods of communicative difficulties in aphasic patients. Furthermore, the "functional" view has led to shifting the focus of therapeutic practice from traditional language tasks to dyadic communicative interaction.

The pragmatic approach to communicative disturbances of aphasic patients has also been concerned with the analysis of communicative behaviour following theoretically oriented taxonomies. The introduction of "pragmatic protocols" in the 1980s has allowed neuropsychologists to examine communicative competence of brain-damaged subjects according to speech-act theory (Austin, 1962, Searle, 1969) or theory of conversational maxims (Grice, 1975). However, proponents of this approach have grappled with a number of difficulties in applying pragmatic concepts to clinical practice. Thus, the majority of clinicians still agree with the claim that application of pragmatic theories has not effected a sea-change in aphasia therapy (Lesser & Milroy, 1993).

In the same years, however, there has been converging evidence that ". . .aphasic people do better when they can capitalise on a verbal message as well as its non-verbal context. . ." and that the reverse is true for subjects with closed head injury, i.e., ". . .he talks better than he communicates. . ." (Holland, 1991, p. 198; see also Penn & Cleary, 1988; and Hartley, 1990). This evidence has led speech / language pathologists to pay increasing attention to the effects of contextual variables on language processing in brain-damaged patients. Cognitive psychologists and psycholinguists, on the other hand, have become interested in using data from brain-damaged subjects to make inferences on human cognitive function. Pathological language in aphasic subjects or in patients with traumatic brain injury, in fact, offers the possibility of describing the effects of disruption at one level of language processing on the others. This analysis may have significant explanatory potential for understanding the interaction between discourse, lexicon, grammar, and psychosocial skills. Thus, researchers in the field of pragmatic competence and neuropsychologists have begun to exchange methodologies to analyse the language/context interaction, and controlled investigations have been made in brain-damaged subjects about referential coherence, shared knowledge, metaphor, indirect requests, and so on.

Our present discussion will bring into focus how experimental paradigms for studying language/context interaction might be incorporated into assessment methods and treatment programmes for aphasic people. This is not because we disregard important contributions from the "functional" or the "taxonomic" views to the analysis of the aphasics' communicative behaviour and to the definition of the related therapeutic hypotheses. There is, in fact, considerable agreement that the two approaches have been successful in defining the concept of communicative disability and in describing how some language disorders are of the pragmatic type while a relative preservation of pragmatic skills may occur in spite of severe linguistic deficits. Moreover, there is experimental support that therapeutic methods which aim to provide aphasic patients with alternative communication strategies may be successful in a number of cases. However, the implications that pragmatic theory has on management procedures remain largely unexplored and we hope to show how experimental models of language/context interaction provide comprehensive framework(s) for incorporating pragmatic concepts into new treatment paradigms.

HISTORICAL BACKGROUND

The development of the pragmatic approach to communicative disorders in aphasic patients originated from recognising the limits of recovery from language deficit. A number of these patients, for instance, do not improve after traditional language stimulation and may not develop functional communication adequate for daily activities. Moreover, some speech pathologists have argued that studying components of language processing in the absence of aspects of natural contexts could not account for functional communication of aphasic subjects in real life (Holland, 1982; Sarno, 1969). By contrast, the pragmatic approach extended the scope of assessment methods and therapy programmes to communicative acts occurring in natural conversation and to non-linguistic modes of communication.

A pioneering attempt to relate pragmatic aspects of communication to evaluation of the aphasics' communicative deficits has been the Functional Communication Profile (FCP, Sarno, 1969). This was the first test to incorporate a core principle of pragmatic evaluation, namely the distinction between natural language use and linguistic performance in artificial testing situations. A similar approach has been developed by Holland in the Communicative Abilities in Daily Life test (CADL, Holland, 1980) which also aims at stimulating natural communicative exchanges. For instance, some CADL items are structured in a "role-playing" situation. The patient is invited to take part as a person visiting the doctor, making a payment in a shop, or looking for information in an office. In this way he or she interacts with the clinician who plays a receptionist or a waiter. Other CADL items investigate knowledge of language rule use, since the patient is requested to show understanding of price lists, common scripts, signboards, or metaphorical sentences. Such a construct makes the CADL test an ecologically valid measure of communicative disability resulting from aphasia. The CADL score, in fact, has been found to predict communicative abilities of aphasics as measured by direct observation of these subjects in everyday activities (Holland, 1980).

This conceptual framework has also dealt with new treatment methods. Schlanger and Schlanger (1970), for instance, have introduced role-play in programmes for rehabilitating patients with aphasia. In one of these exercises, patients are requested to adopt behaviours they would use when seated in an airplane, while the therapist, who plays the person seated alongside, creates a pleasant or unpleasant situation to stimulate spontaneous communicative exchange. The core principle of the programme is that more weight (positive reinforcement) should be given to contextual appropriateness of the patient's spontaneous communicative behaviour than formal adequacy of his or her verbal production.

Role playing has been developed by Aten, Caligiuri, and Holland (1982) into a formal therapy programme called Functional Communication Treatment. This method, in order to compensate for language deficits in familiar contexts, aims to modify the patient's communicative behaviour, e.g., shifting from an ineffective verbal modality to an effective gestural one. The patient is confronted with simulated communicative situations, e.g., shopping or giving information. The therapist puts forward and discusses with the patient the communicative strategy which can supplement defective language skills. Functional Treatment has been shown to be effective in improving communicative effectiveness of chronically non-fluent aphasic patients. Their CADL scores were significantly increased at post-therapy assessment despite their unchanged language scores. Six months later the improvement was found to be stable (Aten et al., 1982). These results indicate that, following Functional Treatment, aphasic patients may have increased communicative success in everyday exchanges.

Such aspects highlight the ecological validity of the "functional" approach to management of communicative deficits in aphasics. However, the "functional" view is strongly limited to the observation that defective language skills can be supplemented by non-verbal modes of communication and that residual linguistic and non-verbal skills can be cued by contextual and situational information. Furthermore, in studies by proponents of the "functional" approach, little or no reference is made to cognitive processes which underly communicative competence, nor to theories of conversation. For instance, the functional hypothesis has been further expanded by Holland (1991) into the "Conversational Coaching" therapy. This method includes preparation of a short monologue which is too difficult for the patient to produce. The clinician and the patient practise the script, with the former suggesting which strategies might be used to get the script content across. Then, the patient's relative or an unfamiliar person who does not know the script is called into the room and the patient tries to communicate the script content while being coached by the clinician. Holland (1991) maintains that "there are several contextual ways in which the difficulty of the task can be modified" (p. 202). These include variation in the listener's familiarity from relatives to unknown persons, and variation in the informativeness of the script from known information to improbable events or gossip. This proposal, however, is not linked to a particular model of conversation in which the interaction between the verbal content of messages and shared knowledge is detailed. Thus, on the one hand, it has been suggested that the pragmatic approach has turned into an "atheoretical approach" to aphasia therapy (Howard & Hatfield, 1987). On the other hand, functional treatments have usually been used with patients with severe aphasia (as a substitute for ineffective language stimulation) or they have been viewed as an additional treatment for generalising to everyday communication which results from the "true" language stimulation therapy.

A second view of pragmatically oriented methods for evaluation and treatment of aphasic deficits emerged in the 1980s. At that time, researchers in the field of pragmatics had spent considerable efforts in defining an appropriate taxonomy of pragmatic behaviours which could cover the interaction between linguistic knowledge, rules of language use in natural contexts, and psychosocial aspects of communication (Bates, 1976; Bloom & Lahey, 1978; Levinson, 1983; Winograd, 1977). Following this line, a number of "pragmatic protocols" have been devised for analysing the range and appropriateness of the communicative behaviours produced by normal subjects in natural conversation. Very soon, the potential of these protocols for clinical use in brain-damaged adults was recognised. In 1983, Prutting and Kirshner, for instance, devised a descriptive taxonomy of 30 pragmatic parameters according to theory of speech acts (Searle, 1969). The taxonomy takes into account verbal, non-verbal and paralinguistic behaviours related to how the message is presented (*utterance act*), the linguistic meaning of the sentence (*propositional act*), the speaker's intention and the effects of the speaker on the listener (*illocutionary / perlocutionary act*), the Pragmatic Protocol (Prutting & Kirchner, 1987). In subsequent studies, however, the classification of parameters according to speech-act theory was abandoned. Prutting and Kirchner, indeed, recognised that there were no precise boundaries that could separate the speech-act categories acknowledged in the model. However, they maintained the need to organise, for clinical purposes, pragmatic aspects of language into a descriptive taxonomy. Thus, pragmatic behaviours were grouped into three main categories: (1) Verbal aspects, which include parameters relating to speech acts, topic management, turn-taking, repair/revision strategies, lexical selection, and stylistic variation; (2) paralinguistic aspects, which include speech intelligibility, prosody and fluency; and (3) non-verbal aspects, which include parameters such as control of body posture, eye gaze, facial expression and arm movement. The modified Pragmatic Protocol has been shown suitable in identifying profiles which distinguish between aphasic patients and other language disordered subjects (Prutting & Kirchner, 1987).

Another checklist for describing communicative competence in language disordered subjects is the Profile of Communicative Appropriateness (Penn, 1983, quoted in Penn, 1988). This analysis takes into account 49 pragmatic parameters grouped into six main sections: Non-verbal communication, socio-linguistic sensitivity, fluency, cohesion, control of semantic content, and responsiveness to the interlocutor. Appropriateness of a single parameter is judged on a 5-point rating scale based on whether the behaviour interferes with conversational flow. Cumulative scores are provided both for overall perfor-mance and the six functional areas.

The Profile of Communicative Appropriateness has been used to describe deficits of communicative competence in patients with aphasia with respect to the syntactic analysis of their language (Penn, 1988). In this study, the syntactic analysis accounted for severity and aphasia type while examination of pragmatic aspects could reveal different profiles of disruption and preserva-tion. Furthermore, there was no one-to-one relation between syntactic deficits and pragmatic profiles. For instance, the degree of aphasia severity constituted an accurate predictor of overall communicative skills. However, there were some patients in whom severe expressive difficulties did not prevent adequate sequential topic management or appropriate discourse structure. By contrast, other patients, despite relatively preserved syntactic competence, were prag-matically inappropriate. These findings allowed the author to note that, following such an assessment method, clinical differences between patients emerged that were obscured by traditional aphasia testing methods. Further-more, it was suggested that describing the complex interaction between parameters of structural and functional aspects of language could lay founda-tions for planning treatment in an individual patient (Penn, 1988; see also Penn, 1984).

The "taxonomic" approach to the study of communicative competence in brain-damaged subjects, in fact, has also been concerned with the development of new therapy programmes. These programmes have been devised according to the hypothesis that pragmatic protocols could be used for careful identifica-tion of conversational weaknesses in adults with aphasia and that such an assessment could result in providing a focus for treatment. An example is the method developed by Doyle, Goldstein, Bourgeois, and Nekles (1989) to train Broca's aphasics to ask questions. This study included a multiple baseline design to examine whether requesting abilities generalised to untrained topics and to unfamiliar persons. Three conversational topics (personal information, leisure, and health) were chosen and a list of prompts was devised for use by the trainers, e.g., "You could ask where I work". These prompts introduced topics and subtopics about which the patients could request information and maintain the topic of conversation. Prompts were randomly used by trainers after a particular topic was introduced. Patients were expected to produce questions and to mark them by means of interrogative structure and/or by rising intonation. Grammatical accuracy was neither required nor particularly reinforced. However, the production of appropriate intonation was given positive feedback. Four patients included in this study received from 36 to 40 therapy sessions, each consisting of 20 trials. Results showed that requesting behaviour generalised and that requesting attempts of all subjects were within a normal level after therapy. Significant changes in talkativeness and conversational success were also observed. A further observation was that the method was more successful for patients talking with unfamiliar persons than with familiar listeners. This indicated an increased pragmatic awareness in the patients. The topics included in the training had, in fact, communicative value for strangers but not for people who already knew the patient. Thus, the patients who had received the training programme were found to act accordingly at the retest (Doyle et al., 1989).

This example illustrates how taxonomies of pragmatic behaviours have been incorporated into new assessment methods. These methods could identify strengths and weaknesses of patients' communicative behaviour. Treatment methods, in turn, could take into account such a detailed analysis in selecting therapy goals and planning therapy content.

However, developing assessment methods and therapies according to the "taxonomic" view has been associated with a number of practical and conceptual problems which have prevented therapists from routinely applying pragmatic protocols and deriving therapy programmes from such an analysis.

From a practical point of view, for instance, most of the protocols require considerable expertise on the part of the therapist to obtain sufficient reliability in observation and rating. Furthermore, they cannot be applied to the analysis of communicative behaviour of severely impaired subjects (Manochiopinig, Sheard, & Read, 1992).

From a theoretical point of view, we have mentioned the difficulties experienced by Prutting and Kirchner (1987) when taking into account the paradigm from speech-act theory in the Pragmatic Protocol. Others have argued that clinical measures of pragmatic competence developed in this framework usually suffer from an abstract, "top-down" definition of categories for analysis (Lesser & Milroy, 1993, p. 154) or that no adequate operational definitions have been developed for a number of pragmatic concepts such as "topic coherence" (Mentis & Prutting, 1987) or "communicative adequacy" (Lesser & Milroy, 1993).

It has also been observed that the direct implications for therapy which can be drawn from an analysis with the pragmatic protocols have been overemphasised by the proponents (Lesser & Milroy, 1993). In the study by Doyle et al. (1989), for instance, the clinicians identified the impaired communicative areas, e.g., difficulties in formulating (syntactically correct) questions and maintaining the topic of conversation. Therefore, it was possible to provide a detailed account of the intervention procedure, e.g., conversation with the therapist modelling what the patient should do and reinforcing the appropriate compensatory behaviour from the patient. However, the majority of aphasic patients do exhibit more complex interrelations between linguistic and pragmatic deficits. Furthermore, language skills are assumed to be unaffected by pragmatically oriented treatments. In the "taxonomic" approach, pragmatic competence is usually regarded as an additional set of language rules (separate from the phonological, lexical, and syntactic) which would be taken into account for the formulation of therapy goals. The therapeutic hypothesis always rests on the development of communicative strategies that substitute for defective language processing, see earlier the programme by Doyle et al. (1989) but see also Penn (1984) for details of this therapeutic paradigm. This aspect may represent a substantial weakness of pragmatically oriented treatments(s) for the therapist, who works to the exclusion of direct intervention on language processing; for the patient, who expects therapies geared to his particular phonological, lexical, or syntactic processing; and for insurance companies who expect improvement on standard language assessment tests (Holland, 1991).

Such a therapeutic hypothesis, however, is quite surprising since the results obtained with another method which incorporates pragmatic concepts into the therapy setting. e.g., the Group Therapy devised by Wertz and co-workers in the framework of the Veteran's Administration Cooperative Study on Aphasia (Wertz et al., 1981; see also Shewan & Kertesz, 1984, for a replication). In this setting, which was designed to improve communication through group interaction and discussion, between three and seven aphasic subjects took part in group discussion on current events or topics selected by therapists. Patients were stimulated to participate in the discussion, to ask questions, and to add relevant information but no attempts were made to their verbal behaviour in terms of isolated words or sentences. Results showed that, following this treatment technique, significant improvement could be found both on standard language scores and functional measures of informativeness even between 26 and 48 weeks post-onset, a period during which no spontaneous recovery usually occurs (Basso, Capitani, & Vignolo, 1979). Furthermore, no differences could be found at the end of the treatment between these patients and those who had received individual language stimulation. These results provide strong support for the view that a therapy setting based on rules of conversation may improve language skills in aphasic patients. Nevertheless, they could not be predicted according to the standard pragmatic paradigm(s) for dealing with language disturbances derived from speech-act theory, see earlier.

In the next section we hope to show how these methodological problems (and related practical difficulties) can be resolved within experimental paradigms for studying relationships between language and context.

THE INTERACTION BETWEEN LANGUAGE PROCESSING AND CONTEXT

In the late 1970s, neuropsychologists started to pay attention to the effects of contextual variables on language processing in brain-damaged subjects. In the study by Stachowiak, Huber, Poeck, & Kerschensteiner (1977) short texts were read to aphasic patients, right brain-damaged, and normal subjects who were asked to choose the picture that illustrated the story from five alternatives. Furthermore, subjects were also given word and sentence comprehension tests. Results indicated that aphasic patients were impaired in word and sentence comprehension. However, they were as effective as controls in identifying the semantic content of the story from which they could indicate the correct pictorial representation. In another study (Wilcox, Davis, & Leonard, 1978), aphasic subjects were given videorecordings of brief communicative inter- actions between two adults. In each episode one adult made an indirect request, e.g., "Can you open the door?". In half the items the listener produced the appropriate response, e.g., opened the door; in the remaining he or she responded inappropriately, e.g., saying "Yes", but remaining seated. The aphasics' performance in judging the listener's behaviour was superior to their performance on the standard sentence auditory comprehension task. In a replication of this study, subjects with Broca's aphasia and right brain-damaged patients were presented with two experimental conditions where a "Can you . . .?" form could have been interpreted in the literal sense (question) or in the non-literal (indirect request) according to contextual infor- mation. Results showed that aphasics had normal performance on items containing indirect requests but had difficulties with questions. Right brain-damaged patients showed the opposite pattern (Hirst, LeDoux, & Stein, 1984).

These studies indicated that, at a neurological level, processing of discrete linguistic units may dissociate from language processing in context: Contex- tual information can cue processing of discrete linguistic units in aphasics, while right brain-damaged subjects have difficulties in integrating linguistic information into coherent wholes. Furthermore, in the study by Stachowiak et al. (1977) explicit reference was made to papers by cognitive psychologists on processes involved in discourse and text comprehension (Brandsford & Johnson, 1972), while in the paper by Wilcox et al. (1978), the distinction between *sentence meaning* and *speaker's meaning* (Searle, 1969) was examined with reference to experimental methodologies to study language comprehension in the context (Clark & Lucy, 1975).

Following this experimental approach, in a number of subsequent works, the study of contextual aspects of communicative disturbances in brain-damaged patients was not conceptualised as a separate level which is independent from other analyses of language deficits, say at the syntactic or lexical level. Instead, the contextual variable was identified as decomposable into discrete aspects which could be manipulated with respect to models of language/context interaction.

For instance, Berko-Gleason and colleagues (1980) had examined narratives produced by aphasic patients describing a cartoon-like picture sequence. Patients looked at the drawings and listened to the examiner's narration so that they could retell the story afterwards. Both non-fluent aphasics and Wernicke's aphasics showed a significant reduction in target lexemes or in number of themes, faulty pronominalisation (producing pronouns without defined antecedents), and inappropriate deixis (verbal pointing with words such as, "that", "this", "there"). The results indicated the pragmatic difficulties of these patients in shaping their utterances in terms of defining topics and focusing information: "This kind of aphasic speech violated ordinary discourse rules . . . (aphasics') speech . . . makes overoptimistic presupposition about the knowledge of the listeners" (Berko-Gleason et al. (1980, p. 380).

However, Bates, Hamby, and Zurif (1983) examined verbal utterances of patients with Broca's or Wernicke's aphasia when describing sets of three figures in each of which one element varied and the others remained constant, e.g.: A mother is giving an apple, toy, or box to a child. In this case, the figures were not visible to the examiner. This task had been shown suitable to examine the pragmatic competence of children in signalling with surface devices the distinction between information which is new and to be focused on and information which has already been given (McWinney & Bates, 1978). Dependent variables included probability of lexicalisation versus ellipsis, pronominalisation, definite and indefinite article use, word order variations, and the use of connectors. Broca's aphasics were found to be competent in lexicalisation and dative structure while Wernicke's aphasics were competent in lexicalisation and article use. It was concluded that subjects with aphasia retain some sensitivity to the pragmatics of natural discourse although this can be masked by semantic or syntactic impairment. In commenting on the substantial difference between the conclusions by Berko-Gleason et al. (1980) and Bates et al. (1983), we should note that structural aspects of the task and the analysis of patient's performance in the latter study takes into account the integrated nature of structural linguistic forms and conversational rules. This probably has allowed Bates and coworkers to examine relationships between lexical/syntactic difficulties and (partially) preserved pragmatic components more accurately than the off-line judgement of definite reference used by Berko-Gleason et al. (1980).

We will not discuss here how long these cognitively oriented methodologies have allowed neuropsychologists to explore aspects of impaired communication in brain-damaged persons or how data from brain-damaged subjects have been used to make inferences about the cognitive organisation underlying communication in context. The interested reader is instead referred, among others, to Brownell and Joanette (1993), Davis and Wilcox (1985), Joanette and Brownell (1989), Lesser and Milroy (1993). Furthermore, similar methodologies have been applied to study other components of functional communication in brain-damaged subjects, e.g., manual activity during speech production (Hadar & Butterworth, 1997; McNeil & Pedelty, 1995).

The question here is whether (and how) this conceptual framework could also influence clinicians when devising diagnostic and therapeutic tools for tapping communicative disturbances of brain-damaged adults. In what follows we illustrate a few examples which could allow us to answer in the affirmative.

We have already mentioned the issues raised by Lesser and Milroy (1993) concerning difficulties in the evaluation of communicative disturbances in adults with aphasia when using pragmatic protocols. These authors have argued that this analysis might benefit from observational techniques developed among sociologists of communication, such as conversation analysis. This method attempts to explain how the speakers direct the course of conversation, and repair its inherent troubles without having recourse to off-line judgement of appropriateness from Searle's (1969) theory or Grice's (1975) maxims. To do so, conversation analysis only searches for patterns of recurring language behaviours in naturally occurring conversation. Milroy and Perkins (1992) have described in detail how this method could be applied to communicative exchanges between an aphasic subject and his or her partner and how it usefully addresses a number of interactional difficulties (pauses, use of discourse markers, hint–guess sequences) resulting from the linguistic deficits of these patients. Lesser and Milroy (1993) have also noted that clinical adaptation of the method offers practical solutions to some difficulties found with pragmatic protocols. For instance, the difficulty in using the formal judgement of communicative appropriateness by an external rater may be overcome since, in conversation analysis, the conversational turn is the observation unit used to rate success or failure in a communicative exchange. The judgement about whether a communicative breakdown occurred or about whether conversational repair was successful is usually made according to the partner's reaction to the patient's communicative attempts (see also Gerber & Gurland, 1989, for such an approach). Furthermore, the method can provide a numerical estimate of the patient's communicative effectiveness which would take into acount the proportion of breakdowns and/or misunderstanding incidents occurring in the communicative interaction, the number of consecutive unsuccessful turns that the breakdown/repair sequences take, and the amount of the partner's help in sustaining the communicative exchange (Clérebaut, Coyette, Feyereisen, & Seron, 1984; Gerber & Gurland, 1989).

Two studies from our group support this hypothesis by having recourse to a model of conversation which is also suitable for describing relationships between language deficit and communicative adequacy in aphasic patients.

Aspects of conversation, such as producing definite reference, can be studied by means of a referential communication task (Krauss & Glucksberg, 1977). In this task, pairs of people talk about arranging picture cards. The participants, separated by an opaque screen, each have a few picture cards in front of them. The cards are in a target order for the speaker and in a random order for the listener who has to rearrange his cards in order to match the target ordering. In the experiment by Clark and Wilkes-Gibbs (1986) it was shown that the speaker usually initiates reference by proposing a noun phrase for the listener to accept. If this does not suffice, however, the participants repair, expand, or replace the noun phrase until they reach a version they mutually consider valid. In so doing they try to minimise the collaborative effort presenting and refashioning the noun phrase as efficiently as possible.

The model allows several predictions to be made about parameters of the conversational exchange between an aphasic speaker and his or her conversational partner. According to previous experiments by Bush, Brookshire, and Nicholas (1988), it is possible to manipulate the amount of information which is crucial to identify each referent. For instance, in the identification of a picture illustrating a man behind a tree presented with distractors illustrating a man in front of a tree, a woman behind a tree and a man behind a chair, it is necessary to send three pieces of information. Thus, the patient's residual lexical and syntactic abilities may be evaluated, by looking at the proportion of the target words and corrected syntactic structures produced in the course of communicative interaction. Then, the number of miniturns or incidents of misunderstanding for a given number of referents may be indicative of the patient's communicative adequacy (Clérebaut et al., 1984, Gerber & Gurland, 1989). When participants are separated by means of a double-faced book-rest instead of the opaque screen used in the Clark and Wilkes-Gibbs' (1986) experiment, another practical advantage of such a task is that it is possible to retain aspects of natural conversation, e.g., gesturing, eye movements, or facial expression. Furthermore, the listener's knowledge about possible referents allows clinicians to control the amount of shared knowledge between speaker and listener. Finally, the resolution of communicative breakdown can be described with a protocol for clinical interaction analysis which takes into account the appropriateness of the patient's compensatory strategies, e.g., appropriate paraphasias, circumlocutions, gesture, and the partner's signals to repair, e.g. vague requests, conversational directives, explicit request of information (Carlomagno, 1994; Clérebaut et al., 1984; Gerber & Gurland, 1989). For instance:

P.:   Man . . . coffee . . .
Th.:   I have two figures with this.
P.:   He . . . the coffee (downward gesture with the hand closed)
Th.:   OK. He is pouring it (shows the picture).

Here, lexical/syntactic difficulties are acknowledged to prevent the patient from communicating effectively since parameters of the task show that he needs two miniturns to identify the referent. However, the patient is shown to retain sensitivity to the listener's request for more information and to supplement defective verbal labelling of the figure with effective gesturing.

In a recent experiment we have given such a referential communication task to normal controls, patients who had recovered from aphasia, and patients with mild to moderate chronic aphasia (Blasi, Faccioli, Losanno, & Carlomagno, 1996). Brain-damaged subjects had previously received comprehensive evaluation by means of a standard language examination (Aachen Aphasia Test, AAT, Huber, Poeck & Willmes, 1984) and the CADL test (Holland, 1980, see earlier). Results showed that a measure of residual verbal abilities (number of target words) and two measures of informative disability (number of incidents of misunderstanding and number of miniturns) were adequate in diagnosing presence and severity of aphasic symptoms. A further analysis showed that the language measure of the test was related to the score on the language production task of the standard language assessment while the two measures of communicative disability were related to the CADL score. Thus, the referential communication task was shown to be suitable in providing valid evaluation both of residual language abilities and communicative effectiveness (Blasi et al., 1996).

The third point of interest was the possibility to describe aspects of pragmatic competence and the effectiveness of compensatory strategies shown by the individual patient. For instance, patients MA and TGe, both suffering from Wernicke's aphasia, produced the same amount of target words but differed greatly in the number of miniturns and incidents of misunderstanding. On the 25 items of the task, for instance, 50 communicative attempts and six incidents of misunderstanding were recorded in the case of MA while 35 attempts were needed for TGe to communicate the 25 referents without errors. This difference corresponded to the difference on CADL score (107 vs. 93), Figure 1. When incidents occurring in the communicative interaction were evaluated by means of a clinical interaction analysis system (Carlomagno, 1994), it was shown that, contrary to TGe, MA showed poor sensitivity to the listener's feedback to add or repair ineffective messages. Finally, TGe succeeded in communicating all the referents by means of context-appropriate compensatory strategies (mainly appropriate paraphasias and informative gestures) while MA did not show appropriate paraphasias nor gestures as a substitute for language (Blasi et al., 1996).

These findings support the hypothesis that experimental methodologies to study features of language/context interaction in normal subjects may be translated into diagnostic tools which allow clinicians to check for relationships between actual communicative effectiveness, residual linguistic skills, and

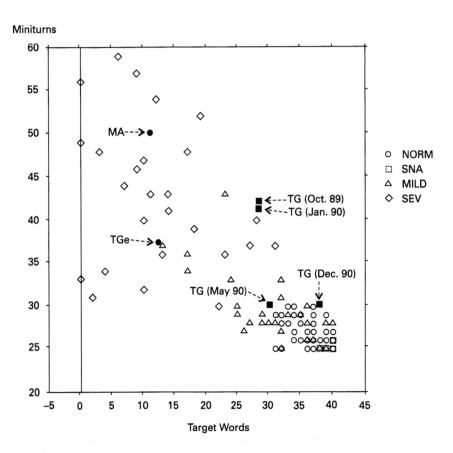

Figure 1. Parameters of performance of 66 normal controls (NORM), 11 left brain-damaged non-aphasics (SNA) and 58 consecutive subjects with mild (MILD) or severe (SEV) aphasia on the referential communication task by Blasi et al. (1996).

Patients MA (CADL score = 93) and TGe (CADL score = 107) are described in the text. Their performance on the referential communication test (filled circle) can be evaluated with respect to performance of subjects with mild (target words $\bar{x}$ = 30.1, SD = 7.1; miniturns $\bar{x}$ = 29.6.6, SD = 4.1; and misunderstanding incidents $\bar{x}$ = 0.1, SD = 0.3) and severe aphasia (target words $\bar{x}$ = 12.4, SD = 8.6; miniturns $\bar{x}$ = 43.0, SD = 8.3; and misunderstanding incidents $\bar{x}$ = 3.2, SD = 2.8), see Blasi et al. (1996).

Patient TG (filled square) received 24 sessions of the modified PACE treatment (see the text) from January 1990 (CADL score = 109) to May 1990 (CADL score = 122). In December 1990 (CADL score = 124) he received a fourth assessment when he was undergoing a therapy for writing disturbances following lexical strategy (Carlomagno et al., 1994). Other behavioural changes in TG's communicative attempts are described in the text.

compensatory strategies. Such an analysis has diagnostic potential since differences emerged between patients with similar aphasic symptoms, e.g., MA vs. TGe. Implications of this assessment method in clinical practice will be illustrated later in the text.

Models of conversation, on the other hand, appear to offer a new framework within which speech pathologists might expand therapeutic settings by taking into account structural aspects of language/context interaction.

An attempt in this direction is the Promoting Aphasics' Communicative Effectiveness therapy (PACE, Davis & Wilcox, 1985). This method was initially devised to familiarise patients with face-to-face communication. For this purpose, parameters of natural conversation were incorporated into the therapy setting. The following are the core principles of PACE therapy:

1. The clinician and the patient participate equally as sender and receiver of messages.
2. The treatment interaction consists of an exchange of new information.
3. The patient is allowed free choice of communicative channels.
4. Feedback from the clinician is based on communicative adequacy of the patient's message.

According to these principles, in the original basic exercise of PACE therapy, clinician and patient sit facing one another across a table on which stimulus cards with printed words or object pictures face downwards. Each participant in turn takes a picture and, without showing it, must convey to the other what it represents. The following example illustrates a typical miniturn sequence in PACE therapy (related pragmatic behaviours are in italics as in Davis and Wilcox, 1985, p. 97).

P.:   (picks up a card) . . . A woman . . . paper . . .
Th.:   A woman with the paper? *Contingent query, article variation*
P.:   No, she's . . . (makes writing gesture) *Pronominalisation, repair*
Th.:   Oh! she's writing? *Pronominalisation, contingent query*
P.:   Yes (shows the card) *Confirmation*
Th.:   She's writing *Confirmation*.

The PACE method has become a popular procedure in many countries as an effective method for managing chronic word finding difficulties. This hypothesis has received experimental support. For instance, in a single case study (Chin Li, Kitselman, Dusatko, & Spinelli, 1988), a patient suffering from chronic severe fluent aphasia received alternating cycles of traditional language stimulation therapy and PACE treatment. At the end of each cycle the patient's ability to identify objects was evaluated. Results showed that traditional therapy did not help while significant improvement could be found following PACE treatment. Analysis of the patient's responses showed that this was due to an increased number of appropriate paraphasias or circumlocutions accompanied by meaningful gestures. Following this approach, other studies have shown the effectiveness of PACE treatment in providing even severe non-fluent aphasic subjects with effective non-gestural behaviour (Carlomagno et al., 1988; Cubelli, Trentini, & Montagna, 1991).

The therapeutic potential of PACE might be no different from that of techniques used for training aphasic subjects in compensating defective language processing (see earlier the Functional Treatment by Aten et al., 1982). Furthermore, PACE has been criticised as being "as far from true communication as one can imagine" and some aspects of the technique have been considered too difficult for more impaired subjects (see Howard & Hatfield, 1987, p. 85, for such a position). However, following the structure of incidents in the clinical setting (see earlier for an example), we would agree with the claim by Davis and Wilcox (1985) that PACE "allows the participants to practice turn-taking, to experience a variety of speech acts, to adopt hint and guess sequences when communication breakdown occurs, to take advantage from linguistic, paralinguistic and extralinguistic contexts, and to make use of conversational rules governing given versus new information". This structure has an important therapeutic potential which has been shown by developments of the PACE method.

Springer, Glindemann, Huber, and Willmes (1991), for instance, presented a modified version of the original PACE setting that incorporates tasks of semantic classification of treatment items. During treatment, semantically correlated items were used, such as a truck, a car, a bus, and a motorcycle. These items were mixed with a few distractors. The patient was supplied with the general category, written on a sheet of paper, and asked to decide whether or not the referent belonged to the category before beginning the exercise of identifying the item. The exercise was structured according to a modified PACE setting where figures are available to both parties on either side of a book-rest (Clérebaut et al., 1984). The authors argued that this modification of the original treatment would lead to greater improvement as compared with standard PACE treatment. Working with a group of four chronic aphasic patients with a marked deficit in identifying objects, they compared the effects of PACE treatment described by David and Wilcox (1985) with those of their modified PACE, used in an ABAB paradigm. At the end of each five-session therapy cycle the responses of patients on control lists were scored with the Language System Score (adapted from Huber et al., 1984) in order to evaluate the lexical–semantic accuracy of the patient's verbal production. The results showed that only in the case of patient HM who was suffering from Broca's aphasia with severe oral aphasia, did the effect of the two treatments coincide. In this case, an increased use of gestural messages and drawings was observed. In the three other participants, by contrast, no effect could be demonstrated for the traditional PACE approach, while the modified PACE therapy led to significant improvement at evaluation with the Language System Score. This indicated increased ability to identify the referent verbally. It is likely that, to communicate "car" from among the vehicle items, the three patients found it more advantageous to resort to verbal labelling (adding information as to whether the vehicle had two or four wheels, was large or small, carried people or goods, etc.) according to the contextual constraints of the task.

These results support the hypothesis we have put forward about the data by Wertz et al. (1981), that a therapy setting which incorporates parameters of natural conversation can exploit aspects of language/context interaction to improve aphasics' language abilities. Further support for this view can be found in the results by Carlomagno et al. (1991a) who studied the effects of PACE on the amount of information produced by aphasic patients in story-retelling. In this trial, the first treatment step involved exercises of picture identification. In one of them, both participants had identical sets of figures in front of them on the two sides of a double-faced book-rest and alternated in the speaker's role. The figures were designed to tackle patient's difficulties in handling agent/recipient relationships and identifying actions or objects. For instance they illustrated a man and a woman, each of whom, depending on the picture, may be threatening the other with a pistol or a rifle or be handing over one of these weapons to the other. The following example will illustrate a typical therapeutic interaction with patient TG (from Carlomagno, 1994).

Example 1

P.: (Looking at the picture, then, without lifting his eyes from it) . . . With the girl . . . (mime of a pistol) . . . with young man and . . . they have the pifle . . . the rifle (mime of pistol) . . . the rufle . . . that they are, that they are (gesturing of stretching out a hand) to the boy . . . the rabble . . . the fiddle.

Th.: Wait please! You must make me understand (raising the voice and lifting a hand to command him to stop, looking into his eyes) . . . you must make me understand which one to which (double gesture pointing right and left, still looking into the patient's eyes).

P.: The girl . . . has her hands . . . (gesture of holding something out) . . . on the right (inclining the head to the right and looking at the thera-pist) . . . the boy is on the left (head to the left, watching the therapist) . . . and the girl . . . offers (gesture of handing something over) . . . to the other (looks at the picture again, then looks up at the therapist) . . . the pistol (mime of pistol) . . . (smiles) . . . now . . . the . . . (mime of pistol).

Th.: OK! The girl hands the pistol to the boy (looks into the patient's eyes and moves one hand from right to left, miming a pistol). Now it's my turn. (Looks at the photo, then looks up at the patient). The boy . . . (pointing to the right)—wait, watch me—the boy is threatening (hands grasping a rifle) the girl, and the girl—watch me carefully!—is raising her hands (gesture).

P.:   (Lifts the corresponding card and smiles) ... This ... this ... (without looking up from the picture) this here ... it's the boy who has *the pistol* (mimes threatening by pistol) ... who ... brings ... to the girl

Th.:   I don't understand! (Looks at him). You must tell me ... (winks, moving his head from right to left, keeping his gaze on the patient).

P.:   (A long look at the photo, then lifts his head and inclines it to the right) Here it's the girl who puts the boy (nods to the left) the boy with his hands ... with his hands up (gesture) ... (looks again at the photo, then looks up at the therapist) ... with the pistol (mime of pistol).

Th.:   OK! (Raises the photo with his left hand and repeats the patient's message, head movements and getures).

P.:   This ... this one here (looks up) ... it's the boy who has ... who brings ... (gesture of offering) ... the pistol (mime) ... (looks at the photo) ... to the girl ... on the right (head inclined to the right).

Th.:   (Shows photo).

In the example, the therapist, both in his replies to messages and when acting as a speaker, proposed to the patient a model of behaviour for overcoming difficulties in producing well-formed utterances. Describing each crucial theme in turn, punctuating the presentation of the different themes (boy, girl, pistol) with deictic head movements, gesturing, and watching the listener's face for possible expressions of incomprehension, was considered effective strategy for overcoming lexical (action and object identification) and syntactic (definition of agent/recipient relationships) difficulties. When no more overt modelling and explicit request of such a behaviour was necessary, the treatment task was changed so that no alteration in the speaker's role was used.

Example 2

P.:   The man is giving! ... she ... no ... tha man is giving ... the ... gun to the ...

Th.:   OK! he is giving it (raises the corresponding card).

P.:   Now he is shooting (gesture) the pistol at the girl.

Th.:   (raises the corresponding card).

P.:   He ... no, she ... she is giving the pistol.

Th.:   Very good! It's the girl who is giving the pistol to the man.

Here, the material designed to train the patient to communicate syntactic relationships served to stimulate pronominalisation strategies, as the figures illustrated the same characters in various situations and the patient, using a pronoun, could identify an agent already known to the listener.

In the following exercises, figures from this set were mixed with those from other series and used in the classical PACE exercise (no picture cards were available to the listener) and the treatment was concerned with describing pictures using the pattern as agent—action—object—place. The therapist first modelled such a behaviour and guided the patient to perform accordingly by means of explicit questions (*Who? What's he doing? Where?*). Then, as quickly as possible, only vague requests for additional information were used to obtain a complete description of the figures from the patient. The exercise was organised in order to familiarise the patient with a response pattern which could fulfil this aim. During the task, two subsequent pictures were used which could have the same characters in two different situations, or the same action performed by two different persons, or different actions performed by the same person, and so on. Or there could be no relationships at all between two or three subsequent pictures.

Example 3

P.:   She . . . she's . . .
Th.:   What do you mean by she?
P.:   There is a girl who pa . . . pa . . . to speak . . . the money . . . the money . . . how do you call it . . . to pay in the shop . . . (writing gesture).
Th.:   She's writing a cheque. OK, the next one?
P.:   There is the girl . . .
Th.:   Is she the same girl?
P.:   Yes, she's with an (gesture around the head) . . . hat . . . hat . . . there is the sun . . .
Th.:   OK! she is going on holiday, maybe . . . the next one?
P.:   Now, . . . there is a man . . . a man who is handling a rifle (gesture), he is threatening a girl (raise hands) . . .

In this way, the therapist can address both lexical–syntactic difficulties and presuppositional-referencing problems of the patient by training him or her to adjust messages (in terms of lexicalisation versus pronoun use, article variation, use of connectors, co-reference, and so on) according to the actual needs of conversational exchange.

These aspects were emphasised in the second treatment step which involved story telling activities in a modified PACE setting. These activities were chosen as they represent a relatively constrained form of conversation where a central aspect of discourse, namely the establishment and maintenance of reference, could be focused on (Marslen-Wilson, Levy, & Komisarjevsky Tyler, 1982). Here, both patient and clinician had in front of them, on the two sides of a double-faced book-rest, identical sets of figures where two or more actors played a number of actions in different places. The pictures of each series were chosen so that they could be arranged in different sequences of episodes. Each speaker had to arrange figures and make up an anecdote to suit the figure arrangement. In this way, the listener could arrange his figure set in the right order. The therapist, when acting as a speaker, modelled redundant discourse. First, he had to get across the main topic, to emphasise the sequence of main events, to display congruent facial expressions and elaborate hand movements, and second, to stress cohesive devices between the episodes of the story. On the other hand, when acting as a listener, the therapist had to make a number of contingent queries and/or general requests for more information so that the patient was forced to produce the complete sequence of episodes, to provide correct cross-reference between sentences, and to supply main themes and details using a variety of communicative channels (verbal, gesturing, writing, and so on). Exercise variations were then introduced by taking away one or more pictures or one of the two participants and by modifying the clinician's support. (For details on these procedures in relation to PACE principles see Carlomagno, 1994).

Eight subjects with aphasia of about 8 months duration took part in the experiment and received 24 treatment sessions. At the pre- and post-therapy evaluations they were given referential communication and story re-telling tasks. Results proved that introducing new tasks in the PACE setting (controlled along with the contextual variable) was suitable to improve the informative behaviour of the patients. The parameters of communicative effectiveness from the referential communication task showed improved performance at re-test (see for instance, performance of patient TG in Figure 1). This corresponded to a slight non-significant increase in the number of target words ($p > .09$) as well as on the standard measures of informativeness (content units, speaking rate, and content units per minute) from the Cookie Theft picture description (Yorkston & Beukelman, 1980). However, it was also noted that patients "were more able . . . to avoid incorrect or irrelevant information" and the number of verbal utterances was found to be reduced (Carlomagno et al., 1991a, p. 423). Taken together these results indicated that *the proportion of words which conveyed information* had increased in the patient's communicative attempts. Note that, in studies on connected speech samples from aphasic subjects, no measure of informative efficiency was found better than joint consideration of measures of speaking rate (words per minute) and percent of correct information (proportion of words that convey relevant information, Nicholas & Brookshire, 1993). This probably accounts for the fact that communicative behaviour of these subjects in the story re-telling task was rated to be more informative than at pre-therapy assessment, i.e., number of words and speaking rate remained unchanged while the percent of correct information increased. In TG's speech samples from the story re-telling task, for instance, percent of correct information increased from 28 to 49. These behavioural changes also resulted in reduced communicative disability at CADL evaluation.

Results by Springer et al. (1991) and Carlomagno et al. (1991a), as well as those obtained by Wertz et al. (1981), seem to indicate that therapy settings based on models of conversation are suitable to address aphasics' language deficits and ineffective informative behaviour. These results deserve further discussion with respect to the relationships between pragmatic theory and a hypothesis about remediating communicative difficulties of these subjects and the relationships between pragmatic theory and the structure of the intervention procedure.

With respect to the study by Carlomagno et al. (1991a), we have already mentioned that language processing by aphasic patients is positively influenced by contextual variables, see earlier, for instance, the study by Stachowiak et al. (1977). This effect was likely put into action in a therapy setting where a large amount of contextual information was provided (see, for example, the familiarity of the listener with picture content in Example 1 of the therapy programme). This information was reduced across the steps of therapy. Situational context from the therapist was modified as well. His behaviour, in fact, moved from guessing and explicit requests for information to vague support for the patient's communicative attempts and from explicit modelling of effective communicative behaviour to a more natural conversational partnership.

This structure of the intervention is in agreement with aspects of functional recovery from language deficit which have been shown by Cannito, Hough, Vogel, and Pierce (1996) in aphasic subjects at different stages of recovery. In their experiments, patients were given reversible passive sentences presented in isolation or preceded by short paragraphs which either predicted or did not predict the subject–object relationships illustrated in the target sentences. Subjects in the early stages of recovery demonstrated no advantage from predictive or non-predictive contextual information; subjects at the intermediate stage of recovery (6 months post-onset) demonstrated advantage only for the predictive narrative condition, while effects of both predictive and non-predictive narrative contexts were found in patients with chronic aphasia (more than 1 year post-onset). We argue that the early steps of the PACE programme by Carlomagno et al. (1991a) corresponded to the intermediate stage of recovery in the case of the study by Cannito et al. (1996). This is not only true for the comparable time post-onset in the two studies but also because the facilitating effects of PACE treatment could be observed only with enriched shared knowledge between the two participants and with redundant situational cues from the therapist. In the more advanced steps of therapy (and at re-test), the patients were able to make use of less explicit contextual information to self cue an appropriate informative behaviour. This might correspond to improved language processing of the chronically aphasic subjects in the study by Cannito et al. (1996) as they took advantage also from non-predictive information about the sentence content.

If further studies support our hypothesis, models of language/context inter-action will produce a considerable shift of the (pragmatic) paradigm from which to view the therapy of language disorders in aphasic adults. The pragmatic approach, in fact, will not be limited to providing patients with communication strategies which are a substitute for defective language or to complementing traditional language stimulation with conversation practice. Instead, it will help in developing therapy programmes which may result in greater communicative effectiveness as well as improved language processing. Davis and Wilcox (1985) indeed, according to models of language/context interaction, have proposed that the development of pragmatic rehabilitation methods must ideally proceed by recognising the contextual variable(s) that influence the language processing of normal and aphasic subjects, then by devising a treatment procedure that might capitalise on this factor and, finally, determining if this procedure has been successful in improving patients' verbal behaviour.

A second observation concerns the implication of pragmatic theory for the structural aspects of the clinical setting. We have described at length how in the experiment by Carlomagno et al. (1991a) the original PACE exercise was modified across the therapy steps. This has not been made to support the claim that these exercises represent a major change in therapy practice. Our aim was only to suggest how aspects of communicating in context could be incorporated into the rules of therapeutic interaction.

Let us, in fact, suppose that we are examining an aphasic subject to be enrolled in therapy. We have already proposed that a model of language/ context interaction which underlies the referential communication task (Blasi et al., 1996), helps to provide description of residual linguistic skills and informative efficacy by means of valid parameters. This information, of course, does not allow, in itself, a comprehensive analysis of linguistic (phonological problems, word-retrieval problems, lexical–syntactic appropriateness) and pragmatic (difficulties in turn taking, presuppositional/referential incompet-ence, problems in topic maintenance or shift and in non-verbal accompanying behaviour) components of functional communication.

In the experiment by Carlomagno et al. (1991a) such an analysis was the core principle which guided clinicians during clinical interaction. As shown in Example 2, the therapist recognised correct pronoun use by the patient and gave positive feedback. The patient continued to use it effectively in the following communicative exchanges. Use of this communicative device was then confronted with another communicative context where, to produce definite reference, pronoun use could be appropriate or lexicalisation was required (see Example 3). This was also made for the compensatory strategy proposed in other steps of the therapy (see Example 1). Thus, the therapist could assess the effectiveness of components of functional communication in the patient "on-line". This assessment, in turn, allowed the therapist to organise the content of the following therapy sessions where establishment and maintenance of the reference was the focus of story-telling activities. The patient, on the other hand, could make practice of aspects of functional communication following the on-line judgement of communicative adequacy from his conversational partner. Finally, the therapist could check the patient's learning by referring to the amount of support provided to patient's communicative attempts and the number of miniturns that the breakdown–repair sequences took. Thus, crucial aspects of the model of referring in conversation (Clark & Wilkes Gibbs, 1986), were used to define treatment tasks and parameters of patient learning.

CONCLUSION

Studies on the application of pragmatic theories to the management of communicatively impaired subjects are notable exceptions in neuropsychological literature. However, Craig (1989) discussed the implications of pragmatic language models for intervention strategies in language-disordered children. She acknowledged that the traditional (symptom-oriented) viewpoint of clinical management usually dichotomises clinical processes into separate diagnosis (goal-setting) and treatment (goal attainment) functions. According to this dichotomy, she noted that the current literature suggests that the pragmatic paradigm has an important impact on the description of language disorders and on the selection of therapy goals. However, in her opinion, the implications of pragmatic theory for intervention procedures remain unexplored. This claim might be extended even to recent pragmatic approaches to communication disturbances in aphasic adults. For instance, in a proposal of combining cognitive neuropsychological and pragmatic approaches to aphasia therapy (Lesser & Algar, 1995), the former was concerned with the psycholinguistic examination of the patients' word-finding difficulties, and the latter with the examination of resulting interactional difficulties by conversation analysis. The intervention strategy, however, only dealt with manipulating the environment, i.e., providing caregivers with facilitating conversational strategies.

We agree with Craig's (1989) claim that this discouraging state of affairs is linked to the fact that pragmatic approached to intervention have usually been "anchored" to the restricted interpretation of pragmatics as a separate set of language rules. Such a paradigm has contributed to a definition of ecologically sound therapy goals for aphasic subjects. However, the related therapeutic procedures mostly consist of stimulation methods, behaviour modification techniques or environmental intervention *separated* from interventions aimed at modifying structural aspects of language processing. Therefore, our major effort was to discuss implications of a model of language/context interaction, i.e., producing definite reference (Clark & Wilkes-Gibbs, 1986; but see also McWinney & Bates, 1978; and Marslen-Wilson et al., 1982), for establishing not only ecological validity but also *construct validity*[1] of a clinical setting where conversational rules do work.

With respect to the last issue it is interesting to point out that the application of cognitive models of communication in context may represent a substantial improvement for conceptualising intervention procedures for aphasic symptoms. In recent years, for instance, a number of single case studies have examined relationships between a theoretically driven interpretation of aphasic symptoms and the development of therapeutic intervention (see also Riddoch & Humphreys, 1994; Seron & Deloche, 1989, and Wilson & Patterson, 1990). In these cases, cognitive models have been shown to provide a detailed description of damaged and intact components of the processing system(s). This analysis has allowed therapists to define a rationale for therapy programmes. It has also been shown that therapies devised in this conceptual framework can be very useful in normal therapeutic practice, i.e., with unselected aphasic patients (Carlomagno, et al., 1991b). However, it has been claimed that identification of the "locus of impairment" within a damaged processing system does not alone provide the identification of an effective treatment strategy (Hillis & Caramazza, 1994). This choice, indeed, would also take into account cognitive factors and neurobiological mechanisms under-lying functional recovery (Hillis & Caramazza, 1994; Carlomagno, Iavarone, & Colombo,1994; Carlomagno, et al., 1997). With respect to this claim, the application of cognitive models of language/context interaction does provide insight to describe not only strengths and weaknesses of functional com-munication in aphasia, i.e., relationships between residual language skills and actual communicative effectiveness (Blasi et al., 1996), but also aspects of functional recovery from language deficits (Cannito et al., 1996). This pragmatic analysis indicates contextual factors which positively affect language processing in these subjects and the way in which these factors have to be manipulated during the therapeutic intervention. In other words, models of communication in context appear to be suitable to define not only what the treatment should focus on but also what the rules of therapeutic intervention should be.

---

[1] With this concept we refer to the extent to which structural aspects of therapeutic programmes and rules of the therapeutic setting concur with the results predicted from the theoretical model underlying both the identification of the impairment and definition of aspects of functional recovery.

REFERENCES

Aten, J.L., (1986). Functional communication treatment. In R. Chapey (Ed.), *Language interven-tion strategies in adult aphasia*. Baltimore: Williams and Wilkins.

Aten, J.L., Cagliuri, M.P., & Holland, A.L., (1982). The efficacy of functional communication therapy for chronic aphasic patients. *Journal of Speech and Hearing Disorders, 47*, 93–96.

Austin, J. (1962). *How to do things with words*. Cambridge, MA: Harvard University Press.

Basso, A., Capitani, E., & Vignolo, L. (1979). Influence of rehabilitation on language skills in aphasic patients: A controlled study. *Archives of Neurology, 36*, 190–196.

Bates, E. (1976). *Language in context*. New York: Academic Press.

Bates, E., Hamby, S., & Zurif, E. (1983). The effects of focal brain damage on pragmatic expres-sion. *Canadian Journal of Psychology, 37*, 59–84.

Berko-Gleason, J., Goodglass, H., Obler, L., Green, E., Hyde, M.R., & Weintraub, S. (1980). Narrative strategies of aphasics and normal speaking subjects. *Journal of Speech and Hearing Research, 23*, 370–382.

Blasi, V., Faccioli, F., Losanno, N., & Carlomango, S. (1996). *Assessing aphasics' communica-tive disability: A referential communication test*. Paper presented at the Seventh International Aphasia Rehabilitation Conference, Boston, MA.

Bloom, L., & Lahey, M. (1978). *Language development and language disorders*. New York: Wiley.

Brandsford, J.D., & Johnson, M.K. (1972). Contextual prerequisites for understanding: Some investigations of comprehension and recall. *Journal of Verbal Learning and Verbal Behav-iour, 11*, 717–726.

Brownell, H.H., & Joanette, Y. (1993). *Narrative discourse in neurologically impaired and normal aging adults*. San Diego, CA: Singular Publishing Group, Inc.

Bush, C.L., Brookshire, R.H., & Nicholas, L.E. (1988). Referential communication by aphasic patients. *Journal of Speech and Hearing Disorders, 53*, 475–482.

Cannito, M.P., Hough, M., Vogel, D., & Pierce, R.S. (1996). Contextual influences on auditory comprehension of reversible passive sentences in aphasia. *Aphasiology, 10*, 217–234.

Carlomagno, S. (1994). *Pragmatic approaches to aphasia therapy*. London: Whurr.

Carlomagno, S., Colombo, A., Emanuelli, S., Casadio, P., & Razzano, C. (1991b). Cognitive approaches to writing rehabilitation in aphasics: evaluation of two treatment strategies. *Aphasiology, 5*, 355–360.

Carlomagno, S., Iavarone, A., & Colombo, A. (1994). Cognitive approaches to writing rehabilita-tion: From single case to group studies. In J. Riddoch & G. Humphreys (Eds.), *Cognitive neuropsychology and cognitive rehabilitation*. Hove, UK: Lawrence Erlbaum Associates Ltd..

Carlomagno, S., Losanno, N., Belfiore, A., Casadio, P., Emanuelli, S., & Razzano, C. (1988). *Evaluation of PACE effect in severe chronic aphasia*. Proceeding of IIIrd International Aphasia Rehabilitation Congress, Firenze, Omega Edizioni.

Carlomagno, S., Losanno, N., Emanuelli, S., & Razzano, C. (1991a). Expressive language recovery or improved communicative skills: Effects of PACE therapy on aphasics' referential communication and story telling. *Aphasiology, 5*, 419–423.

Carlomagno, S., Van Eeckhout, P., Blasi, V., Belin, P., Samson, Y., & Deloche, G. (1997). The impact of functional neuroimaging methods on the development of a theory of cognitive remediation. *Journal of Neuropsychological Rehabilitation, 7*, 311–326.

Chin Li, E., Kitselman, K., Dusatko, D., & Spinelli, C. (1988). The efficacy of PACE in the remediation of naming deficits. *Journal of Communicative Disorders, 21*, 491–503.

Clark, H., & Lucy, P. (1975). Understanding what is meant from what is said: A study in con-versationally conveyed requests. *Journal of Verbal Learning and Verbal Behaviour, 14*, 56–72.

Clark, H.H., & Wilkes-Gibbs, D. (1986). Referring as a collaborative process. *Cognition, 22,* 1–39.

Clérebaut, N., Coyette, F., Feyereisen, P., & Seron, X. (1984). Une méthode de réeducation functionelle des aphasiques: La PACE *Réeducation Orthophonique, 22,* 329–345.

Craig, H. (1983). Application of pragmatic language models for intervention. In T. Gallagher & C. Prutting (Eds.), *Pragmatic assessment and intervention, issues in language.* San Diego: College-Hill.

Cubelli, R., Trentini, P., & Montagna, C.G. (1991). Re-education of gestural communication in a case of chronic global aphasia and limb apraxia. *Cognitive Neuropsychology, 9,* 369–380.

Davis, G., & Wilcox, M. (1985). *Adult aphasia rehabilitation: Applied pragmatics.* Windsor: NFER-Nelson.

Doyle, P.J., Goldstein, H., Burgeois, M.S., & Nekles, K. (1989). Facilitating generalized requesting behaviour in Broca's aphasia: An experimental analysis of a generalization training procedure. *Journal of Applied Behaviour Analysis, 22,* 157–170.

Gerber, S., & Gurland, G.B. (1989). Applied pragmatics in the assessment of aphasia. *Seminars in Speech and Language, 10,* 263–280.

Grice, H. (1975). Logic and conversation. In P. Cole & Morgan (Eds.), *Syntax and semantics: speech acts.* New York: Academic Press.

Hadar, U., & Butterworth, B. (1997). Iconic gestures, imagery, and word retrieval in speech. *Semiotica, 112,* 147–172.

Hartley, L.L. (1990). Assessment of functional communication. In K.D. Cicerone (Ed.), *Neuropsychology of everyday life.* Boston: Kluwer Academic.

Hillis, A.E., & Caramazza, A. (1994). Theories of lexical processing and rehabilitation of lexical deficits. In J. Riddoch & G. Humphreys (Eds.), *Cognitive neuropsychology and cognitive rehabilitation.* Hove, UK: Lawrence Erlbaum Associates Ltd.

Hirst, W., LeDoux, J., & Stein, S. (1984). Constrains on the processing of indirect speech acts: Evidence from aphasiology. *Brain and Language, 23,* 26–33.

Holland, A. (1980). *Communicative abilities in daily living.* Baltimore: University Park Press.

Holland, A. (1982). Observing functional communication of aphasic adults. *Journal of Speech and Hearing Disorders, 47,* 50–56.

Holland, A. (1991). Pragmatic aspects of intervention in aphasia. *Journal of Neurolinguistics, 6,* 197–211.

Howard, D., & Hatfield, F.M. (1987). *Aphasia therapy: Historical and contemporary issues.* Hove, UK: Lawrence Erlbaum Associates Ltd.

Huber, W., Poeck, K., & Willmes, K. (1984). The Aachen Aphasia Test. In C. Rose (Ed.), *Advances in neurology. Vol 42: Progress in aphasiology.* New York: Raven Press.

Joanette, Y., & Brownell, H.H. (1990). *Discourse ability and brain damage: Theoretical and empirical perspectives.* New York: Springer-Verlag.

Lesser, R., & Algar, L. (1995). Towards combining the cognitive neuropsychological and the pragmatic in aphasia therapy. *Neuropsychological Rehabilitation, 5,* 67–91.

Krauss, R.M., & Glucksberg, S. (1977). Social and non-social speech. *Scientific American, 236,* 100–105.

Lesser, R., & Milroy, L. (1993). *Linguistics and aphasia. Psycholinguistic and pragmatic aspects of intervention.* London: Longman.

Levinson, S.C. (1983). *Pragmatics.* Cambridge: Cambridge University Press.

Manochiopinig, S., Sheard, C., & Read, V.A. (1992). Pragmatic assessment in adult aphasia: A clinical review. *Aphasiology, 6,* 519–533.

Marslen-Wilson, W., Levy, E., & Komisarjevsky Tyler, L. (1982). Producing interpretable discourse: The establishment and maintenance of reference. In R.J. Jarvella, & W. Klein (Eds.), *Speech, place and action.* London: Wiley.

Mentis, M., & Prutting, C.A. (1987). Analysis of topic as illustrated in a head-injured and a normal adult. *Journal of Speech and Hearing Research, 34,* 583–595.

McNeil, D., & Pedelty, L. (1995). Right brain damage and gestures. In K. Emmorey and J. Reilly (Eds.), *Language, gestures and space.* Hillsdale, NJ: Erlbaum.

McWinney, B., & Bates, E. (1978). Sentential devices for conveying givenness and newness: A cross-cultural developmental study. *Journal of Verbal Learning and Verbal Behaviour, 17,* 539–558.

Milroy, L., & Perkins, L. (1992). Repair strategies in aphasic discourse; towards a collaborative model. *Clinical Linguistics and Phonetics, 6,* 27–40.

Nicholas, L.E., & Brookshire, R.H. (1993). A system for quantifying the informativeness and efficiency of the connected speech samples of adults with aphasia. *Journal of Speech and Hearing Research, 36,* 338–350.

Penn, C. (1984). Compensatory strategies in aphasia: Behavioural and neurological correlates. In K.M. Grieve & D. Griesel (Eds.), *Neuropsycology.* University of South Africa Press.

Penn, C. (1988). The profiling of syntax and pragmatics in aphasia. *Clinical Linguistic & Phonetics, 2,* 179–207.

Penn, C., & Cleary, J. (1988). Compensatory strategies in the language of closed head injured patients. *Brain Injury, 2,* 3–17.

Prutting, C., & Kirchner, D. (1987). A clinical appraisal of the pragmatic aspects of language. *Journal of Speech and Hearing Disorders, 52,* 105–119.

Riddoch, J., & Humphreys, G. (Eds.) (1994). *Cognitive neuropsychology and cognitive rehabilitation.* Hove, UK: Lawrence Erlbaum Associates Ltd.

Sarno, M.T. (1969). *The functional communication profiles: Manual of directions.* Rehabilitation Monograph number 42. New York Medical Center: Institute of Rehabilitation Medicine.

Schlanger, P., & Schlanger, B. (1970). Adapting role playing activities with aphasic patients. *Journal of Speech and Hearing Disorders, 35,* 229–235.

Searle, J. (1969). *Speech acts: An essay in the philosophy of language.* Cambridge, UK: Cambridge University Press.

Seron, X., & Deloche, G. (1989). *Cognitive approaches to neuropsychological rehabilitation.* Hillsdale: Erlbaum.

Shewan, C.M., & Kertesz, A. (1984). Effects of speech and language treatment on recovery from aphasia. *Brain and Language, 23,* 272–299.

Springer, L., Glindemann, R., Huber, W., & Willmes, K. (1991). How efficacious is PACE therapy when "language systematic training" is incorporated. *Aphasiology, 5,* 391–399.

Stachowiak, F., Huber, W., Poeck, W., & Kerschensteiner, M. (1977). Text comprehension in aphasia. *Brain and Language, 4,* 177–195.

Wertz, T.R., Collins, M.J., Weiss, d., Kurtzke, J.F., Friden, T., Brookshire, R.H., Pierce, J., Holtzapple, P., Hubbard, D.J., Porch, B.E., West, J.A., Davis, L., Matovitch, V., Morley, G.K., & Ressurreccion, E. (1981). Veterans Administration cooperative study on aphasia: A comparison of individual and group treatment. *Journal of Speech and Hearing Research, 24,* 580–594.

Wilcox, M., Davis, G., & Leonard, L. (1978). Aphasics' comprehension of contextually conveyed meaning. *Brain and Language, 6,* 362–377.

Wilson, B., & Patterson, K. (1990). Rehabilitation for cognitive impairments. Does cognitive psychology apply? *Applied Cognitive Psychology, 4,* 247–260.

Winograd. (1977). A framework for understanding discourse. In M. Just & P. Carpenter (Eds.), *Cognitive processes in comprehension.* Hillsdale: Erlbaum.

Yorkston, K.M., & Beukelman, D.R. (1980). An analysis of connected speech samples of aphasics and normal speakers. *Journal of Speech and Hearing Disorders, 45,* 27–36.

Manuscript received October 1999

NEUROPSYCHOLOGICAL REHABILITATION, 2000, *10* (3), 365–376

Neuroimaging of recovery from aphasia

Stefano F. Cappa

University of Brescia Medical School, Brescia, Italy

This paper is a selective review of neuroimaging studies about recovery from aphasia. Two basic mechanisms, i.e., regression of diaschisis and functional reorganisation, have been considered to play an important role in language recovery. The results of recent investigations using positron emission tomography and other functional imaging modalities are reviewed, from the point of view of their contribution to the understanding of the respective role of these mechanisms. Finally, an integration is attempted between these findings and general theories of functional recovery, underlining the crucial role of the spared areas in the language-dominant hemisphere, and the limits to brain plasticity in the adult brain.

In most patients with aphasia due to non-progressive neurological damage to the brain, such as in the case of stroke or head injury, a variable degree of "spontaneous" recovery can be expected, even in the absence of specific therapeutic interventions (see Cappa, 1998, for a recent review of the factors affecting recovery of aphasia). The neural mechanisms underlying the spontaneous recuperation of aphasia, as well as, in general, the recovery of neurological function after acute brain injury, are only incompletely understood. Even less is known about the effects of therapeutic interventions aiming at the rehabilitation of neurological dysfunction. It must be underlined that, in the case of aphasia, the obvious lack of an animal model, which can be applied to the investigation of the neurological mechanisms of recovery, makes the situation particularly challenging.

Notwithstanding these problems, it must be underlined that some important insights have been gained in recent years, in particular by the utilisation of functional imaging methods, which allow the *in vivo* assessment of brain function in humans during or after neurological recovery. These methods can

---

Requests for reprints should be sent to Stefano F. Cappa, Dept of Psychology, Vita Salute S. Raffaele University, Via Olgettina 58, 20132 Milano, Italy. Email: cappa.stefano@hsr.it

© 2000 Psychology Press Ltd
http://www.tandf.co.uk/journals/pp/09602011.html

be employed to explore what happens in the brain of aphasic patients after their stroke, and to track the modifications of brain function, which may be correlated to recovery. Brain function can be studied with neurophysiological techniques, such as EEG (electroencephalogram) and evoked potentials, as well as with the newer methods for the assessment of regional cerebral blood flow and metabolism, such as the positron emission tomography (PET) and functional magnetic resonance (fMR). The present review is limited to recent developments in the application of these techniques to the investigation of aphasia recovery; a discussion of the older clinical literature can be found in Cappa and Vallar (1992).

THE MECHANISMS UNDERLYING FUNCTIONAL RECOVERY

A proper interpretation of these results of the neuroimaging studies of recovery from aphasia requires an understanding of the neurological mechanisms which could theoretically be responsible for functional recovery after acute brain damage in humans. The starting point is the well-known fact that the adult human central nervous system has a very limited potential for regeneration. The repair of nervous tissue and the re-growth of neuronal connections do not appear to play a major role in restitution of function after damage. In some cases the recovery from the consequences of brain damage, i.e., from neurological disability, appears to take place only at the behavioural level, for example as the consequence of a "strategic" reorganisation in the way a task can be accomplished. The patient can spontaneously attain these behavioural modifications, or specific training can induce them. However, this is not the only mechanism which can account for recovery. There is considerable evidence that, also, the direct consequences of brain damage, i.e., the neurological impairment, may show considerable modifications (recovery) over time. In the case of cognitive dysfunctions, the relative contributions of behavioural adaptation to the consequences of brain damage, and of "true" neurological recovery are different in specific neuropsychological conditions. For example, in the case of severe episodic memory loss (amnesia), most of the recovery appears to take place at the functional (disability) level, through the use of memory aids and of other "substitutive" methodologies. Memory impairment *per se*, as reflected, for example, by the scores of episodic memory tests, remains usually quite stable over time, and does not appear to be significantly affected by rehabilitation treatment (Wilson, 1987). On the contrary, in the case of aphasia, there is uncontroversial evidence that specific linguistic impairments, such as phonological disorders or lexical–semantic impairment may show substantial recovery, both spontaneously and because of rehabilitation. This may be taken to indicate that, in the case of aphasia, but not of amnesia, significant modifications are taking place at the neural level, i.e., in the patient's brain functioning.

The difference in recovery between conditions usually associated with bihemispheric damage, such as amnesia, and those which follow unilateral lesions, such as aphasia, suggests that in the latter case the undamaged contralateral hemisphere may have an important role in the development of compensatory mechanisms. This hypothesis of the role of the right hemisphere in recovery from aphasia has a long history (a review can be found in Cappa & Vallar, 1992), and is still the leading issue in the interpretation of the results of neuroimaging investigations.

A considerable number of functional imaging studies addressing the question of aphasia recovery are now available. They have indicated that two basic, probably complementary mechanisms may be involved: regression of diaschisis and brain plasticity.

REGRESSION OF DIASCHISIS

The term diaschisis was originally introduced by Von Monakow (1914) to define the loss or decrease of function which can be observed in the period following an acute brain lesion in structurally unaffected brain regions connected to the directly damaged area. This "distant effect" of a unilateral hemispheric lesion can affect both ipsilateral and contralateral brain regions. The presence of diaschisis has been considered to contribute to the global severity of the clinical picture in the acute period after a stroke. A regression of diaschisis usually takes place in the following months, and may be related to the clinical recovery which is generally observed in the period after a stroke. In humans, the presence of diaschisis can be assessed using functional imaging methods, such as PET or single photon emission tomography (SPET), which allow the measurement of regional brain function (perfusion or metabolism) in the resting state, i.e., while the subject is not engaged in any specific cognitive task. What has been repeatedly found with this methodology is that the area of brain dysfunction is much larger than the structural (anatomical) lesion as shown by CT (computed tomography) or MRI (magnetic resonance imaging).

One of the first observations supporting a role of the regression of these distant effects in recovery after an acute brain lesion came from a study using a semi-quantitative method for the assessment of brain perfusion, i.e., single photon emission computerised tomography (SPECT). A series of patients with aphasia or neglect due to a stroke involving the subcortical areas were studied twice, in the early phase after stroke and after recovery. The regression of hypoperfusion in the ipsilesional, structurally unaffected cortical areas was found to parallel the recovery of neuropsychological disorders (Vallar et al., 1988). Whether the results of this study could be generalised to the much more frequent condition of aphasia due to a cortical stroke was unknown. However, in the following years, several PET studies of resting-state glucose metabolism in aphasic patients suggested that similar mechanisms may also be involved in patients with "standard" cortical aphasia. A large series of investigations has been devoted to the assessment of regional cerebral metabolic abnormalities in structurally affected and unaffected brain areas in aphasic patients by Metter and his co-workers (Metter, Jackson, Kempler, & Hanson, 1992). They reported significant positive correlations between, respectively, changes of left and right temporoparietal glucose metabolism, and the improvement of the auditory comprehension score of the Western Aphasia Battery. With a similar methodology, Heiss and coworkers (1993) found that the value of left hemispheric glucose metabolism outside the infarcted area in the acute stage after a left hemispheric lesion was the best predictor of recovery of auditory comprehension, as assessed by Token Test scores, after 4 months. These studies concur in suggesting an important role of intrahemispheric diaschisis in determining the severity of the aphasic picture in the acute stage. The Heiss et al. study also included an "activation" procedure: The day following the first PET examination, a subset of patients with mild aphasia was submitted to a second study with (^{18}F) fluorodeoxyglucose in an "activated" state, i.e., while they were engaged in an open conversation. It must be underlined that the (^{18}F) fluorodeoxyglucose is not well-suited for activation studies, because of the long time required for the measurement of regional glucose metabolism (in the order of 30 minutes). Keeping this limitation in mind, the results of this precursor study are of interest. The metabolic values during activation in the "infarcted" region (i.e., most likely in perilesional tissue), in the contralateral homotopic area and in the left Broca's area, were all highly predictive of the recovery of auditory comprehension. This finding suggested that the possibility of activating an extensive, bihemispheric neural network during language task was a crucial factor for recovery. Confirming evidence came from a follow-up investigation by the same group (Karbe et al., 1995). Two years post-stroke, the metabolic rates of the classical language areas in the left hemisphere (left superior temporal and left prefrontal cortex) were still the best predictors of, respectively, language comprehension and word fluency. A further study by the same group (Karbe et al., 1998) has corroborated the conclusion that the functional state of left hemispheric regions (and in particular, of Wernicke's area) has a close relationship to recovery. The regression of functional deactivation in brain regions remote, but connected to the primarily injured areas in patients with aphasia due to cortical lesions has also been investigated by Cappa et al. (1997). This study focused on the early period after an acute stroke involving the cerebral cortex of the left hemisphere, and included only patients with lesions of limited size and mild aphasia, in which a significant spontaneous recovery can in general be expected. The patients were submitted to a first PET measurement of regional glucose metabolism two weeks after stroke, i.e., when the clinical picture of aphasia can be considered "stable". The follow-up PET study was performed 6 months later, when considerable language recovery had taken place, as expected. An extensive metabolic depression was present in structurally unaffected areas in the acute phase. The reduction of glucose metabolism was not limited to the ipsilateral hemisphere, but also involved the contralateral hemisphere. The regression of this bihemispheric functional deactivation in structurally unaffected brain regions was related to language recovery. Taken together, these findings suggest that in the first months after a stroke the regression of intrahemispheric and transhemispheric diaschisis may be associated with the recovery of a function, such as language, which is subserved by an extensive network of interconnected regions in both hemispheres. A recent SPECT study (Mimura et al., 1998) reported a significant correlation between the increase in left hemisphere perfusion and aphasia recovery in the first year after a stroke; however, in a retrospective study, it was the right hemisphere cerebral blood flow that was higher in the patients with good recovery.

The hypothesis of a correlation between recovery and increase in rCBF (regional cerebral blood flow) in unaffected brain areas is, however, not uncontroversial. Different results have been reported by Iglesias et al. (1996). These authors studied a group of 19 patients in the acute period after an ischaemic stroke. The comparison between a first PET study, within 18 hours of onset, and a follow-up one 15–30 days later did not indicate a significant change in the overall oxygen consumption in the contralateral hemisphere. On the other hand, the global neurological deficit was significantly improved in the patient group. The discrepancy between the results of this study and the other reports may be due to the different time window. In the Iglesias et al. study both PET examinations were performed within 1 month, while the other investigations reporting positive correlations between regression of diaschisis and recovery generally spanned a longer time period. Furthermore, the utilisation of a global neurological scale rather than a more detailed examination does not allow any conclusions to be drawn about the presence of significant language recovery during the time of the study in this patient sample.

BRAIN PLASTICITY

The general concept of brain plasticity refers to the reorganisation of the brain structures responsible for a specific function. In neuropsychology, one of the earliest hypotheses about plasticity was actually formulated in order to account for aphasia recovery. The "right hemisphere theory of recovery", i.e., the hypothesis of a take-over of the linguistic functions of the language-dominant left hemisphere by the contralateral hemisphere was originally proposed by Gowers (1887). Making reference to the theoretical model of brain function developed by Hughlings Jackson (York & Steinberg, 1995), this take-over was attributed to the "unmasking" of pre-existing, functionally committed areas of the right hemisphere, which are normally inhibited by the contralateral "dominant" hemisphere (Moscovitch, 1997). There is substantial evidence for a linguistic role of the right hemisphere, coming, for example, from the investigation of patients with callosal disconnection (see Zaidel, 1998, for a review). A "release" of the right hemisphere has been suggested to be responsible for peculiar qualitative features of aphasics' performance, such as the production of semantic errors in reading (Landis, Regard, Graves, & Goodglass, 1983).

This "functional reorganisation" of the cerebral substrate of language function can be considered as an instance of cerebral plasticity. The study of neural plasticity has an important role in contemporary neuroscience. However, it must be clearly acknowledged that the term covers a wide range of extremely diverse experimental phenomena. Broadly summarising, there are two main applications of the concept of plasticity. The first refers to modifications, which take place in normal, undamaged brain tissue. These modifications include both molecular phenomena, such as, for example, the activity-enhanced presynaptic facilitation subserving classical conditioning in aplysia, as well as anatomical rearrangements, such as the modifications of somatotopic maps which can be induced by specific training in monkeys (Kandel, Schwartz, & Jessel, 1991). The second application is more strictly related to the topic of this review, and refers to he modifications which take place in neural tissue after a lesion. In the latter case, plasticity is generally indicated by the reorganisation of the cortical representation of functions, responsible for behavioural recovery. The experimental evidence for plasticity in the latter sense is limited, and comes largely from lesion studies in infant animals. An exception is the study of experimental stroke in monkeys by Nudo, Wise, SiFuentes, and Millikan (1996), who were able to demonstrate post-lesional plastic changes in cortical motor representations induced by exercise in monkeys with experimental stroke.

In the case of human studies, plasticity often refers to modifications in the normal brain induced by learning. For example, using fMR it has been possible to demonstrate that the prolonged performance of a complex motor task is associated with plastic changes in the motor cortex, persisting for several months (Karni et al., 1995). In the same vein, it has been shown that the increased use of the left-hand fingers in string players is associated with a permanent enlargement of the cortical representation in the contralateral somatosensory area. This enlargement is proportional to the number of years devoted to the musical activity (Elbert, et al., 1995). Several studies in amputees have shown persistent plastic changes in the representation of the phantom limb in the somatosensory cortex. The amplitude of the cortical reorganisation was correlated to the intensity of pain sensation experienced (Flor et al., 1995). These examples clearly indicate that an appropriate training, or a persistent sensory stimulation, can induce a structural reorganisation of the normal cerebral cortex. However, this aspect of neural plasticity has only indirect implications for the understanding of functional recovery, as it does not involve the crucial issue at stake, i.e., cerebral plasticity after brain damage in humans.

Functional brain activation methods have provided a tool to investigate this aspect of plasticity. The basic idea behind this approach is to compare the pattern of brain activation observed in normal subjects engaged in a cognitive task, with the cerebral activity observed in recovered patients performing the same task. Any difference in the "functional landscape" of brain activation can then be considered to reflect reorganisation phenomena. This approach is fraught with formidable methodological difficulties. One of the first activation studies in aphasic patients was performed by Knopman et al. in 1983, using the two-dimensional (non-tomographic) Xenon 133 method for the measurement of cerebral blood flow. These authors reported that aphasic patients who had a good recovery of auditory comprehension showed a "reactivation" of left temporoparietal areas during language processing. The first PET studies of recovery deal with the recuperation of hemiparesis in patients with striatocapsular ischaemic lesions (Weiller et al., 1992), and showed an extensive functional reorganisation, including both ipsilateral and contralateral regions, when the subjects were performing a motor task with the affected hand. The choice of patients with subcortical lesions was dictated by the requirements of the PET activation technique, which at the time of the study was based on the averaging of data from multiple subjects, in order to detect the cerebral activations associated with the performance of a specific task. The variability in the location of lesions in patients with cortical strokes was considered to constitute a major problem for data analysis. A similar procedure was nevertheless applied to aphasia by Weiller et al. (1995) in a group study of six partially recovered patients with Wernicke's aphasia. The patients' cerebral perfusion was measured at rest and during non-word repetition and verb generation. According to a classical "subtractive" design, each language condition was compared with rest in order to detect the areas of significant task-related activation. The same activation paradigm was applied to a group of normal controls, and the results provided the baseline to evaluate the presence of functional reorganisation. The main conclusion was that, in comparison to control subjects, the patient group had a more extensive recruitment of frontal and temporal right hemispheric regions, homotopic to the language areas of the left hemisphere. This study opened new perspectives for the investigation of the neurological correlates of recovery from aphasia; however, the interpretation that the increased right hemispheric activation was responsible for aphasia recovery must be considered with caution. While the patients were largely recovered, as shown by the change in their aphasia test scores, the verb generation task is very demanding, and calls for an extensive activation of the right hemisphere, as it does in many normal right-handed subjects (Frackowiak, 1997). Furthermore, the use of a group analysis decreases the likelihood of detecting activation in perilesional areas, which will necessarily vary in individual subjects because of differences in lesion size and location. Another PET activation study in a group of 16 aphasic patients (10 fluent, 6 non-fluent) has been reported by Ohyama et al. (1996). The patients were studied at different times post-stroke (from 1 month to 5 years), had a wide range of lesion sizes and sites, and different levels of recovery, as reflected by their Western Aphasia Battery (WAB) scores. In order to be included in the study, they had to be able to repeat single words (phonemic paraphasias were discounted), as the activation task was single word repetition. In normals, the study was analysed with the standard methodology of intersubject averaging. The repetition task, when compared to rest, resulted in a largely bilateral activation, including the classical language areas, with a left-sided prevalence. A "region of interest" approach was then used in the patients, in order to avoid the major problems related to the variations in individual anatomy. The regions of interest were placed on co-registered PET–MRI images of individual subjects and the magnitude of the activations were calculated. The main result of the analysis was that the percentage change induced by repetition was larger on the left side in all language areas. A greater right-sided increase was observed in the frontal areas in non-fluent patients; in the fluent group, the increase was more symmetrical than in normal subjects. The implications of these findings for a right hemispheric role in recovery are difficult to interpret, as it is unclear whether the structurally damaged region in the left hemisphere was excluded from the analysis. Furthermore, the only significant correlation between rCBF increase and the WAB scores involved the left frontal areas.

Two other studies provided relevant information. Belin et al. (1996) reported a PET activation study in seven patients with chronic non-fluent aphasia, who had shown considerable improvement after the introduction of Melodic Intonation Therapy (MIT). The pattern of brain activation in comparison with rest was analysed with a region of interest approach, excluding the structurally damaged areas. The results of this analysis indicated extensive right-sided activation during single word repetition. However, in the other active task, which required repetition of words with MIT intonation, the right hemisphere was actually deactivated, and a significant increase was found in the left frontal areas. The author argue that the right-sided activations might reflect a "maladaptive" functional reorganisation, due to the presence of the lesion itself, while actual recovery may be associated with the reactivation of left-hemispheric structures. Thomas and coworkers (1997) report an interesting study based on the assessment of the shifts of the cortical direct current potential during cognitive tasks. In normal right-handers this potential is lateralised to the left during language processing. Eleven aphasic patients were studied with this methodology twice, before and after some degree of recovery had taken place. In patients with Broca's aphasia, an initial shift towards right hemisphere prevalence reverted to the "normal" left frontal asymmetry with recovery. A similar pattern was present in anomic patients, but not in the three cases of Wernicke's aphasia, which showed a persistent right hemispheric prevalence.

The latter investigations cast some doubt on the relationship between right hemisphere activation and recovery, and suggest that the "reactivation" of the left hemispheric area may be a crucial variable. This hypothesis is compatible with the results of a large proportion of the studies of resting cerebral metabolism, reviewed in the previous section, which have underlined the predictive value of the functional status of the left hemispheric language areas in predicting recovery. Converging evidence is starting to be provided by single case studies. The investigation of individual patients has become possible only recently, thanks to the developments in PET technology and to the introduction of functional MRI. A series of patients studied at the Wellcome Institute of Cognitive Neurology (Warburton et al., 1999) suggests an important role of the perilesional areas in mediating recovery. The presence of increased right-hemispheric activation appears to be less consistent, and may be related to the pre-existing pattern of language lateralisation. Our experience with fMR has given similar results (Perani et al., in preparation). Studies of recovered aphasic subjects indicate that the pattern of reorganisation observed during word fluency tasks is heterogeneous, but shows mainly left hemispheric activation, in the same areas activated in normal subjects, or in other language-related regions. It is interesting to observe that a PET study of recovery in another condition associated with unilateral hemispheric damage, i.e., unilateral neglect, has given similar results (Pizzamiglio et al., 1998). The brain areas activated by the performance of a visuospatial task in three recovered patients were largely in the right hemisphere, i.e., ipsilateral to the lesion. The activations were largely overlapping with those observed in normal subjects performing the same visuospatial task, but included additional parietal and frontal areas, involved in attentional and oculomotor functions. The reorganisation thus appears to be mostly interhemispheric, and to involve areas, which are to some degree dedicated to other aspects of the same function.

CONCLUSIONS

The fact that the potential for reorganisation of language function after injury in adults appears to be limited should come as no surprise to anyone who has been working with aphasic patients. Imaging studies have provided strong support for the notion that bihemispheric activations are associated with language processing; a left-sided prevalence is normally observed in right-handed individuals, but there appear to be considerable individual differences, probably related to variable patterns of cerebral lateralisation. An increased activation of the right-sided component of this bilateral network appears to be frequently present in aphasic subjects engaged in language tasks. What the functional role of this right-sided activation is, remains an open question. One possibility is that it represents a "back-up" resource, with a high degree of interindividual variability. In some subjects, a premorbid cerebral language organisation characterised by a relevant functional involvement of the right hemisphere may be associated with an unexpectedly rapid recovery. This hypothesis is difficult to test, because it would require knowledge of the pattern of language lateralisation prior to the stroke. In others, the recruitment of the right hemisphere may be less useful, and simply reflect the pathological performance. In this case, the recovery process may be associated with the reactivation of the dedicated left hemispheric structures which have not been irreversibly destroyed by the lesion. Given this complex set of hypotheses, it is clear that group studies cannot be expected to provide useful information: A multiple single case methodology appears to be a more appropriate approach. The increasing corpus of knowledge about the patterns of brain activity during the multiple aspects of linguistic processing in normal subjects may in the near future provide a better baseline to evaluate the complex patterns of functional reorganisation observed in aphasic subjects engaged in linguistic tasks. It might well be that the question of the neurological correlates of recovery is ill-posed, as it has not a single, or a small set of answers, applicable to broad, clinically defined categories, such as Broca's and Wernicke's aphasia. What we can image in individual patients are the patterns of brain activation associated with specific linguistic performances, and compare them to what is seen in normal subjects (see, for example, the study of deep dyslexic reading by Price et al., 1998). This type of evidence can then be used to constrain models of normal language processing, and of the specific modifications induced by aphasia. Future research should of course include another crucial variable, i.e., rehabilitation. The specific treatment methodologies which are discussed in several papers of this special issue might be expected to influence the neural processes of reorganisation in different ways: At the moment, however, there is no firm evidence to be reviewed about this important topic.

REFERENCES

Belin, P., Van Eeckhout, P., Zilbovicius, M., Remy, P., François, C., Guillaume, S., Chain, F., Rancurel, G., & Samson, Y. (1996). Recovery from nonfluent aphasia after melodic intonation therapy: A PET study. *Neurology, 47,* 1504–1511.

Cappa, S.F. (1998). Spontaneous recovery from aphasia. In B. Stemmer & H. Withaker (Eds.), *Handbook of neurolinguistics.* San Diego: Academic Press.

Cappa, S.F., Perani, D., Grassi, F., Bressi, S., Alberoni, M., Franceschi, M., Bettinardi, V., Todde, S., & Fazio, F. (1997) A PET follow-up study of recovery after stroke in acute aphasics. *Brain and Language, 56,* 5567.

Cappa, S.F., & Vallar, G. (1992). Neurological correlates of recover in aphasia. *Aphasiology, 6,* 359–372.

Elbert, T., Pantev, C., Weinbruch, C., Rockstroh, B., & Taub, E. (1995). Measured cortical representation of the fingers of the left hand in string players. *Science, 270,* 305–307.

Flor, H., Elbert, T., Knecht, S., Weinbruch, C., Pantev, C., Birbaumer, N., Larbig, W., & Taub, E. (1995). Phantom-limb pain as a perceptual correlate of cortical reorganization following arm amputation. *Nature, 375,* 482–484.

Gowers, W. (1887). *Lectures in the diagnosis of diseases of the brain.* Philadelphia: Blakiston.

Heiss, W.-D., Kessler, J., Karbe, H., Fink, G.R., & Pawlik, G. (1993). Cerebral glucose metabolism as a predictor of recovery from aphasia in ischemic stroke. *Archives of Neurology, 50,* 958–964.

Iglesias, S., Marchal, G., Rioux, P., Beaudouin, V., Hauttement, J.L., De la Sayette, V., Le Doze, F., Derlon, J.M., Viader, F., & Baron, J.C. (1996). Do changes in oxygen metabolism in the unaffected cerebral hemisphere underlie early neurological recovery after stroke? *Stroke, 27,* 1192–1199.

Kandel, E.R., Schwartz, J.H., & Jessel, T.M. (1991). *Principles of neural science* (III ed.). New York: Elsevier.

Karbe, H., Kessler, J., Herholz, K., Fink, G.R., & Heiss, W.-D. (1995). Long-term prognosis of post-stroke aphasia studied with positron emission tomography. *Archives of Neurology, 52,* 186–190.

Karbe, H., Thiel, A., Weber-Luzenburger, G., Herholz, K., Kessler, J., & Heiss, W.D. (1998). Brain plasticity in poststroke aphasia: What is the contribution of the right hemisphere? *Brain and Language, 64, 215*–230.

Karni, A., Meyer, G., Jezzard, P., Adams, M.M., Turner, R., & Ungerleider, L. (1995). Functional MRI evidence for adult motor artex plasticity during motor skill learning. *Nature, 377,* 155–158.

Knopman, D.S., Selnes, O.A., Niccum, N., Rubens, A.B., Yock, D., & Larson, D. (1983). A longitudinal study of speech fluency in aphasia: CT correlates of recovery and persistent non fluency. *Neurology, 33,* 1170–1178.

Landis, T., Regard, M., Graves, R., & Goodglass, H. (1983). Semantic paralexia: A release of right hemispheric function from left hemispheric control. *Neuropsychologia, 21,* 359–364.

Metter, E.J., Jackson, C.A., Kempler, D., & Hanson, W.R. (1992). Temporoparietal cortex and the recovery of language comprehension in aphasia. *Aphasiology, 6,* 349–358.

Mimura, M., Kato, M., Sano, Y., Kojima, T., Naeser, M., & Kashima, H. (1998). Prospective and retrospective studies of recovery in aphasia. Changes in cerebral blood flow and language functions. *Brain, 121,* 2083–2094.

Moscovitch, M. (1997). The development of lateralisation of language and its relation to cognitive and linguistic development. A review and some theoretical speculations. In S.J. Segalowitz & F.A. Gruber (Eds.), *Language development and neurological theory* (pp. 193–211). New York: Academic Press.

Nudo, R.J., Wise, B.M., SiFuentes, F., & Millikan, G.W. (1996). Neural substrates for the effects of rehabilitative training on motor recovery after ischemic infarct. *Science, 272,* 1791–1794.

Ohyama, M., Senda, M., Kitamura, S., Ishii, K., Mishina, M., & Terashi, A. (1996). Role of the nondominant hemisphere and undamaged area during word repetition in poststroke aphasics. A PET activation study. *Stroke, 27,* 897–903.

Pizzamiglio, L., Perani, D., Cappa, S.F., Vallar, G., Paolucci, S., Grassi, F., Paulesu, E., & Fazio, F. (1998). Recovery of neglect after right hemispheric damage: A H215O PET activation study. *Archives of Neurology, 55,* 561–568.

Price, C., Howard, D., Patterson, K., Warburton, E.A., Friston, K.J., & Frackowiak, R.S.J. (1998). A functional neuroimaging description of deep dyslexic patients. *Journal of Cognitive Neuroscience, 10,* 303–315.

Thomas, C., Altenmueller, E., Marckmann, G., Kahrs, J., & Dichgans, J. (1997). Language processing in aphasia: Changes in lateralization patterns during recovery reflect cerebral plasticity in adults. *Electroencephalography and Clinical Neurophysiology, 102,* 86–97.

Vallar, G., Perani, D., Cappa, S.F., Messa, C., Lenzi, G.L., & Fazio, F. (1988). Recovery from aphasia and neglect after subcortical stroke: Neuropsychological and cerebral perfusion study. *Journal of Neurology, Neurosurgery and Psychiatry, 51,* 1269–1276.

von Monakow, C. (1914). *Die Lokalisation in Grosshirn und der Abbau der Funktion durch Kortikale Herde.* Wiesbaden: Bergmann.

Warburton, E., Price, C.J., Swinburn, K., Wise, R.J. (1999). Mechanisms of recovery from aphasia: Evidence from positron emission tomography studies. *Journal of Neurology, Neurosurgery and Psychiatry, 66*, 155–161.

Weiller, C., Chollet, F., Friston, K.J., Wise, R.J.S., & Frackowiak, R.S.J. (1992). Functional reorganization of the brain in recovery from striatocapsular infarction in man. *Annals of Neurology, 31,* 463–472.

Weiller, C., Isensee, C., Rijintjes, M., Huber, W., Mueller, S., Bier, D., Dutschka, K., Woods, R.P., Noth, J., & Diener, H.C. (1995). Recovery from Wernicke's aphasia—a PET study. *Annals of Neurology, 37,* 723–732.

Wilson, B.A. (1987). *Rehabilitation of memory.* New York: Guilford Press.

York, G.K., & Steinberg, D.A. (1995). Hughlings Jackson's theory of recovery. *Neurology, 45,* 834–838.

Zaidel, E. (1998). Language in the right hemisphere following callosal disconnection. In: B. Stemmer, & H.A. Whitaker, (Eds.), *Handbook of neurolinguistics.* (pp. 366–383). San Diego: Academic Press.

Manuscript received October 1999

NEUROPSYCHOLOGICAL REHABILITATION
Notes for Authors

Manuscript submission. Please send the original copy of a manuscript and its figures, plus three photocopies to Editorial Administrator, Neuropsychological Rehabilitation, 27 Church Road, Hove, East Sussex BN3 2FA, UK. Authors should include their electronic mail and facsimile numbers if available. The manuscript should be typed throughout in <u>double spacing</u> on <u>one</u> side of A4 paper with wide margins. It should contain a title page, followed by a separate page for an abstract of 50-200 words, and end with separate pages containing a complete list of references followed by a list of figure legends also typed in double spacing.

Submission of an article is taken as acceptance by the author that the publisher will hold copyright on all material published in the journal, including printed, electronic, and other publication formats, in all languages.

Manuscript presentation. Papers should be prepared in the format prescribed by the American Psychological Association; see the Publication Manual of the APA (4th edition) for details.
Title. This should be concise, and typed on a separate sheet, together with the name(s) of the author(s) and the full postal address(es) of their institution(s). Proofs and requests for reprints will be sent to the first author unless otherwise indicated. A short running title of no more than 40 characters (including spaces) should also be indicated.
Abstracts. An abstract of 50-200 words should follow the title page on a separate sheet.
Headings. Indicate headings and sub-headings for different sections of the paper clearly do not number headings.
Acknowledgements. These should be as brief as possible and typed on a separate sheet.
Permission to Quote. Any direct quotation, regardless of length, must be accompanied by a reference citation and include a page number. Any quote over six manuscript lines should have formal written permission to quote from the copyright owner. It is the author's responsibility to determine whether permission is required from the copyright owner, and if so, to obtain it.
Footnotes. These should be avoided unless absolutely necessary. Essential footnotes should be indicated by superscript figures in the text typed in a separate section at the end of the manuscript.
Reference citations within the text. Use authors' last names, with the year of publication in parentheses after the author's name, for example: Jones and Smith (1987). Alternatively: (Brown, 1989; Jones & Smith, 1987; White, Johnson, & Thomas, 1990). On first citation of references with three or more authors, give all names in full, thereafter use first author et al. If more than one article by the same author(s) in the same year is cited, the letters a, b, c etc. should follow the year.
Unpublished work cited. (Conference presentations, for example) should be included in alphabetical order in the reference list. The citation of unpublished reports of empirical investigations is strongly discouraged.
Reference list. A full list of references quoted in the text should be given at the end of the paper in alphabetical order of author's names, commencing as a new sheet, typed double spaced.
Titles of journals and books should be given in full, as in the following examples:
Books
Cronbach, L.J., & Gleser, G.C. (1965*)*. <u>Psychological tests and personnel decisions</u> (2nd ed.). Urbana, IL: Glencoe Press.
Chapter in Edited Book
Jones, R.R., Reid, J.B., & Patterson, G.R. (1975). Naturalistic observation in clinical assessment. In P. McReynolds (Ed.), <u>Advances in psychological assessment</u> (Vol.3). San Francisco: Jossey-Bass.

Journal Article

McReynolds, P. (1979). Interactional assessment. <u>Behavioural Assessment</u>, 1, 237–247.

Tables. These should be kept to the minimum. Each table should be typed double spaced on a separate sheet, giving the heading, e.g., Table 2, in Arabic numerals, followed by the legend, followed by the table. Make sure that appropriate units are given. Instructions for placing the table should be given in parentheses in the text, e.g. (Table 2 about here).

Figures. Figures are expensive to reproduce and should only be used when essential. The same data should not be presented both as a figure and in a table. Where possible, related diagrams should be grouped together to form a single figure. Figures should be drawn to professional standards, and it is recommended that the linear dimensions of figures be approximately twice those intended for the final printed version. (Maximum printed figure size 182 mm x 114 mm, including caption.) Make sure that axes of graphs are properly labelled, and that appropriate units are given. The figure captions should be typed in a separate section, headed e.g., Figure 2, in Arabic numerals. Instructions for placing the figure should be given in parentheses in the text, e.g. (Figure 2 about here).

Statistics. Results of statistical tests should be given in the following form:

$\underline{F}(1, 9) = 25.35, \underline{p} < .01$

similarly for t, and other tests. The logic of significance testing implies that only a small number of conventional levels of p should be quoted (e.g., .05, .01, .001): Authors should depart from this convention only if a special point is being made, for example if a result just fails to reach significance at the .05 level.

Abbreviations. Abbreviations should be avoided except in the most standard of cases. Experimental conditions should be named in full, except in tables and figures.

Submission procedures. Authors will normally receive a decision on their papers within three months of receipt, and if accepted they will normally be published six to nine months later. The date of receipt of the manuscript will be printed. Where minor revision of a paper is requested the original date of receipt will appear, provided that a satisfactory revision is received within one month of the request. Otherwise it will bear the revised version date.

Offprints. Contributors receive 50 copies of their paper free. Additional copies may be ordered on a form provided by the publishers at the time proofs are sent to authors. Please note there are no offprints of any plate sections published in the journal.

NEUROPSYCHOLOGICAL REHABILITATION

Editor: Barbara A. Wilson

Deputy Editor: Ian H. Robertson

Executive Editors

Max Coltheart • Guido Gainotti • Elizabeth Glisky • George Prigatano

Associate Board of Editors

Alan Baddeley, UK; Anna Basso, Italy; Rita Sloan Berndt, USA; Corwin Boake, USA; Anne-Lise Christensen, Denmark; G. Deloche, France; Leonard Diller, USA; Elaine Funnell, UK; Peter Halligan, UK; Glynda Kinsella, Australia; Pamella Klonoff, USA; Michael Kopelman, UK; Jeffrey Kreutzer, USA; Muriel Lezak, USA; Nadina B. Lincoln, UK; Catherine Mateer, USA; Anna Mazzucchi, Italy; T. McMillan, UK; Karalyn Patterson, UK; Luigi Pizzamiglio, Italy; Jennie Ponsford, Australia; Jane Riddoch, UK; Dan Schacter, USA; Myrna F. Schwartz, USA; Xavier Seron, Belgium; Donald Stein, USA; Toshiko Watamori, Japan; Klaus Willmes, Germany; Jill Winegardner, USA; Y. Ben Yishay, USA; J. Zihl, Germany; A.H. van Zomeren, The Netherlands.

Aims and Scope

Neuropsychological Rehabilitation provides an international forum for the publication of well-designed and properly evaluated intervention strategies, surveys and observational procedures, which are clinically relevant and may also back up theoretical arguments.

Research Digest

Editors: Janet Cockburn, Rivermead Rehabilitation Centre, Abingdon Road, Oxford OX1 4XD.

Jon Evans, The Oliver Zangwill Centre for Neuropsychological Rehabilitation, Princess of Wales Hospital, Lynn Road, Ely, Cambridge, CB6 1DN.

The Research Digest features in every issue of *Neuropsychological Rehabilitation*. The digest editors regularly scan a wide range of journals and other publications for material of particular interest to those working in rehabilitation. This section is an invaluable resource providing both bibliographic references and informal comment and discussion.

Book Reviews

Neuropsychological Rehabilitation publishes a variety of book reviews, either wholly or partly dealing with matters related to rehabilitation issues. These may examine new publications or volumes now regarded as classics, compare and contrast similar publications or those with opposing viewpoints, and discuss one or more publications in relation to the discipline as a whole. Correspondence should be sent to Barbara Wilson, MRC Cognition and Brain Sciences Unit, Box 58, Addenbrooke's Hospital, Hills Road, Cambridge CB2 2QQ.

Neuropsychological Rehabilitation is published by Psychology Press Ltd., a member of the Taylor & Francis Group. Correspondence for the publisher and submissions should be addressed to *Neuropsychological Rehabilitation*, Psychology Press, 27 Church Road, Hove, East Sussex, BN3 2FA, UK.

Subscription rates to Volume 10, 2000 (5 issues) are as follows:

To individuals: UK £90.00 / Rest of World $149.00

To institutions: UK £189.00 / Rest of World $312.00

Periodicals postage is paid at Jamaica, NY 11431, USA. US Postmasters: send address changes to *Neuropsychological Rehabilitation*, Publications Expediting Inc., 200 Meacham Avenue, Elmont, NY 11003, USA. Air freight and mailing in the USA by Publications Expediting Inc.

New subscriptions and changes of address should be sent to, Psychology Press, c/o Taylor & Francis, Rankine Road, Basingstoke, Hants, RG24 8PR, UK. Please send change of address notices at least six weeks in advance, and include both old and new addresses.

Advertising enquiries should be sent to Philip Law, Advertising Assistant, Taylor & Francis Ltd, P.O. Box 25, Abingdon, OX14 3UE, UK. Tel: +44 (0) 1235 401000; Fax: +44 (0) 1235 401550; Email: philip.law@CARFAX.CO.UK

Information about Psychology Press journals and other publications is available from http://www.psypress.co.uk. Go to http://www.tandf.co.uk/journals/pp/09602011.html for current information about this journal, including how to access the online version or to register for the free table of contents alerting service.

Neuropsychological Rehabilitation is covered by the following index/abstracting services: ASSIA; Excerpta Medica/Embase; MLA International Bibliography; Neuroscience Citation Index (ISI); PsycINFO; Research Alert (ISI); SciSearch (ISI), Social Services Abstracts, Sociological Abstracts.

Copyright: The material in this journal is copyright. No Part of this journal may be reproduced in any form, by photostat, retrieval system, or any other means, without written permission of the publisher.

© 2000 Psychology Press Ltd.

Submission of Manuscripts

Please send the original copy of a manuscript and its figures, plus three photocopies to the Editorial Assistant, 27 Church Road, Hove, East Sussex BN3 2FA, UK. Authors should include their electronic mail and facsimile numbers if available. The manuscript should be typed throughout in double spacing on one side of the paper with wide margins, contain a title page, followed by a separate page for an abstract of 50-200 words, and end with separate pages containing a complete list of references followed by a list of figure legends in double spacing.

The manuscript and references should be presented in accordance with APA style (see APA manual, fourth edition). Tables and figures should be kept to a minimum consistent with clear exposition, while abbreviations should be avoided except in the most standard of cases.

Submission of Accepted Manuscripts on Disk: Final versions of articles which have been accepted for publication may be submitted on disk to the Editorial Office. Guidelines for preparation of text and artwork for final electronic submission are available from the Editorial Assistant (address above) or from Kirsten Buchanan at kirsten.buchanan@psypress.co.uk

Submission of an article is taken as acceptance by the author that the publisher will hold copyright on all material published in the journal, including printed, electronic and other publication formats, in all languages. Detailed 'Notes for Authors' are available on request from the publisher and are published from time to time in the journal.

Preparation of Figure Artwork

Please submit the best possible figure artwork, i.e. an original, not a photocopy.

1. Size: The text area of the journal is 114mm wide x 182mm deep. Each figure and its caption must fit into this area. If submitted figures are larger than this, they have to be reduced to fit.
2. Proportion: When any figure is reduced for publication, its proportions don't change. For example, a very shallow figure measuring 228mm wide and 30mm deep will be printed 114mm wide and 15mm deep (a 50% reduction). If your figure has several elements, for instance, two graphs and a common key, consider arranging them vertically rather than horizontally so that the figure is closer to the proportions of the text page. Including the key inside the area of the graph increases the amount of space available for the graph itself.
3. Labelling: Labelling works best if kept to a minimum and it should be consistent both within and between figures. It is particularly important to remember size when preparing labels. If your figure is going to be reduced in size before printing, its labels will be reduced as well.
4. Line Weights: Computer graphics programmes can produce very fine lines, which may look nice on the original figure when it comes off the laser printer, but there is a risk that in the printing processes these lines may break up or even disappear completely. It is far safer to select a line which appears quite black and definite.
5. Data Points on Graphs: Several data lines on the same graph are often distinguished by using different sorts of symbols to mark the data points-such as, open and closed circles, boxes and triangles. If these are small they blur during the printing processes making it impossible to tell which is which.
6. Tones and Shading:
   • Don't combine lettering and tone at all.
   • Only use tones that (in the case of dots) produce very clear distinct black dots with clear white areas between them creating more of a pattern effect than a grey. In the case of line patterns make sure that there is plenty of white space on both sides of each line.
   • Don't use tones if you figures is going to be greatly reduced.
   • If you're using several tones on the same figure, for example to distinguish types of data in a bar chart, make sure that they are significantly different from each other and that they are identified in a large, clear key.

Detailed *Guidelines for Preparation of Figure Artwork* are available from the publisher. Please contact Psychology Press, 27 Church Road, Hove, BN3 2FA, UK.

For Product Safety Concerns and Information please contact our EU
representative GPSR@taylorandfrancis.com Taylor & Francis Verlag GmbH,
Kaufingerstraße 24, 80331 München, Germany

Batch number: 08153778

Printed by Printforce, the Netherlands